Canadian
Semantic Web

SEMANTIC WEB AND BEYOND
Computing for Human Experience

Series Editors:

Ramesh Jain
University of California, Irvine
http://jain.faculty.gatech.edu/

Amit Sheth
University of Georgia
http://lsdis.cs.uga.edu/~amit

As computing becomes ubiquitous and pervasive, computing is increasingly becoming an extension of human, modifying or enhancing human experience. Today's car reacts to human perception of danger with a series of computers participating in how to handle the vehicle for human command and environmental conditions. Proliferating sensors help with observations, decision making as well as sensory modifications. The emergent semantic web will lead to machine understanding of data and help exploit heterogeneous, multi-source digital media. Emerging applications in situation monitoring and entertainment applications are resulting in development of experiential environments.

SEMANTIC WEB AND BEYOND
Computing for Human Experience
addresses the following goals:

➤ brings together forward looking research and technology that will shape our world more intimately than ever before as computing becomes an extension of human experience;
➤ covers all aspects of computing that is very closely tied to human perception, understanding and experience;
➤ brings together computing that deal with semantics, perception and experience;
➤ serves as the platform for exchange of both practical technologies and far reaching research.

Additional information about this series can be obtained from
http://www.springer.com

Additional Title in the Series:

Semantic Management of Middleware by Daniel Oberle; ISBN-10: 0-387-27630-0

Canadian Semantic Web

edited by

Mamadou Tadiou Koné
Université Laval, Québec, Canada

Daniel Lemire
Université du Québec à Montréal, Canada

 Springer

Mamadou Tadiou Koné
Université Laval
Faculty of Science & Engineering
Dept. of Computer Science
Pavillon Adrien-Pouliot
QUÉBEC G1K 7P4
CANADA
Kone.Mamadou@ift.ulaval.ca

Daniel Lemire
Université du Québec à Montréal
UER Sciences and Technologies
Télé-Université
100 Sherbrooke West
MONTRÉAL QC H2X 3P2
CANADA
lemire@acm.org

Canadian Semantic Web
edited by Mamadou Tadiou Koné and Daniel Lemire

ISBN-13: 978-1-4419-4004-9

e-ISBN-13: 978-0-387-34347-1
e-ISBN-10: 0-387-34347-4

Printed on acid-free paper.

© 2006 Springer Science+Business Media, LLC
Softcover reprint of the hardcover 1st edition 2006

9 8 7 6 5 4 3 2 1

springer.com

Table of Contents

Keynote session

Service-Oriented Computing: Multiagent Foundation, Robust Applications, and Research Agenda
Michael N. Huhns

Technical session: Applications I

Technical session: Applications II

Technical session: Ontologies I

Technical session: Ontologies II

Preface

The Canadian Semantic Web Working Symposium (CSWWS) 2006 is the first major event in Canada on the theme of semantic Web. It is the initiative of the Canadian Semantic Web Interest Group (SWIG) which gathers researchers supported by the Canadian Society for the Computational Studies of Intelligence (CSCSI). The SWIG is made of academic, government and industry representatives promoting emerging Semantic Web research initiatives in academia and industries in Canada with connections to similar groups world-wide.

Given the attention the one day event CSWWS 2006 received, we are pleased to say that the *short term objective* of this symposium has been acheived. That is to say, many players in the community have acknowledged its contribution to the advancement of the semantic Web by facilitating the exchange of scientific knowledge among researchers in academia, industry and government in Canada. Based on this success, the *long term objective* of the SWIG is to develop a strong presence within the international Semantic Web community and foster a Canadian semantic Web industry.

The CSWWS received a total of 29 contributions of which 25 where short/long papers, 2 positions papers and 2 tutorials. Although the majority came from Canada, we received contributions from several countries around the world like Austria, France, Iran, India, Netherland, Pakistan Switzerland, Turkey, and USA. After careful review of these contribution by the international program committee members, 13 papers, two tutorials on "MDA Standards for Ontology Development" and "State of Affairs in Semantic Web Services" were accepted for presentation of this one day event. In addition, positions papers were also included in the symposium for a birds of feather session.

The program of this symposium covers a variety of well known topics of interest to the semantic Web community. They are Languages, tools and methodologies for the Semantic Web, Semantic Web-based ontology management and engineering, Semantic Web Services (description, discovery, invocation, composition), Semantic Web-based Knowledge Management, Semantic Grid and semantic Grid services, Semantic Web for databases, Semantic Web Mining , Trust, privacy, security on the Semantic Web, Practical applications of the Semantic Web techniques in e-business, e-commerce, e-government and e-learning, Artificial intelligence methods and tools for the Semantic Web, Software agents on the Semantic Web, Visualization and modeling of the semantic Web.

We sincerely thank the people without whom this event would not have been possible in the first place. First, our gratitude goes to the program committee members who actively took part in the evaluation process of the contributions submitted. Their frank criticisms, insightful comments and suggestions were indeed outstanding. Then, we need to acknowledge that this publication has been possible thanks to the recommendations of Michael Huhns at the University of South Carolina, Munindar Singh at University of North Carolina USA, Dieter Fensel at Vrije Universiteit in Netherland, Will Fitzgerald at NASA AMES Research Center, and Bruce Spencer at N.R.C, New Brunswick,Canada.

April 3 2006

Mamadou Tadiou Koné

Daniel Lemire

Program Committee

Chairs

Koné Mamadou Tadiou, Université Laval, Canada

Daniel Lemire, Université du Québec à Montréal, Canada

Program committee members

Abdolreza Abhari (Ryerson University, Toronto, Canada)

Ahmad Kayed (SNCMonash University, Australia),

Alain Auger (Defence R&D Canada, Canada),

Alain Léger (France Telecom R&D, Tech. et Direct. de la Recherche, France),

Aldo Gangemi (Institute of Cognitive Sc. and Technologies, Roma, Italy),

Alessio Bertone (Inst. for Applied Math. and Info. Tech., N.R.C., Italy),

Alexander Wahler (NIWA-WEB Solutions, Austria),

Ali A. Ghorbani (University of New Brunswick, Canada),

Althea Liang Qianhui (Singapore Management University, Singapore),

André Trudel (Acadia University, Nova Scotia, Canada),

Andre Valente, (Knowledge Systems Ventures, LLC, USA),

Andreas Hotho (University of Kassel, Germany),

Anupriya Ankolekar (Carnegie Mellon University, USA),

Arash Shaban-Nejad (Concordia Univesrity, Montréal, Canada),

Ashok U. Mallya (North Carolina State University, USA),

Atanas Kiryakov (Ontotext Lab, Sirma Group, Bulgaria),

Atilla Elçi (Eastern Mediterranean University, Turkey),

Axel Polleres (DERI Innsbruck, Austria),

Bernard Moulin (Laval University, Québec, Canada),

Bettina Berendt (Humboldt University Berlin, Germany),

Bill Andersen (Ontology Works, Inc., MD, USA),

Bruce Spencer (National Research Council, New Brunswick, Canada),

Carlos Viegas Damásio (Informática, Universidade Nova de Lisboa, Portugal),

Christopher Baker (Concordia University, Montréal, Québec, Canada),

Curtis Gittens (Info~Tech Research Group, Canada),

Daniela Berardi (Università di Roma La Sapienza, Roma, Italy),

David Sadek (France Telecom R&D, Paris, France),

Deborah L. McGuinness (Stanford U., Knowledge Systems Laboratory, USA),

Demetrios G. Sampson (University of Piraeus, Greece),

Dieter Fensel (Vrije U. and DERI International, Amsterdam, Netherland),

Dimitris Plexousakis (University of Crete, Greece),

Dogac Asuman (Middle Eastern Technical University, METU, Turkey),

Dumitru Roman (DERI Innsbruck, Austria),

Eero Hyvönen (Helsinki University of Technology (TKK), Finland),

Fabien Gandon (Inst. Nat. de Recherche en Info. et Automatique, France),

Francesco Guerra (U. di Modena e Reggio E., Italy),

Fred Popowich (Simon Fraser U., British Columbia, Canada),

Glen Newton (National Research Council (CISTI), Canada),

Gregoris Mentzas (National Technical University of Athens, Greece),

Gregory Butler (Concordia University, Montreal, Canada),

Hai Zhuge (Inst. of Comp. Tech. & Chinese Academy of Sc., Beijing, China),

Heiner Stuckenschmidt (Vrije Universiteit Amsterdam, Netherland),

Hideaki Takeda (National Institute of Informatics, Tokyo, Japan),

Ian Dickinson (Hewlett-Packard Laboratories, UK),

Jae Kyu LEE (Singapore Management U.),

Jan Maluszynski (Linköping University, Sweden),

Jean Charlet (Université Paris 6, France),

Jinan Fiaidhi (Lakehead University, Thunder Bay, Ontario, Canada),

Jingwei Huang (Enterprise Integration Lab., University of Toronto, Canada),

Joel Sachs (University of Maryland, Baltimore County, USA),

Joerg Evermann (Victoria University Wellington, New Zealand),

Jorge Cardoso (University of Madeira, Portugal),

Jos de Bruijn (DERI, University of Innsbruck, Innsbruck, Austria),

Khalil Abuosba (The Arab Academy, Jordan),

Krishnaprasad Thirunarayan (Wright State University, Dayton, USA),

Leo Obrst (The MITRE Corporation, VA, USA),

Leonid A. Kalinichenko (Russian Academy of Sciences, Moscow, Russia),

Li Ding (University of Maryland Baltimore County, USA),

Li Qin (Western New England College, USA),

Ludger van Elst (German Research Center for Artificial Intelligence [DFKI],

Luis Llana (U. Complutense de Madrid, Spain),

Germany), Magdalini Eirinaki (Athens U. of Eco. and Business, Greece),

Manuel Núñez García with Luis Llana (U. Complutense de Madrid, Spain),

Marek Hatala (Simon Fraser U., Canada),

Riccardo Albertoni (National Research Council [CNR-IMATI-GE], Italy),

Richard Benjamins (Intelligent Software Components, S.A., Spain),

Riichiro Mizoguchi (ISIR, Osaka University, Japan),

Robin Cohen (University of Waterloo, Canada),

Robert M. Colomb (University of Queensland, Australia),

Rose Dieng-Kuntz (INRIA Sophia Antipolis, France),

Sabah Mohammed (Lakehead University, Thunder Bay, Ontario, Canada),

Sandy Liu (National Research Council, Canada),

Sehl Mellouli (Laval University, Québec, Canada),

Sergio F. Castillo Castelblanco (UIS Universitè Industrielle du Santander, Colombia),

Sergio Tessaris (Free University of Bozen-Bolzano, Italy),

Sheila McIlraith (University of Toronto, Canada),

Sonia Bergamaschi (U. di Modena e Reggio E., Italy),

Stephen Downes (National Research Council, Canada),

Stephen Harris (IAM, University of Southampton, UK),

Steve Cayzer (Hewlett-Packard Laboratories, Bristol, UK),

Sven Casteleyn (Vrije Universiteit Brussel, Belgium),

Vipul Kashyap (Clinical Info. R&D, Partners HealthCare System, MA, USA),

Virendra C. Bhavsar (University of New Brunswick, Canada),

Volker Haarslev (Concordia University, Montréal, Québec, Canada),

Weiming Shen (National Research Council, IMTI Canada),

Yevgen Biletskiy (University of New Brunswick, Canada),

Ying Ding (Digital Enterprise Res. Inst [DERI], Austria),

Ying Chen (IBM China ResearchLab,China),

York Sure (Institute AIFB, University of Karlsruhe, Germany),

Yoshinobu Kitamura (Osaka University, Japan),

Vladimir Geroimenko (University of Plymouth, UK).

Service-Oriented Computing: Multiagent Foundation, Robust Applications, and Research Agenda

Michael N. Huhns

Center of Information Technology at the University of South Carolina, USA.
huhns@sc.edu

Description of Talk

In contrast to the original Web's content, which was designed for human use and comprehension, the Semantic Web's content is for computer use and understanding. Many organizations are attempting to make the Web computer-friendly via Web services, but current incarnations of these technologies are subject to several limitations:

- · A Web service knows only about itself — not about its users, clients, or customers.
- · Web services are not designed to use and reconcile ontologies among each other or with their clients.
- · Web services are passive until invoked; they can't provide alerts or updates when new information becomes available.
- · Web services do not cooperate with each other or self-organize, although they can be composed by external systems.

Overcoming the limitations appears to require agent-like capabilities. Agents have the potential to harmonize Web services' behaviors and reconcile and exploit Web sources' semantics. This talk focuses on the role of agents as next-generation Web services and the business advantages that will result. It also specifies the research that is needed to achieve the results.

A Semantic Web Mediation Architecture

Michael Stollberg[1], Emilia Cimpian[1], Adrian Mocan[1], and Dieter Fensel[1,2]

[1] Digital Enterprise Research Institute Innsbruck (DERI Austria), Institute for Computer Science, University of Innsbruck, Technikerstrasse 21a, A-6020 Innsbruck, Austria.
[2] Digital Enterprise Research Institute (DERI Ireland), IDA Business Park, Lower Dangan, Galway, Ireland

Abstract. Heterogeneity is an inherent characteristic of open and distributed environments like the Internet that can hamper Web resources and Web services from successful interoperation. Mediation can be used to resolve these issues, which are critical problems in the Semantic Web. Appropriate technologies for mediation need to cover two aspects: first, techniques for handling the different kinds of heterogeneity that can occur between Web resources, and secondly logical components that connect resources and apply required mediation technique along with invocation and execution facilities. This paper presents an integrated model for mediation on the Semantic Web with special attention to Semantic Web services that is developed around the Web Service Modeling Ontology WSMO. Covering both dimensions, we explain the techniques developed for handling different types of heterogeneity as well as the components and architecture for establishing interoperability on the Semantic Web if not given a priori.

1 Introduction

Due to its design principle of decentralization, the World Wide Web is a network of decoupled, independently working computers. This makes the Web heterogeneous by nature: people create web sites and applications independently, resulting in mismatches that hamper information interchange and interoperability 4. In consequence, the Semantic Web - envisioned for better supporting information processing and computing over the Web on basis of on-tologies and Web services as an augmentation of the existing Internet 3 - will be heterogeneous as well. Techniques for handling and resolving mismatches that hamper interoperability of Web resources require mediation, which be-comes a central pillar of next generation Web technologies 8.

In the early 1990ies, Wiederhold propagated so-called *mediator-orientated architectures* for heterogeneity handling in IT systems 26. In these architectures, mediators are integrated components capable of dynamically handling heterogeneities that hamper system components from successful interoperation. For generic, application independent mediation, the mechanisms for mismatch resolution need to work on a structural level based on declarative resource descriptions. A main merit of the Semantic Web is that resources carry semantic descriptions, which allows mediation techniques to be defined on a semantic level. Understanding Semantic Web services as an integrated technology for realizing the Semantic Web 24, OWL-S 14 defines an ontology for semantically describing Web services while remaining orthogonal to mediation 19. In contrast, the Web Service Modeling Ontology WSMO 13 identifies mediation as a first class citizen and in consequence defines mediators as a core element of Semantic Web services.

This paper presents the mediation framework and techniques developed within WSMO as an integrated technology for handling and resolving all kinds of heterogeneity that potentially occur on the Semantic Web. In order to attain a mediator-oriented architecture in accordance to Wiederhold's conception, our approach distinguishes two dimensions: (1) the *mediation techniques* for resolving different kinds of heterogeneities that can arise within the Semantic Web, (2) *logical components* that connect resources and apply required mediation techniques; these are embedded in a software architecture for dynamic invocation and execution. Figure 1 shows the structure of the mediation model that we subsequently explicate and position within related work in this paper.

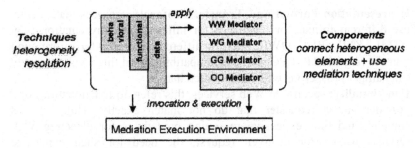

Fig.1 Dimensions of Mediation

Throughout the paper we apply the well-studied Virtual Travel Agency use case for illustration. Referring to 25 for a detailed specification, a Web service provider VTA offers end-user travel services by dynamically using and aggregating other Web services. Requesters can define several different goals, e.g. buying train or flight tickets, booking hotels, as well as combination of these or similar travel related requests. For resource modelling, we use the Web Service Modeling Ontology Language WSML that provides a structural and logical language for WSMO 7.

2 Mediation Levels and Techniques

The first dimension of our model is concerned with the types of heterogeneities that can occur within the Semantic Web. Each heterogeneity type requires a specific technique for mismatch resolution, which we refer to as *levels of mediation*. Extending the heterogeneity types and corresponding mediation levels first identified in 8, developing Semantic Web technology has revealed the four types of heterogeneity enlisted below. We explain this categorization and then reveal mediation techniques for each level developed around WSMO.

1. **Terminology:** Web services or other Web resources use different terminologies; e.g. one entity understands 'name' to be the full name of a person, and another one defines 'name' to only denote the family name. This can hamper successful interoperation on the semantic level, i.e. concerning the meaning of information.

2. **Representation Format and Transfer Protocol:** resources that interact use different formats or languages for information representation (e.g. HTML, XML, RDF, OWL, etc.), or different protocols for information transfer (e.g. HTTP, RPC, etc.); incompatibilities on this level obviously can hamper prosperous information interchange.
3. **Functionality:** specific to Web services, this refers to functionalities of a provider and a requester that do not match exactly. This enforces complex and thus expensive reasoning procedures for detecting Web services usable for a given request; the need for such expensive operations can be reduced by gaining and utilizing knowledge on the functional heterogeneities, as explained below in more detail.
4. **Business Process:** also specific to Web services, this denotes mismatches in the supported interaction behavior of Web services and clients. This can hamper successful interaction on a behavioral level for consumption or interaction of Web services.

2.1 Data Level Mediation

The first mediation level addresses the first two types of mediation identified above. As these are strongly interconnected and can be handled by similar techniques, they are consolidated as *data level mediation* 16. This provides a general mediation technique for Semantic Web applications.

The most common type of mismatch in the Semantic Web occurs due to usage of different terminologies by entities that shall interchange information. Within ontology-based environments like the Semantic Web, this results from usage of heterogeneous ontologies as the terminological basis for resource or information descriptions. A main merit of ontologies is that such mismatches can be handled on a semantic level by so-called *ontology integration techniques* explained below in more detail. Regarding the second type of heterogeneity on representation formats and transfer protocols, a suitable way of resolving such heterogeneities is to lift the data from the syntactic to a semantic level on basis of ontologies, and then resolve the mismatches on this level 17 .

Techniques Used.

The central mediation techniques for the data level are semantically enabled information integration techniques. Collectively referred to as ontology integration 1, the main techniques are ontology mapping, alignment, and merging that we briefly summarize in accordance to 18.

- *Ontology mapping* involves the creation of a set of rules and axioms that precisely define how terms from one ontology relate with terms from the other ontology. These rules and axioms are expressed using a mapping language, as in the example given below. Ontology mapping refers to mapping definitions only, while none of the involved ontologies is changed or altered.
- *Ontology alignment* has the role of bringing the involved ontologies in a mutual agreement. As for the ontology mapping technique, the ontologies are kept separately but at least one of them has to be altered such as the involved ontologies are "aligned" (i.e. they match) in their overlapping
- *Ontology merging* results in creation of a new ontology that replaces the original ontologies. The merging can be done either by unification (all the terms from the involved ontologies are included and mismatches between the overlapping ones are resolved) or by intersection (only the overlapping terms are included and their mismatches reconciliated).

Illustrative Example.

Within the VTA use case, consider that a client uses a different ontology than the VTA Web service description. We consider the following example for illustrating one terminology mismatch handling: the ontology used by the requestor contains the concept station, and the one used by the provider contains the concept route:

```
concept station
  startLocation impliesType boolean
  destinationLocation impliesType boolean
  name impliesType string
concept route
  from hasType (0 1) string
  to hasType (0 1) string
```

There are two terminological mismatches: (1) the attribute startLocation of the concept station corresponds to the attribute from in the route concept;

(2) the attribute `destinationLocation` of the concept `station` corresponds to the attribute `to` of the `route` concept. In order to allow automated processing by ontology mapping, we need to create three mapping rules: one for stating the relation between the two concepts and two for imposing the mappings between their attributes. The following shows this using an *abstract* mapping language, propagated in 21 for higher flexibility and easier maintenance of mappings.

```
Mapping(http://www.example.org/ontologies/TravelRequestOntology#station
       http://www.example.org/ontologies/TravelOfferOntology#route
       classMapping(one-way station route))
Mapping(http://www.example.org/ontologies/TravelRequestOntology#destination_Location
       http://www.example.org/ontologies/TravelOfferOntology#to
       attributeMapping( one-way
        [(station) destination_Location => city]  [(route) to => string]))
        valueCondition(station [(station) destination_Location => boolean] true)
Mapping(http://www.example.org/ontologies/TravelRequestOntology#start_Location
       http://www.example.org/ontologies/TravelOfferOntology#from
       attributeMapping( one-way
        [(station) start_Location => boolean]   [(route) from => string]))
        valueCondition(station [(station) start_Location => boolean] true)
```

2.2 Functional Level Mediation

Heterogeneities on the functional level arise when the functionality provided by a Web service does not precisely match with the one requested by a client. For instance, in our VTA scenario a requester defines a goal for purchasing a ticket to travel from Innsbruck to Vienna without specifying the type of ticket (i.e. for a bus, train, or plane); an available Web service offers train tickets from Innsbruck to Vienna. Here, the Web service is only usable for solving the request under the condition that the ticket is a train ticket.

We expect situations like this to be the common case for Web service usage. In order to determine the usability of a Web service for a given request - commonly referred to as functional discovery, a central reasoning task for automated Web service usage - complex and thus expensive reasoning procedures are required 11. As this hampers efficiency of Semantic Web technologies with regard to Web scalability, we use so-called *Δ-relations* for denoting functional heterogeneities and allow omitting or reducing the need for such expensive operations.

Techniques Used

The central technique for functional level mediation are Δ-relations that denote the explicit logical relationship between functional descriptions of Web services and goals. Functional descriptions are a central pillar of comprehensive Web service description frameworks like OWL-S and WSMO. Defined as conditions on pre- and post-states in some first-order logic derivate, they provide a black box description of normal runs of a Web service omitting information on how technical service invocation 12.

Following 9, the desired relationship can most adequately be described as the logical difference between functional descriptions. For two given functional descriptions α and β as first-order logic formulas, the Δ-relation between them is defined as $Δ(α, β) = (α \wedge ¬β) \vee (¬α \wedge β)$; this means that Δ contains those elements that are models for either α or β and not common to them. A Δ-relation defines a symmetric relation between α and β; when concatenating $Δ(α, β)$ with either α or β we obtain logical equality with the respective other formula. This allows definition of beneficial algorithmic procedures for omitting or reducing the need of expensive reasoning operations in functional Web service discovery. We refer to 23 for details on this technique.

Illustrative Example.

For purpose of illustration, we consider the Δ-relation between functional descriptions of the goal and the Web service in the example outlined above. The following gives the WSMO element definitions for (1) the postcondition of the goal capability (capabilities denote functional descriptions in WSMO 13), and (2) the capability postcondition of the VTA Web service description.

```
goal _"http://www.example.org/goals/goal1"
capability
postcondition
definedBy
?x memberOf ticket[passenger hasValue "Michael Stollberg,
    origin hasValue innsbruck, destination hasValue vienna,
    date hasValue 2006-01-20].

webService _"http://www.example.org/webservices/ws1"
capability
postcondition
definedBy
?x memberOf trainTicket[passenger hasValue ?pass,
```

```
origin hasValue ?ori, destination hasValue ?dest,
date hasValue ?date] and
?pass memberOf person and
?ori memberOf city and ?dest memberOf city
?date memberOf date and (?date >= currentdate).
```

The Δ-relation between the postconditions is given below. It basically states defines all tickets that are not tickets to be models of Δ, and so forth for the attribute value types. Computable by the above formula, this explicates the Δ-relation to denote the logical difference between the source and target component.

```
?x memberOf ticket and not(?x memberOf trainTicket) and
?x[passenger hasValue ?pass,
   origin hasValue ?ori, destination hasValue ?dest,
   date hasValue ?date] and
?pass memberOf person and
?ori memberOf city and ?dest memberOf city and
?date memberOf date.
concept route
  from hasType (0 1) string
  to hasType (0 1) string
```

2.3 Process Level Mediation

The third mediation technique is concerned with mismatches on the behavioral level that can occur during the Web service consumption or interaction. For instance, at some point during the consumption of a Web service S by a requester R, R expects an acknowledgement while S waits for the next input; so, the interaction process between R and S runs into a deadlock situation.

Within the WSMO framework, this mediation level refers to the interaction behavior described in the so-called interfaces of a Web services 22. These specify the interaction behavior supported or expected by the Web service for consuming its functionality (choreography), and for interacting with other Web services that are aggregated in order to achieve the service functionality (orchestration). WSMO defines a formal description language that integrates ontologies with Abstract State Machines 5 for representing the dynamics of service interface descriptions.

Techniques Used

Business process level mismatches can occur in every interaction a Web service is involved in. These heterogeneities can be resolved by inspecting the individual business processes of the entities that interact and trying to establish a valid process for interaction on basis of pre-defined mediation operations on business processes. 6 presents a prototype that supports the patterns for process level mismatch resolution shown in Figure 2.

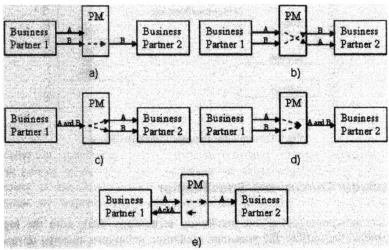

Fig.2 Process Mediation Patterns - (a) Unexpected Message Stop, (b) Order Inversion, (c) Splitting, (d) Merging, (e) Dummy Acknowledgement

Illustrative Example.

The following exemplifies how the process mediation patterns can be applied for resolving a communication mismatch in the VTA scenario. A requestor R wants to first send information about the travel date, followed by the start location and end location of the trip; the provider P wants to receive first the route, and then the data of the trip. R and P use the ontologies with the concepts introduced in Section 2.1.

Figure 3 gives an overview of this situation. The interaction between the requester and the provider is initialized by an outgoing message from R with content of type date. But P expects an incoming message with a route. The

Process Mediator inspects the interaction behavior of *R*, determining that the second and third outgoing messages contain instances of `station` that can be mediated to `route` by the mappings defined above. Hence, the Process Mediator applies the order inversion pattern in order to hold the first message from *R*, and then - after data level mediation - uses the merging pattern; now, the information can be submitted to *P* in the expected order and terminology.

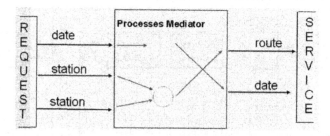

Fig.3 Example for Process Level Mediation

3 Mediator Component Specification

The second dimension of our mediation technology deals with the logical components that utilize the presented mediation techniques in order to resolve mismatches. With respect to the dynamic and evolving nature of the Semantic Web, essential design principles for a comprehensive mediation architecture are *minimality*, i.e. modularized mediation in distinct components, and *strong decoupling* with respect to reusability of mediation facilities 8. The following describes how this is realized within the concept of mediators in WSMO, explaining the conceptual model and the explicit logical definition of mediator components.

3.1 Mediator Typology

WSMO defines four top level notions and provides a structure for semantic description of each 13. Understood to be the general elements of Semantic Web service technology, these are *Ontologies* that provide the formal terminology definition for the domain of discourse, *Goals* that specify the objective a client wants to achieve, *Web services* as the functionality implementation accessible over the Web, and *Mediators* for resolving possibly occurring mismatches.

Four different types of mediators are distinguished that appear to be applicable within the Web service usage process 24. The mediator type is indicated by a prefix denoting the type of the source and the target component; each mediator type applies those mediation technique required for resolving the heterogeneities that can possibly occur between the connected components. Figure 4 gives an overview of the WSMO mediator typology further explained below.

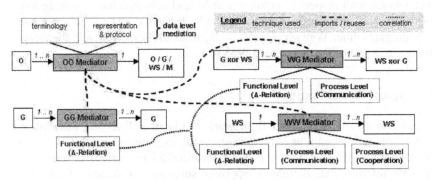

Fig. 4 WSMO Mediator Typology

OO Mediators provide the data level mediation component. The source elements are ontologies or other OO Mediators, while the target can be any WSMO top level element. The only mediation technique used is data level mediation. OO Mediators provide a general mediation component for ontology-based applications.

GG Mediators connect WSMO goals, i.e. both the source and target are goals. The mediation techniques used are (1) data mediation by usage of OO Mediators, and (2) functional level mediation on basis of Δ-relations that precisely define the logical relationship between source and target goals. As outlined in Section 2.2, the purpose of the latter is increasing the efficiency of functional discovery.

WG Mediators connect Web services and goals in case a Web service is not usable for solving a goal a priori. WG Mediators can be defined in two directions: either the source elements are one or more Web Services and the target is a Goal, or the other way around. The used mediation techniques are (1) data level mediation by usage of OO Mediators, (2) functional level mediation for establishing usability of a Web service for solving a Goal if not given a priori, and (3) process level mediation for resolving potential mismatches on the communication level between the source and target component.

WW Mediators connect Web services that interact but are not compatible a priori. Its source and target components are Web services. The related mediation techniques are (1) data level mediation by usage of OO Mediators, (2) functional level mediation for handling functional heterogeneities, and (3) process level mediation for resolving mismatches between the source and target service with respect to communication and coordination of interaction. Most commonly, the source component of a WW Mediator is a Web service W that aggregates other Web services $W_1 \ldots W_n$ in its orchestration, and the target component is one of the aggregated Web services W_j.

3.2 Logical Specification

A main feature of the WSMO framework is that it defines the description structure of its elements as a meta-layer ontology, following OMG's Meta-Object Facility 13. This allows explicit meta-model definitions of elements and their interrelation, thereby supporting semantic validation of element definitions and providing an unambiguous specification for execution.

The meta-model ontological description of WSMO mediators consists of a superclass mediator that is refined within the distinct mediator types. It defines the source and target component of a mediator, the mediation techniques used for mismatch resolution, the imported other mediators, and non-functional properties as the means for element descriptions used in WSMO. While referring to 15 for detailed meta-model definitions of each WSMO mediator type, the following inspects a concrete mediator definition in detail in order to explicate the presented model.

The listing below shows a WG mediator from the VTA usage scenario that connects the Web service ws1 and the Goal goal1 for ticket purchasing as introduced in Section 2.2. Apart from the Δ-relation for functional level mediation, imagine that the goal and the Web service use heterogeneous ontologies, so we need to apply data level mediation. Therefore, we use an OO Mediator oom1 that contains the mapping definitions outlined in Section 2.1. As the facility for executing the mappings, the data mediator provided in WSMX is used (see next section); this is defined in the `mediationService` description slot. Moreover, process level mismatches might occur when the goal and Web service start interacting. Hence, the `mediationService` description slot indicates that the WSMX Process Mediator (also see next section) is used for handling these.

```
wgMediator _"http://www.example.org/mediators/wgm1"
source _"http://www.example.org/webservices/ws1"
target _"http://www.example.org/goals/goal1"
importsOntology
         {_"http://www.example.org/ontologies/TravelRequestOntolo
          gy"
    _"http://www.example.org/ontologies/TravelOfferOntology"}
usedMediators _"http://www.example.org/mediators/oom1"
deltarelation
definedBy
?x memberOf ... // omitted here (see section 2.2)
mediationService {_"http://www.wsmx.org/datamediator"
    _"http://www.wsmx.org/processmediator"}
```

This example reveals that WSMO mediators explicitly specify elements that are needed in order to establish interoperability between Web services if not given a priori. Apart from the source and target components, all mediation definitions (i.e. mappings and Δ-relations) are explicitly specified as well as the components used for executing the mediation. Consequently, WSMO mediators provide a specification framework for mediation definition and execution whereby each element definition is modularized and decoupled to the maximum possible extent in order to achieve a flexible mediation technology. In conclusion, the most important feature of mediator components is that they are *minimal* and *modular* components, meaning that each mediator only covers a minimal aspect of heterogeneity handling while several mediators might be used within a specific application scenario. Additionally, the model of WSMO mediators exhibits the following properties:

- OO Mediators provide a data level mediation component generally applicable for the Semantic Web; all data level mismatches are handled by OO Mediators via re-use in the Web service specific mediator types;
- In case that the same Goals and Web services are connected by GG, WG, and WW Mediators, specific logical correlations exist between the Δ-relations defined in the respective mediators.

4 Reference Implementation

In order to demonstrate the implementability of the presented mediation framework and technology, the following outlines its realization within the Web Service Execution Environment WSMX 10, a reference implementation of the overall WSMO framework (homepage: www.wsmx.org).

4.1   The Web Service Execution Environment WSMX

The Web Service Execution Environment WSMX is a platform for automated discovery, selection, composition, invocation and execution of Semantic Web services. In order to enable automated usage of Semantic Web services, WSMX takes a WSMO goal specification as input and dynamically utilizes components required for resolving the goal.

The WSMX architecture depicted in Figure 5 consists of two types of services: application services and base services. The former provide components for central reasoning tasks for Semantic Web services like discovery, as required for automated goal resolution on the Problem Solving Layer. The base services offer low-level support such as reasoning or semantic based storage/retrieval mechanisms. For instance, the Process Mediator service may use a reasoner when analyzing candidate web services, previously retrieved from the repository. Dependent on the concrete goal to be solved and on available Web services, WSMX invokes respective application services.

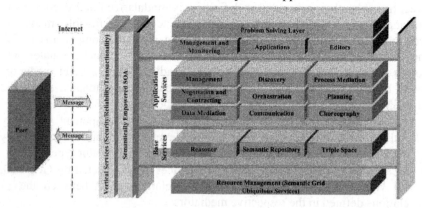

Fig.5 WSMX Architecture

4.2 Dynamic Mediation Invocation

The WSMX Data Mediator 16 is invoked in two situations: during the discovery phase and during the communication phase. The need for data mediation is necessary when the ontologies of the goal and of the candidate or selected web service are different - in both the discovery or the communication phase. For data level heterogeneity handling, it uses the ontology mapping technique described above to resolve the mismatches that can appear between two given ontologies. The mappings between ontologies are created in a semi-automatic manner during design time and stored in a persistent storage. That is, these mappings are retrieved during run-time by WSMX and applied on the incoming data (i.e. ontology instances) to transform it from the terms of one ontology in the terms of another ontology (this process in known as instance transformation). The same mappings can also be used for determining which concepts from the mapped ontologies are semantically related (and how). The former functionality is required to enable the process level mediation (it solves the data heterogeneity for the communication stage), while the latter is required to enable the functional level mediation (solves the data heterogeneity that appears in the functional descriptions).

The WSMX Process Mediator 6 works on the behavior interface descriptions of goals and the Web services (i.e. WSMO choreographies) to determine if the communication is interrupted by behavioral mismatches. As a consequence, the process mediator acts as an intermediary and maintains instances of the two choreographies analyzing what messages are expected and in what order. Following this analysis, the order of messages might be change by delaying, suppressing or even generating of fake messages as described in Section 2.3. It is worth noting that the analysis of sent and expected messages is done with the support of the data mediation level when the two choreographies use different ontologies.

5 Related Work

We are not aware of any other comprehensive model for mediation on the Semantic Web, as most existing approaches for heterogeneity handling only address partial aspects of mediation. However, while related work on the distinct mediation techniques is discussed elsewhere (see references in Section 2), the following examines works on mediation architectures and positions our approach therein.

An early approach for realizing a mediation technology that follows Wiederhold's propagation has been presented in the MedMaker project in the mid 1990s 20. The approach is based on a proprietary, not ontology-based description language for resources called the Object Exchange Model (OEM), and a Mediator Specification Language (MSL), which are both defined in first-order logic. The latter is used for specifying rules that integrate heterogeneous OEM resource descriptions, thereby enabling information interchange between heterogeneous resources. The referenced paper further presents a system implementation Mediator Specification Interpreter (MSI) that is capable of reading and executing MSL specifications. This work can be seen as a predecessor of data level mediation as realized in OO Mediators (see Section 3). OEM refers to ontologies, respectively WSMO descriptions of goals and Web Services, while MSL refers to ontology mapping languages for data level mediation.

A more recent approach concerned with the formal specification of mediators as software components is presented in 2. Addressing process level mediation, the approach proposes eight basic mediation patterns - four for bilateral communication and four for the multilateral mediation patterns, along with combinations and refinements of the basic patterns. However, all these basic patterns as well as their combinations and refinements are defined as hard-coded Abstract State Machines, and pre-defined predicates, obtaining in this way an inflexible, rigid model. In our approach we aim at being more flexible and support extensions of the process mediation patterns addressed.

Concerning the needs for mediation within Semantic Web services, the Web Service Modeling Framework WSMF - the conceptual basis of WSMO - distinguishes three levels of mediation 8: (1) Data Level Mediation - mediation between heterogeneous data sources; (2) Protocol Level Mediation - mediation between heterogeneous communication protocols, and (3) Process Level Mediation - mediation between heterogeneous business processes. While we have adopted these levels and realized respective semantically techniques for mismatch resolution, the framework presented here introduces functional mediation as a novel level. On basis of Δ-relations that explicitly denote the logical relationship between functional descriptions of goals and Web services, this allows increasing the efficiency of Semantic Web service technologies.

6 Conclusions and Future Work

In this paper we have presented an integrated technology for mediation on the Semantic Web developed around WSMO. Heterogeneity being an inherent characteristic of the Web and hence its successors, the presented approach covers all aspects relevant for heterogeneity handling on the Web while remaining open to future developments on mismatch resolution techniques.

The first dimension of the mediation model identifies the types of heterogeneity that potentially can occur on the Semantic Web - that is general Semantic Web applications and Web services in particular. With respect to the suitable techniques for mismatch resolution, we distinguish three levels of mediation: the data level, the functional level, and the process level. For each of these, we have outlined ongoing developments for semantically enabled mismatch resolution techniques. The second dimension of our model deals with components for heterogeneity handling for which we provide WSMO mediators. Defined as logical elements, the four types of WSMO mediators allow explicitly specifying the elements and components for establishing interoperability if not given a priori, whereby each mediator remains a minimal and modularized element itself. In order to demonstrate the realizability of the presented model, we have outlined its implementation within WSMX.

The presented approach realizes Wiederhold's conception of mediator-oriented architectures as follows. While Semantic Web and especially Semantic Web services by definition have declarative resource descriptions, we have presented semantically enabled mediation techniques that allow general purpose, application independent heterogeneity handling and resolution. Furthermore, WSMO mediators provide unambiguous logical definitions of the mediation components that can be executed dynamically with respect to the goal that is to be solved.

In conclusion, we consider the presented mediation model to be sufficient for the Semantic Web as it defines architectural components that applies appropriate mediation facilities for the types of heterogeneity that can appear between the core elements of Semantic Web service systems. The main merit of this model is that each mediator is *minimal* (i.e., it covers only a minimal aspect of heterogeneity handling), and *modular* (i.e., several mediators are combined for specific application purposes). This enables reuse of mediation facilities and eases their maintenance within dynamic and evolving environments like the Internet.

Acknowledgement

This material is based upon works supported by the EU funding under the DIP project (FP6 - 507483), and by the Science Foundation Ireland under Grant No. SFI/02/CE1/I131. The authors would like to thank the members of the WSMO working group (www.wsmo.org) for fruitful input and discussion.

References

1. Alexiev, V. et al. *Information Integration with Ontologies*. Wiley, West Sussex, UK, 2005.
2. Barros, A. and E. Börger. *A Compositional Framework for Service Interaction Patterns and Interaction Flows*. Technical Report, 2005.
3. Berners-Lee, T.; Hendler, J., and Lassila, O. The Semantic Web. In *Scientific American*, 284(5), 2001.
4. Berners-Lee, T. *Weaving the Web*. Harper, San Francisco, USA, 1999.
5. Börger, E. and Stärk, R. *Abstract State Machines. A Method for High-Level System Design and Analysis*. Springer, Berlin, Heidelberg, 2003.
6. Cimpian, E. and Mocan, A. *WSMX Process Mediation Based on Choreographies*. In Proceedings of the 1st International Workshop on Web Service Choreography and Orchestration for Business Process Management at the BPM 2005, Nancy, France, 2005.
7. de Bruijn, J. (ed.). *The Web Service Modeling Language WSML*. WSML Deliverable D16.1 final version 0.2, 2005. available from http://www.wsmo.org/TR/d16/d16.1/v0.2/.
8. Fensel, D. and Bussler, C.. The Web Service Modeling Framework WSMF. *Electronic Commerce Research and Applications*, 1(2), 2002.
9. Fensel. D. and Straatman, R. *The Essence of Problem-Solving Methods: Making Assumptions to Gain Efficiency*. International Journal of Human-Computer Studies, 48(2):181--215, 1998.
10. Haller, E. Cimpian, A. Mocan, E. Oren, and C. Bussler. *WSMX - A Semantic Service-Oriented Architecture*. In Proceedings of the International Conference on Web Service (ICWS 2005), Orlando, Florida, 2005.
11. Keller, U. et al.. *Automatic Location of Services*. In Proceedings of the 2nd European Semantic Web Conference (ESWC 2005), Crete, Greece, 2005.

12. Lausen, H. (ed). *Functional Description of Web Services*. Deliverable D28.1v0.1 Oct 20 2005, WSML Working Group. online: http://www.wsmo.org/TR/.
13. Lausen, H. and Polleres, A. and Roman, D. (eds.). *Web Service Modeling Ontology (WSMO)*. W3C Member Submission 3 June 2005, 2005. online: http://www.w3.org/Submission/WSMO/.
14. Martin, D. (ed.). *OWL-S: Semantic Markup for Web Services*. W3C Member Submission 22 November 2004, http://www.w3.org/Submission/OWL-S.
15. Mocan, A.; Cimpian, E., and Stollberg, M. (eds.). *WSMO Mediators*. Deliverable D29, 2005. Most recent version at: http://www.wsmo.org/TR/d29/.
16. Mocan, A. (ed.). *WSMX Data Mediation*. WSMX Working Draft D13.3, 2005. available at: http://www.wsmo.org/TR/d13/d13.3/v0.2/.
17. Moran, M. and Mocan, A. *Towards Translating between XML and WSML based on mappings between XML Schema and an equivalent WSMO Ontology*. In Proc. of the WIW 2005 Workshop on WSMO Implementations, Innsbruck, Austria, 2005.
18. Noy., N. *Semantic Integration: a Survey of Ontology-based Approaches*. ACM SIGMOD Record, 33(4):65-70, 2004.
19. Paolucci, M. ; Srinivasan, N., and Sycara, K. *Expressing WSMO Mediators in OWL-S*. In Proceedings of the workshop on Semantic Web Services: Preparing to meet the world of Business Applications held at ISWC 2004, Hiroshima, Japan.
20. Papakonstantinou, Y.; Garcia-Molina, H., and Ullman, J. D. *MedMaker: A Mediation System Based on Declarative Specifications*. In Proceedings of the 12th International Conference on Data Engineering, pages 132-141, 1996.
21. Scharffe, F. and de Bruijn, J. *A Language to Specify Mappings between Ontologies*. In Proc. of the Internet Based Systems IEEE Conference (SITIS05), 2005.
22. Scicluna, J.; Polleres, A., and Roman, D.(eds.). *Ontology-based Choreography and Orchestration of WSMO Services*. Deliverable D14, 2005. available at: http://www.wsmo.org/TR/d14/.
23. Stollberg, M.; Cimpian, E., and Fensel, D. *Mediating Capabilities with Delta-Relations*. In Proceedings of the First International Workshop on Mediation in Semantic Web Services at the 3rd International Conference

on Service Oriented Computing (ICSOC 2005), Amsterdam, the Netherlands, 2005.

24. Stollberg, M. et al. *Semantic Web Services - Concepts and Technology*. In N. Ide, D. Cristea, and D. Tufis, editors, Language Technology, Ontologies, and the Semantic Web. Kluwer Publishers (to appear), 2006.

25. Stollberg, M. and Lara, R. (eds.). *WSMO Use Case "Virtual Travel Agency"*. Deliverable D3.3, 2004, http://www.wsmo.org/2004/d3/d3.3/v0.1/.

26. Wiederhold, G. *Mediators in the Architecture of Future Information Systems*. In Computer, 25(3):38-49, 1994.

Applying and Inferring Fuzzy Trust in Semantic Web Social Networks

Mohsen Lesani and Saeed Bagheri

Computer Engineering Department, Sharif University of Technology, Tehran, Iran.
mohsen_lesani@mehr.sharif.edu and bagheri@sharif.edu

Abstract. Social networks let the people find and know other people and benefit form their information. Semantic Web standard ontologies support social network sites for making use of other social networks information and hence help their expansion and unification, making them a huge social network. As social networks are public virtual social places much information may exist in them that may not be trustworthy to all. A mechanism in needed to rate coming news, reviews and opinions about a definite subject from users, according to each user preference. There should be a feature for users to specify how much they trust a friend and a mechanism to infer the trust from one user to another that is not directly a friend of the user so that a recommender site can benefit from these trust ratings for showing trustworthy information to each user from her or his point of view from not only her or his directly trusted friends but also the other indirectly trusted users. This work suggests using fuzzy linguistic terms to specify trust to other users and proposes an algorithm for inferring trust from a person to another person that may be not directly connected in the trust graph of a social network. The algorithm is implemented and compared to an algorithm that let the users to specify their trust with a number in a definite range. While according to the imprecise nature of the trust concept writing and reading a linguistic expression for trust is much more natural than a number for users, the results show that the algorithm offers more precise information than the previously used algorithm especially when contradictory beliefs should be composed and also when a more precise inference is potentially possible in searching deeper paths. As the trust graphs and inference are viewed abstractly, they can be well employed in other multi agent systems.

1 Introduction

All the information that we have is what we ourselves have devised or we have gotten from the others. The information we get from others about different subjects is obviously an important part of our knowledge bases. The social networks such as LiveJournal (http://www.livejournal.com), Orkut (http://www.orkut.com) and so on are growing and becoming more popular day by day. Web based social network sites offer many facilities to their users to find their friends, make new ones and specify their relationships. Some of them let their users to rate and write reviews about films, shows, events and so on. Millions of people are connected to each other in each of such social networks making a large relationship graph. Semantic Web community has proposed a general ontology for people relationships in FOAF (friend of a friend) project (http://www.foaf-project.org/) and many social network sites also offer their user relationship information in accordance to this vocabulary in RDF (http://www.w3.org/RDF/) or OWL (http://www.w3.org/2004/OWL/) files. This makes the foundation for a large distributed social network comprising those individual social networks information. A person may know and be connected to hundreds of people but may not know many others. The user may know how much she or he should rely on the persons she or he directly knows but how about the others? How much does she or he trust a review that is written by a person she or he does not directly know? Recommender sites are favored that offer individualized recommendation for each user about a subject e.g. a film and also an ordered list of reviews from the other users that are directly or indirectly reliable for the user. There is a need to infer how much a person trusts another person in the social network that is not directly connected to the person provided that a person can only specify her or his trust to his direct friends.

Golbeck [1] has researched on trust in social networks and deduced some trust graphs properties from real networks and proposed an algorithm that has called TidalTrust algorithm for inferring trust in trust graphs the trust ratings in which can be numbers in a continuous range.

While the users should specify their trusts to other persons as numbers in TidalTrust [1] algorithm, people naturally use linguistic expressions when they are asked about their trust to other individuals. People tend to specify their trust in expressions like very low, medium or high and so on and specifying trust in crisp numbers may seem odd to them. A user that trusts another user by a medium high value may find no or little difference between 6 and 7 trust values in a trust value scale of 10. Similarly people like to hear linguistic expressions when they ask others about their trust to an unknown person, although this can be told more strongly when a subjective study of users supports it. In connection with the crisp nature of the TidalTrust algorithm, its averaging scheme for composition sometimes infers incorrect trust values. It seems that a crisp number is not enough for conveying accurate information especially contradictory information. Aside form the crisp view of trust, TidalTrust does not report the inference preciseness while the inference along a lowly trusted path even if yielding the same inferred trust value is less precise than the inference done along a highly trusted path. Also TidalTrust confines the search to shortest paths while the information inferred from a long chain of people with high trust between them may be much more precise than the information inferred from a short chain of people with low trust between them.

According to the aforementioned considerations about crisp view of trust and as trust is generally an ambiguous concept fuzzy logic seems an ideal for trust modeling and inference. This research proposes using fuzzy linguistic terms for specifying trust and offers an algorithm called FuzzyTrust algorithm for inferring trust in social networks with such linguistic terms trust ratings. The inference preciseness is also computed for each inference. The FuzzyTrust algorithm results agree well with the results of TidalTrust algorithm for corresponding trust graphs while it outperforms the TidalTrust in reporting richer information especially in contradictory composition situations. A modified version of FuzzyTrust considers not only the shortest paths but also all the longer ones to find the strongest of all the possible paths and results show inference preciseness improvement when longer paths are more trusted sources.

This paper presents some properties of trust first and then the Golbeck's TidalTrust algorithm is explained and then the proposed FuzzyTrust algorithm is offered. Simulation and Results present the experiments and comparisons of the two algorithms and at the end conclusion and future works sections will conclude the paper.

2   Properties of Trust and Trust Graphs

Although trust can be used in different contexts but its meaning is intuitive in each case. Modeling the persons as nodes and friendships or acquaintances as directed edges and trust values as edge labels, social networks are viewed as large directed graphs. The trust rating on an edge is the trust that the source node has to the sink or equally to the information coming from the sink.

2.1   Asymmetry

As two friends have different beliefs and have seen different behaviour form each other, although not usually, the trust they have to each other may be different. This is what makes the trust graph asymmetric.

2.2 Transitivity

Trust may seem not to be transitive i.e. if A highly trusts B and B highly trusts C it does not mean that A also highly trusts C. But it is usual that you ask one of your highly trusted friends about an unknown person and take his opinion as your own. Consider a case when A asks B about a film because A highly trusts B and B does not know about the film so B asks her or his highly trusted friend C that knows about the film while A is unaware of this relationship. B takes C's opinion as her or his own and gives it to A that will also take it as her or his own. A finally takes C's opinion. It is seen that trust is transitive in this sense. Transitivity lets the trust to a person to pass back through a chain of people.

2.3 Composability

If A does not know C, she or he asks her or his friends (Bs) about C. Different friends (Bs) may have different ideas about that person (C). Person A should compose the different ideas she or he receives about C from Bs to infer a unique idea about C. People naturally compose trust value when they receive them from different sources maybe giving higher importance to more trusted sources.

2.4 The Stronger Paths, the More Accurate Inference

When you are to infer the trust to a person and you have the choice of two people chains that have the same depth, you certainly choose the chain that more trust is between the people along it. Golbeck [1] showed that paths with higher trust ratings cause better trust inference.

2.5 The Shorter Paths, the More Accurate Inference

When you hear news from a witness of an event you believe it more than when you hear from some one who has heard from a witness or when you get the news from a deeper chain of people. Similarly when the trust should be inferred it is more desirable to be inferred from a shorter chain of people. Golbeck showed that shorter paths lead to more accurate trust inference results.

She also has presented the following properties. People tend to use higher values of trust when they rate their connections. This is because people are naturally friend with people that they trust more. The people that are connected with high trust ratings agree more and rate other people more similarly than people that are connected with low trust ratings. Also people with high trust rating connections have more common friends than people with lower ones.

3 Tidal Trust Algorithm

The TidalTrust algorithm supports the trust values to be numbers in a continuous range. A simple algorithm for inferring trust in binary trust networks in which only 0 or 1 trust values are allowed where 1 indicates having trust to and 0 indicates having no idea of another person is presented first as a basis for the TidalTrust algorithm. While the pseudo code is a brief explanation, some simplified code snippets were prepared that were reviewed and simplified for reading while their formal object oriented structure were preserved. Contact the authors for them for more clarity as there is not enough room in the current text. The reader is recommended to follow these simplified codes along the algorithm explanation.

```
If source is adjacent to the sink
   return trust rating in the trust graph from the
source to the sink.
else
   compute the trust from the trusted neighbors of
   the source to the sink recursively.
   compute the inferred trust as a rounded average
   between the trust of the trusted neighbors to the
   sink.
```

This algorithm simply returns the trust rating from the source to the sink if they are directly connected and if not, all the trusted neighbors trust to the sink are computed recursively and then an average of them and rounding makes the result. It should be noted that the neighbors with 1 trust rating participate in average computation and all 0 trust rated neighbors are ignored as they are believed to convey no trustworthy information. An extension to this algorithm is to round the trust only at the original source and retain the intermediate trust results as numbers in [0, 1] range.

In order to extend the mentioned average to continuous trust ratings, weighted average is used. If $trust_{sr}$ represents trust rating and $iTrust_{sr}$ represent the inferred trust from s to r, $iTrust_{sr}$ is given by:

$$iTrust_{sr} = \frac{\sum\limits_{i \in adjacent(s)} trust_{si} \times iTrust_{ir}}{\sum\limits_{i \in adjacent(s)} trust_{si}}$$

TidalTrust makes use of the aforementioned properties of the shorter and the stronger paths. The most trustworthy information comes from highest trusted paths and lower trusted ones give lower trustworthy information. The strength property for a path is defined as the minimum trust rating along the path excluding the last trust rating in the path. The path strength from one node to another (considering all paths) is defined as the maximum path strength in all the paths between them and equally the path from source to sink strength value is the maximum trust value that at least one path from source to the sink with all the trust ratings along it excluding the last greater than or equal to the value can be found; this strength will be called the required strength. The reason behind excluding the last trust rating in path strength computation is that although its value is of trust nature but it is the information that we get from the path and all the previous trust ratings along the path contribute to the trust we have to this information. The strength of a path with zero length is the max value by definition.

While the computation excluding the last trust rating is called strength computation, the counterpart including the last trust rating is called the complete strength computation. Note that strength computation in the manner defined is only for the strength from the source to the sink computation and all the strength from the source to midway nodes computations in the incremental strength computation as presented in the algorithm are complete strength computations. The algorithm presented in Golbeck dissertation does not attention to the difference of the last rating but the algorithm presented here for Tidal-Trust has fixed this.

TidalTrust algorithm proposes to limit the information used in averaging to higher trusted paths i.e. giving zero weight to neighbors along lower trusted ones. For inferring trust from a node to the sink, from the node's neighbors that have a path to the sink with a strength greater than or equal to the required strength and hence the trust from them to the sink can be inferred sufficiently strongly those with trust ratings to them greater than or equal to the required strength participate in averaging in TidalTrust algorithm so the weighted averaging equation will become.

$$iTrust_{sr} = \frac{\sum\limits_{i \in Participating(s)} trust_{si} \times iTrust_{ir}}{\sum\limits_{i \in Participating(s)} trust_{si}}$$

Where
Participating(s) =
{n ∈ Nodes |
adjacent(s, n) and trust(s, n) ≥ RequiredStrength
and
pathFromTo(p, n, r) and strength(p) ≥ RequiredStrength}

As it is mentioned shorter paths lead to more accurate inference so Tidal-Trust seeks the shortest paths from the source to the sink by an algorithm similar to breadth first search and any other paths longer than the shortest ones are ignored and the nodes along them do not participate in the inference.

The TidalTrust algorithm which supports inference in trust graphs with continuous trust rating is as follows. Firstly the pseudo code is presented that conveys the main ideas and then a more delved explanation will come afterwards. Here is the pseudo code.

```
The TidalTrust algorithm pseudo code
Forward wave: The required strength computation
        Iterate the nodes from the source to the sink
        similar to the breadth first search level by level
        to find shortest paths.
        Set the path strength from source to any node in
        the next level using the previously set path
        strengths from the source to current level nodes.
Backward wave: The trust from nodes to the sink infer-
ence
        Iterate the nodes form the sink to the source
        level by level.
        If the node is adjacent to the sink then its in-
        ferred trust is simply its trust rating to the
        sink in the trust graph.
        Else (If the node is not adjacent to the sink) do
        weighted averaging on the neighbors with trust
        ratings to them greater than or equal to the re-
        quired strength and that also have a path to the
        sink with a strength greater than or equal to the
        required strength and hence the trust from them to
        the sink is previously inferred strongly enough.
```

The algorithm is named TidalTrust because computation flows from source to sink and then back from sink to source. The algorithm starts with the source node and iterates the adjacent nodes level by level similar to the breadth first search algorithm. Whenever a node is seen it is pushed to a stack to take the nodes in reverse order later. When a node that is not adjacent to the sink is visited, all its neighbors are marked visited and added to the next level search queue if they are not visited before. No previously visited nodes are placed in the next level queue nodes since they have been placed in the previous level queues and shorter paths to them are considered. The path strength to each of the next level search queue nodes are updated whenever a new path containing the current node from the source to them is found and as all the current level nodes are iterated before next level nodes, path strength values for next level nodes is finalized before they are iterated and hence can be used in updating their next level nodes path strength values. Note that the trust ratings from the last level nodes directly to the sink do not contribute to the strength computation form the source to the sink.

If a node is seen that is adjacent to the sink the minimum path length from the source to the sink is set and path strength from source to sink is updated. The functions min and max are supposed to return the minimum and maximum of their parameters respectively and the other parameter when one of the parameters has an invalid value. When all the current level nodes are iterated, depth variable is incremented, the next level search queue replaces the current one and iteration proceeds until all the nodes with a depth below or equal to the minimum depth are iterated. If the depth is equal to max integer value after the loop it means that it is never updated i.e. all the nodes in the connected component containing the source are iterated and no path from the source to the sink could be found, the trust can not be inferred and a dummy value is returned instead of an inferred trust value.

The nodes are popped from the stack and iterated in the reverse order. If a node is adjacent to the sink then its inferred trust to the sink is simply its trust rating to the sink in the trust graph. If not, the trust to the sink is computed from the inferred trusts of its neighbors to the sink according to the aforementioned weighted averaging formula. As the nodes are reversely iterated level by level from the sink to the source, the trusts values from all of a node neighbors to sink that are required for the trust inference of that node are set before the trust to sink value for the node is inferred. Only the neighbor nodes that the trust rating to them is greater than or equal to the required strength and are along a path to the sink stronger or as strong as the required strength should participate in the trust computation. If a neighbor node has a path to the sink with its strength greater than or equal to the required strength, its trust to the sink value is previously set to a trust value other than the dummy initial value. Aside with checking the inequality of the neighbor's trust to the sink to the dummy value, the trust rating from the node to the neighbor should also be higher than or equal to the required strength. The last trust value that is computed is the source inferred trust to the sink that is returned as the result.

4 Fuzzy Trust Algorithm

Fuzzy Trust algorithm supports the linguistic terms as trust rating of a node for another in the trust graph. The fuzzy membership functions for the linguistic terms such as low, medium, medium low, medium high and high can be defined as depicted in Fig. 1.

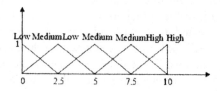

Fig. 1. Fuzzy membership functions of trust linguistic terms

The algorithm tries to compute trust from stronger and shorter paths similar to the TidalTrust algorithm so it performs a breadth-first-like search through the nodes to find shortest paths and also to find the path from source to sink strength fuzzy set. The path from source to sink strength fuzzy set is the maximum trust term fuzzy set that at least a path from the source to the sink with all the trust rating fuzzy sets along it excluding the last larger than or equal to that fuzzy set can be found; this will be called the required strength fuzzy set. It is considered that low, medium, medium low, medium, medium high and high fuzzy sets are in ascending order.

```
The FuzzyTrust algorithm pseudo code
Forward wave: The required strength fuzzy set computa-
tion
        Iterate the nodes from the source to the sink
        similar to the breadth first search level by level
        to find shortest paths.
        Set the path strength fuzzy set from source to any
        node in the next level using the previously set
        path strengths fuzzy sets from the source to cur-
        rent level nodes.
Backward wave: The trust from nodes to the sink infer-
ence
        Iterate the nodes form the sink to the source
        level by level.
```

> If the node is adjacent to the sink then its in-
> ferred trust fuzzy set is simply its trust rating
> fuzzy set to the sink in the fuzzy trust graph.
> Else (If the node is not adjacent to the sink) use
> fuzzy inference procedure on the neighbors with
> trust ratings to them greater than or equal to the
> required strength fuzzy set and that also have a
> path to the sink with a strength greater than or
> equal to the required strength fuzzy set and hence
> the trust from them to the sink is previously in-
> ferred strongly enough.

The algorithm is structurally similar to the TidalTrust algorithm excluding the inference. When the nodes are popped and iterated in the reverse order if a node is adjacent to the sink its inferred trust to the sink is simply its trust rating to the sink in the fuzzy trust graph. If the node is not adjacent to the sink, its inferred trust fuzzy set to the sink should be computed from all the neighbors that have a sufficiently strong path to the sink and the trust rating from the node to them is larger than the required strength fuzzy set. Only the neighbors that satisfy these two conditions participate in the trust inference. If a node's neighbor has an enough strong path i.e. a path with the strength fuzzy set of larger than or equal to the required strength fuzzy set, its trust to the sink is set to a value other than the dummy initial value before the trust inference for the node is performed.

For the fuzzy inference a fuzzy set named Acceptable trust fuzzy set is defined according to the required strength fuzzy set with a linear membership function having value 0 at 0 and value 1 at 10. The Acceptable fuzzy set for medium low required strength is shown in Fig. 2.

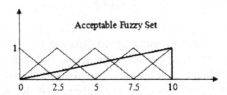

Fig. 2. Acceptable Fuzzy Set

The fuzzy inference is done according to the fuzzy inference rules. If the trust rating fuzzy set from the node to the neighbor is denoted by Trust-ToNeighbor and the neighbor's trust fuzzy set to the sink is denoted by NeighborTrustToSink, the only fuzzy rule is as follows:

$$if \; (TrustToNeighbor \; is \; Acceptable)$$

$$then \; (TrustToSink \; is \; NeighborTrustToSink)$$

Note the similarity of the rule to how people get a friend opinion as their own about an unknown matter if they acceptably trust the friend. The Acceptable fuzzy set is defined so that the firing rate plays the same role as the weight in weighed averaging that is giving an importance to the neighbor trust to the sink proportional to the node trust rating to the neighbor. The inference with different neighbors' data yields different experiences and the fuzzy union of them makes the final result fuzzy set.

What the FuzzyTrust algorithm returns is the inferred trust fuzzy set. To make the inferred trust value comprehendible to the user the result fuzzy set should be approximated to the most similar fuzzy set of the known terms fuzzy sets or the known terms with hedges such as very, more or less, more than and so on fuzzy sets or a disjunction of them and report the corresponding linguistic expression such as "medium or more or less high" to the user. The similarity of two fuzzy sets A and B is defined as:

$$S = \frac{|A \cap B|}{|A \cup B|}$$

Where || is the cardinality of a fuzzy set that is defined as:

$$|A| = \int_{x \in SupportSet} \mu_A(x)$$

A simple procedure for yielding approximating linguistic expressions is to prepare all the possible combination of the terms and hedges and find the most similar one by an exhaustive similarity computation for them and the inferred fuzzy set although more intelligent algorithms may be possible. The whole fuzzy inference procedure can be summarized as in Fig. 3.

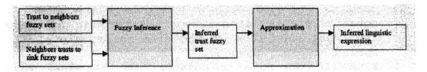

Fig. 3. The fuzzy trust inference

As inference is done along the paths with at least the required strength, the minimum trust rating to any neighbor node participating in the trust inference is the required strength so the inference is trusted at least by the required strength value. Therefore the required strength computed along the inference procedure is reported as the inference preciseness.

The basic algorithm is modified to benefit from longer paths. The AllLengthFuzzyTrust algorithm does not stop the search when the sink node is visited for the first time but the search continues until no other unvisited nodes can be found. Allowing longer paths to participate in the trust inference makes information from other nodes available aside from its own trust rating to the sink for trust inference from a source that the sink is its direct neighbor. This corresponds to the situation when someone knows another but also gets help about his trusted friends about him. So the pseudo code for AllLengthFuzzy-Trust algorithm is:

```
The AllLengthFuzzyTrust algorithm pseudo code
Forward wave: The required strength fuzzy set computa-
tion
        Iterate the nodes from the source to the sink
        similar to the breadth first search level by level
        to find all the paths.
        Set the path strength fuzzy set from source to any
        node in the next level using the previously set
        path strengths fuzzy sets from the source to cur-
        rent level nodes.
Backward wave: The trust from nodes to the sink infer-
ence
        Iterate the nodes form the sink to the source
        level by level.
        If the node is not adjacent to the sink use fuzzy
        inference procedure on the neighbors with trust
        ratings to them greater than or equal to the re-
        quired strength fuzzy set and that also have a
```

```
path to the sink with a strength greater than or
equal to the required strength fuzzy set and hence
the trust from them to the sink is previously in-
ferred strongly enough.
Else (If the node is adjacent to the sink) then
its inferred trust fuzzy set is the result of
fuzzy inference on its direct trust rating fuzzy
set to the sink in the fuzzy trust graph with a
high trust to it among information coming from the
qualified neighbors with conditions of the same as
in the if part.
```

This algorithm leads to more precise inference when deeper paths conduct more trusted information.

5 Simulation and Results

The graph depicted in Fig. 4 is used as the graph for TidalTrust Algorithm simulation. All the trust values are 0, 2.5, 5, 7.5 or 10 although they could be any number in the [0, 10] range. These values are selected deliberately because all of them are only and completely belonging to one of the terms fuzzy sets and so the corresponding fuzzy trust graph of the trust graph in Fig. 4 is the fuzzy trust graph in Fig. 5. This correspondence helps in comparing the two algorithms. The trust inference is reported for every node from A to L to any other one form A to L in the simulations for brevity.

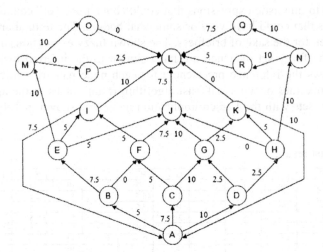

Fig. 4. Trust Graph for TidalTrust Algorithm

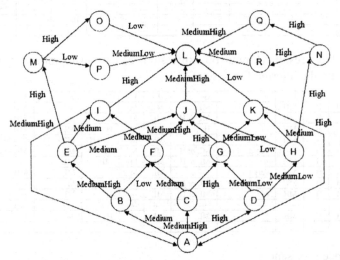

Fig. 5. Trust Graph for FuzzyTrust Algorithm

The result values of TidalTrust algorithm is shown in Table 1. The linguistic expressions of approximating fuzzy sets of FuzzyTrust algorithm result fuzzy sets by Larsen implication method is shown in Table 2. The inferred fuzzy sets are approximated to linguistic expressions that could contain one "or" connective on trust terms that could have very or somewhat hedges. The term abbreviations are written for the sake of briefness. The shown fuzzy expressions are the expressions the fuzzy set of which are most similar to the inferred fuzzy sets. Table 3 shows the inference preciseness for each node pair trust inference. Membership values of the TidalTrust algorithm result values in the approximating fuzzy sets with the Larsen implication method is shown in Table 4.

Table 1. TidalTrust results

	A	B	C	D	E	F	G	H	I	J	K	L
A	----	5	7.5	10	7.5	5	2.5	2.5	5	10	2.5	7.5
B	7.5	----	7.5	10	7.5	0	5.7	2.5	5	5	2.5	8.8
C	7.5	5	----	10	7.5	5	10	2.5	5	10	2.5	7.5
D	10	5	7.5	----	7.5	3	2.5	2.5	5	5	3.8	3
E	7.5	5	7.5	10	----	3	5.7	2.5	5	5	2.5	8.8
F	7.5	5	7.5	10	7.5	----	5.7	2.5	5	7.5	2.5	7.5
G	10	5	7.5	10	7.5	3	----	2.5	5	10	2.5	7.5
H	10	5	7.5	10	7.5	3	5.7	----	5	0	5	0
I	7.5	5	7.5	10	7.5	5	5.7	2.5	----	10	2.5	10
J	----	----	----	----	----	----	----	----	----	----	----	7.5
K	10	5	7.5	10	7.5	5	2.5	2.5	5	10	----	0
L	----	----	----	----	----	----	----	----	----	----	----	----

Table 2. FuzzyTrust results (Linguistic expressions of the most similar fuzzy sets approximating the inferred fuzzy sets)

	A	B	C	D	E	F	G	H	I	J	K	L
A	----	M	MH	H	MH	M	ML	ML	M	H	ML	MH
B	MH	----	MH	H	MH	L	ML or H	ML	M	M	ML	MH or H
C	MH	M	----	H	MH	M	H	ML	M	H	ML	MH
D	H	M	MH	----	MH	very L or M	ML	ML	M	L or H	ML or M	L or MH
E	MH	M	MH	H	----	very L or M	ML or H	ML	M	M	ML	MH or H
F	MH	M	MH	H	MH	----	ML or H	ML	M	MH	ML	MH
G	H	M	MH	H	MH	very L or M	----	ML	M	H	ML	MH
H	H	M	MH	H	MH	very L or M	ML or H	----	M	L	M	L
I	MH	M	MH	H	MH	M	ML or H	ML	----	H	ML	H
J	----	----	----	----	----	----	----	----	----	----	----	MH
K	H	M	MH	H	MH	M	ML	ML	M	H	----	L
L	----	----	----	----	----	----	----	----	----	----	----	----

Table 3. Inference preciseness

	A	B	C	D	E	F	G	H	I	J	K	L
A	----	H	H	H	M	MH	H	H	M	MH	MH	MH
B	M	----	M	M	H	H	M	M	MH	MH	M	M
C	M	M	----	M	M	H	H	M	M	H	H	H
D	ML	ML	ML	----	ML	ML	H	H	ML	ML	ML	ML
E	M	M	M	M	----	M	M	M	H	H	M	M

F	M	M	M	M	M	----	M	M	H	H	M	MH
G	ML	ML	ML	ML	ML	ML	----	ML	ML	H	H	H
H	M	M	M	M	M	M	M	----	M	H	H	M
I	H	MH	MH	MH	M	MH	MH	MH	----	MH	MH	H
J	----	----	----	----	----	----	----	----	----	----	----	H
K	H	H	H	H	M	MH	H	H	M	MH	----	H
L	----	----	----	----	----	----	----	----	----	----	----	----

Table 4. TidalTrust result values membership in FuzzyTrust result fuzzy sets

	A	B	C	D	E	F	G	H	I	J	K	L
A	----	1	1	1	1	1	1	1	1	1	1	1
B	1	----	1	1	1	1	0	1	1	1	1	0.5
C	1	1	----	1	1	1	1	1	1	1	1	1
D	1	1	1	----	1	0	1	1	1	0	0.5	0
E	1	1	1	1	----	0	0	1	1	1	1	0.5
F	1	1	1	1	1	----	0	1	1	1	1	1
G	1	1	1	1	1	0	----	1	1	1	1	1
H	1	1	1	1	1	0	0	----	1	1	1	1
I	1	1	1	1	1	1	0	1	----	1	1	1
J	----	----	----	----	----	----	----	----	----	----	----	1
K	1	1	1	1	1	1	1	1	1	1	----	1
L	----	----	----	----	----	----	----	----	----	----	----	----
Average = 0.8945945945945947												

Table 5. Absolute difference between TidalTrust values and defuzzified values of FuzzyTrust inferred fuzzy sets

	A	B	C	D	E	F	G	H	I	J	K	L
A	----	0	0	1	0	0	0	0	0	0.8	0	0
B	0	----	0	1	0	1	1.3	0	0	0	0	0.8
C	0	0	----	1	0	0	0.8	0	0	0.8	0	0
D	0.8	0	0	----	0	1	0	0	0	0	0	2.3
E	0	0	0	1	----	1	1.3	0	0	0	0	0.8
F	0	0	0	1	0	----	1.3	0	0	0	0	0
G	0.8	0	0	1	0	1	----	0	0	0.8	0	0
H	0.8	0	0	1	0	1	1.3	----	0	0.8	0	0.8
I	0	0	0	1	0	0	1.3	0	----	0.8	0	0.8
J	----	----	----	----	----	----	----	----	----	----	----	0
K	0.8	0	0	1	0	0	0	0	0	0.8	----	0.8
L	----	----	----	----	----	----	----	----	----	----	----	----
Average = 0.3058253058253062												

Table 6. AllLengthFuzzyTrust algorithm

	FuzzyTrust	FuzzyTrust preciseness	AllLengthFuzzyTrust	AllLengthFuzzyTrust preciseness
A to L	MH	MH	MH	MH
B to L	MH or H	M	*L	*MH
C to L	MH	H	MH	H
D to L	L or MH	ML	*M or MH	ML

E to L	MH or H	M	*L	*H
F to L	MH	MH	MH	MH
G to L	MH	H	MH	H
H to L	L	M	*M or MH	*H
I to L	H	H	H	H
J to L	MH	H	MH	H
K to L	L	H	L	H
L to L	----	----	----	----
M to L	L	H	L	H
N to L	M or MH	H	M or MH	H
O to L	L	H	L	H
P to L	ML	H	ML	H
Q to L	MH	H	MH	H
R to L	M	H	M	H

The average near one shows that the two algorithms agree generally in the results. The two algorithm results differ more when contradictory information should be composed for trust inference. One of the membership values in Table 4 that is 0 is the membership value from D to J meaning that the two algorithms results are completely different. There are two shortest paths from D to J that both participate in trust computations. The two neighbors G and H are trusted to the same amount so they take part the same in D to J trust value inference. The neighbor nodes G and H have contrary trust recommendations for node J that is trust of one of them to J is high (10) while the other one's is low (0). The TidalTrust algorithm simply takes the average of 0 and 10, yielding the 5 value that is a value just in between (medium), none of the neighbors believe in it in fact. The FuzzyTrust algorithm with Larsen method result linguistic expression is "Low or high". While FuzzyTrust result is exactly the information that exists in the trust graph, TidalTrust algorithm fails to exactly convey the information existing in the trust graph due to its improper composition scheme that is averaging. A crisp number is incapable of conveying enough information in fact. Similar arguments can be brought for other node pairs that two algorithm results do not completely agree. That averaging as the composition strategy infers trust wrongly when the neighbors give contradictory information is mainly why these differences occur.

The Absolute difference between TidalTrust results and defuzzified Fuzzy-Trust inferred fuzzy sets are shown in Table 5. Note that the difference for D to J is zero meaning that the result of TidalTrust algorithm can be gotten from the FuzzyTrust algorithm result. The average of 0.3 in the [0, 10] range of trust indicates very little difference. This little average difference suggests that the TidalTrust results are contained in or can be computed from FuzzyTrust results by defuzzification.

As TidalTrust crisp trust values can also be approximated to the trust term fuzzy set with the maximum membership function value, the two heterogeneous trust inference systems that one of them computes trust with TidalTrust algorithm and the other one with FuzzyTrust algorithm can also cooperate successfully and benefit from each other's trust graph information and inference.

The AllLengthFuzzyTrust algorithm is compared to the FuzzyTrust algorithm in Table 6. The FuzzyTrust algorithm results and their preciseness are written in column two and three and the AllLengthFuzzyTrust algorithm results and preciseness are in fourth and fifth respectively where star depicts a result difference between the algorithms. The three stars in the fifth column correspond to the node pairs (B to L, E to L and H to L) that more strong paths than the shortest ones exist for them that are well utilized for a more precise inference by the AllLengthFuzzyTrust algorithm.

6 Conclusion and Future Work

The inference simulations show that the FuzzyTrust algorithm results generally agree with TidalTrust results but FuzzyTrust algorithm reports richer expressions that match more with the information existing in the trust graph than TidalTrust algorithm especially when contradictory information should be composed for the trust inference. Also the fuzzy linguistic expressions are much more desirable for the user to write and read about trust values. The inference preciseness values that are also reported for each inference are improved by AllLengthFuzzyTrust algorithm that searches not only the shortest paths but also any other to perform the inference from the most trusted existing paths.

The algorithms make use of strongest paths while other path may also have useful information. Less strong paths are pruned in the algorithms while they have even little information. The future work of this research involves benefiting from weaker paths in the inference (AllLengthAllStrengthFuzzyTrust algorithm).

Besides the advantages it should be mentioned that fuzzy inference has a more computational load that averaging. The simulations show that FuzzyTrust infers trust well theoretically but a study of real world network of users will show clearly if the fuzzy calculated trust values superior in with real users.

Although the work targeted the social networks, ideas are proposed abstractly enough in trust graph modeling. The abstract node can be a social network user, a software mobile agent, a robot of a cooperating team or a semantic web URI. TidalTrust and FuzzyTrust that are structurally similar need global trust information in the trust graph format. This need can be satisfied in a society of social networks size but not easily for network of the web size. The most important issue to address before deploying the algorithm in semantic web trust layer may be distributiveness. The two algorithms can be distributively employed if the nodes are computational entities and each compute path strength form the source to it, convey it to its neighbors and infer its own trust to the sink but a lot of synchronization that is needed for the algorithms level by level computations should be done that seems highly impractical in the web. Although investigating different paths is valuable for the sake of more trusted information and better inference but scalability may be more important. A model and algorithm should be well distributed to become the trust modeling and inference algorithm for the semantic web trust layer. The path searching can be eliminated towards localization and each computational node can infer its trust from all the information coming from all the neighbors according to its trust to them using the same fuzzy inference rule or other fuzzy information composition procedures that are under study.

References

1. Golbeck J. (2005). Computing and Applying Trust in Web-based Social Networks. Doctor of Philosophy Dissertation, University of Maryland, College Park, 200 pages.
2. Golbeck J. (2005). Semantic Web Interaction through Trust Network Recommender Systems: End User Semantic Web Interaction Workshop at the 4th International Semantic Web Conference, November 2005.
3. Golbeck J., Hendler J., Inferring Trust Relationships in Web-based Social Networks. ACM Transactions on Internet Technology, 2005 (in press).
4. Golbeck J., Hendler J. (2004) Reputation network analysis for email filtering: Proceedings of the First Conference on Email and Anti-Spam, July 2004, Mountain View, California.

5. Golbeck J., Hendler J. (2004) Accuracy of Metrics for Inferring Trust and Reputation in Semantic Web-based Social Networks: Proceedings of EKAW 04.
6. Golbeck J., Parsia B., Hendler J. (2003) Trust Networks on the Semantic Web: Proceedings of Cooperative Intelligent Agents, 2003, Helsinki, Finland.
7. Ziegler C., Golbeck J. (2005) Investigating Correlations of Trust and Interest Similarity - Do Birds of a Feather Really Flock Together?: Submitted to the Journal of Artificial Intelligence Research.

A Trust Model for Sharing Ratings of Information Providers on the Semantic Web

Jie Zhang and Robin Cohen

David R. Cheriton School of Computer Science, University of Waterloo
Waterloo, Ontario, N2L 3G1, Canada

Abstract. In the context of the Semantic Web, it may be beneficial for a user (consumer) to receive ratings from other users (advisors) regarding the reliability of an information source (provider). We offer a method for building more effective social networks of trust by critiquing the ratings provided by the advisors. Our approach models the consumer's private reputations of advisors based on ratings for providers whom the consumer has had experience with. It models public reputations of the advisors according to all ratings from these advisors for providers, including those that are unknown to the consumer. Our approach then combines private and public reputations by assigning weights for each of them. Experimental results demonstrate that our approach is robust even when there are large numbers of advisors providing large numbers of unfair ratings. As such, we present a framework for sharing ratings of possibly unreliable sources, of value as users on the Semantic Web attempt to critique the trustworthiness of the information they seek.

1 Introduction

The vision of the Semantic Web is to construct a common semantic interpretation for World Wide Web pages, in order to one day reliably run software to understand the information conveyed in any of its documents. In building the Semantic Web, however, information may be supplied by a wide selection of sources, with the result that a user seeking information will need to judge whether the content of any given source is in fact trustworthy. It is therefore important to develop models for trust in the context of the Semantic Web. Various approaches to date have been formulated about how best to form a Web of Trust, in order to share information and selectively choose trustworthy partners from whom information may be obtained. In our research, we are considering a problem that arises when social networks are formed in order to share trust ratings - that of unfair ratings. Dellarocas [2] distinguishes unfair ratings as unfairly high ratings and unfairly low ratings. Unfairly high ratings may be used to increase the trustworthiness of others and promote their services. They are often referred to as "ballot stuffing". Unfairly low ratings of others are often referred to as "bad-mouthing". In brief, the ratings of the trustworthiness of others, obtained from third parties, may in fact be suspect. What is required therefore is a mechanism for effectively adjusting the basis on which decisions of trust are made, to discount these possibly unfair ratings.

In this paper, we discuss our research in the context of sharing ratings of sources (called information providers) among users on the Semantic Web. We present an approach for modeling the trustworthiness of advisors - those users providing reputation ratings for potential providers from whom information may be obtained. We refer to the user seeking advice as the consumer. We first represent private reputation values, based on what is known about the advisors' ratings for providers with whom the consumer has already had some experience. We then describe how to construct a public model of trustworthiness of advisors based on common, centrally held knowledge of providers and the ratings provided by advisors, including the reputation ratings of providers totally unknown to the consumer. We then outline how both private and public models can be combined, in order to obtain a value for the trustworthiness of each possible advisor. In summary, we offer a method for building more effective social networks of trust, by critiquing the advice provided by advisors.

In Section 2 we introduce the Semantic Web setting for sharing information about sources, and present some current research on modeling the trustworthiness of information sources based on ratings provided by advisors. Section 3 presents our approach for modeling the trustworthiness of advisors according to the ratings provided by them in the context of the Semantic Web. Section 4 provides an example that goes through each step of our approach. Section 5 includes some experimental results demonstrating what happens when there are large numbers of advisors providing large numbers of unfair ratings. Conclusions and future work are outlined in Section 6.

2 Background and Related Work

In this section, we discuss the setting of sharing information about sources, on the Semantic Web. We motivate the need to acquire information about the reliability of sources and then briefly outline some current research on modeling the trustworthiness of sources. This includes some discussion of approaches to communicate with other users to obtain advice about sources, sometimes referred to as a Web of Trust [4], as well as an approach for addressing the problem that some users may provide untruthful advice.

The challenge of trusting information providers in a Web-based environment is discussed in [10]. Paolucci et al. provide in [10] valuable insights into the need for trust on the Web, in the context of Web services, where Web sites dynamically exchange information using XML descriptions, but where it is difficult to ensure that the meaning of the messages being sent is well understood, without human intervention. The Semantic Web contributes by providing ontologies for Web services to interpret meanings in exchanged messages. According to [10], with the Semantic Web, the interaction between users and providers needs a process of capability matching to link users with providers of Web services. Specifically, providers advertise their capabilities, a user sends a request for the type of service she requires, a registry matches the capabilities of providers and the capabilities expected by the user, and finally the user selects the most suitable provider. However, in their advertisements, providers may lie about their capabilities in order to be selected by the user. To avoid selection of an untruthful provider, there is a need to properly model the trustworthiness of providers. In [4] this problem is reinforced for the Semantic Web: whether to trust the content of a Web resource, depending on the source. Richardson et al. [11] explain further that due to the great diversity of the Web, it is difficult to expect the content to be consistent and of high quality. It then becomes important to decide how trustworthy each information source is.

Maximilien and Singh [7,8] adopt an agent-based approach for modeling trust on the Semantic Web. Their work focuses on representing multiple qualities of services (QoS) for automatic runtime Web service selection. This trust model is based on a shared conceptualization of QoS and takes into account providers' quality advertisement, consumers' quality preferences, quality relationships, and consumers' quality tradeoffs. In order to select a Web service implementation, a consumer dynamically associates a trust value with each service implementation and selects the service implementation with the highest assigned level of trust. The trust value of each service implementation partially depends on its reputation value, which is determined by the set of quality values from other users who previously selected that provider.

Kagal et al. [6] use a DAML+OIL trust ontology in a multi-agent system, which is based on a distributed trust and delegation mechanism verifying that a user's credentials are acceptable. The trust ontology is built for specifying credentials and checking if the credentials conform to policies. A policy maps credentials to a certain ability or right. The mechanism allows propagation of trust beliefs exchanged between users and avoids repeated checking of users' credentials.

The research of Gil and Ratnaker [4] provides a framework for users to express their trust about a source and the statements it contains, by annotating each part of a source to indicate their views. The focus of the work is on how to provide an effective interface for users to record their annotations. This TRELLIS system ultimately averages the ratings provided over many users and many analysis, to present a reflection of the trustworthiness of the source. A credibility-reliability pair emerges for each source-statement pair, to derive an overall rating of a single source, based on each of its associated statements.

Modeling trust on the Semantic Web, as discussed so far in this section, includes a reliance on the beliefs or ratings provided by third parties to be truthful. In fact, it is important to address the problem of possibly unfair or unreliable ratings. One approach that explores this possibility is that of Richardson et al. [11]. In this work, each user first explicitly specifies a small set of users whom she trusts, leading to a Web of Trust. This arrangement allows any user to compute the trustworthiness of a possible provider, based on the ratings supplied by others in her social network. The trust value of a provider is computed locally by combining the trust ratings provided by other users. One feature of this approach is to recursively propagate trust through the user's social network. In effect, trust in a provider is derived using some aggregating functions along each possible chain of trust from the user to the provider. One concern with this approach, however, is that this method of propagating trust may be computationally intractable, as there may be many different paths, of various lengths, which need to be aggregated.

In our own research, we are developing a model for representing the reliability of advisors from whom advice may be sought, when a user seeks to evaluate the trustworthiness of a provider. This framework is sufficiently general to operate in a variety of environments including electronic commerce, where buyers may make decisions about sellers by soliciting input on those sellers from other buyers in the marketplace.

In the context of the Semantic Web, our model is useful for the problem of determining the reliability of a provider being evaluated by a consumer by virtue of reputation ratings provided by advisors. Our focus is on addressing the problem of advisors who may be untrustworthy. The existence of malicious advisors is in fact acknowledged in [11]. But in contrast to the model of Richardson et al. [11], we provide a more direct evaluation of each possible advisor in a Web of Trust, leading to an evaluation about how best to make use of that advisor's ratings of a possible provider being examined by a consumer.

As will be seen in the sections that follow, we make various limiting assumptions (which are revisited as future work) in order to examine more clearly the need to adjust for possibly unfair ratings from advisors. In particular, we do not envisage entire chains of trust from advisor to advisor, instead evaluating independently the trustworthiness of each advisor, based in part on the user's own past experience. In addition, we represent the input from each advisor as a summary rating of a possible source as simply reliable or unreliable. We also allow an advisor to rate a source several times. In so doing, we are able to weight more heavily more recent evaluations of the source, allowing for dynamically varying trustworthiness of the source.

3 Modeling Trustworthiness of Advisors

In the discussion below, we use the following terminology:
- **User/Consumer:** person seeking information from various sources
- **Provider:** an information source, providing information
- **Advisor:** other users providing ratings of providers to consumers
- **Private reputation:** a determination of the reputation of an advisor by a user, based on commonly rated providers
- **Public reputation:** a determination of the reputation of an advisor by a user, based on a centrally held model of the advisor, from interactions with a whole set of providers

Our method for determining the trustworthiness of advisors is to employ a combination of what we refer to as private and public reputation values. To explain, the private reputation of an advisor is calculated by a consumer, based on ratings the advisor supplies of providers with whom the consumer has already had some experience. If the advisor is reputable and has similar preferences as the consumer, the consumer and advisor will likely have many ratings in common. This can then be used as the basis for assessing the trustworthiness of the advisor. In cases where the consumer has little private knowledge of the advisor, a public reputation will be elicited, reflecting the trustworthiness of that advisor, based on his ratings of all providers in the system. A weighted combination of private and public reputations is derived, based on the estimated reliability of the private reputation value. This combined value then represents the trustworthiness of the advisor.

3.1 Private Reputation

Our approach allows a consumer C to evaluate the private reputation of an advisor A by comparing their ratings for commonly rated providers $\{P_1, P_2, ..., P_m\}$. For one of the commonly rated providers P_i ($1 \leq i \leq m$ and $m \geq 1$), A has the rating vector R_{A,P_i} and C has the rating vector R_{C,P_i}. A rating for P_i from C and A is binary ("1" or "0", for example), in which "1" means that P_i is trustworthy and "0" means that P_i is untrustworthy. For the purpose of simplicity, we assume ratings for providers are binary. Possible ways of extending our approach to accept ratings in different ranges will be investigated as future work. Further discussion can be found in Section 6.

The ratings in R_{A,P_i} and R_{C,P_i} are ordered according to the time when they are provided. The ratings are then partitioned into different elemental time windows. The length of an elemental time window may be fixed (e.g. three days) or adapted by the frequency of the ratings to the provider P_i, similar to the way proposed in [2]. It should also be considerably small so that there is no need to worry about the changes of providers' behavior within each elemental time window. We define a pair of ratings (r_{A,P_i}, r_{C,P_i}), such that r_{A,P_i} is one of the ratings of R_{A,P_i}, r_{C,P_i} is one of the ratings of R_{C,P_i}, and r_{A,P_i} corresponds to r_{C,P_i}. The two ratings, r_{A,P_i} and r_{C,P_i}, are correspondent only if they are in the same elemental time window, the rating r_{C,P_i} is the most recent rating in its time window, and the rating r_{A,P_i} is the closest and prior to the rating r_{C,P_i}. We consider ratings provided by C after those by A in the same time window, in order to incorporate into C's rating anything learned from A during that time window, before taking an action. According to the solution proposed by Zacharia et al. [14], by keeping only the most recent ratings, we can avoid the issue of advisors "flooding" the system. No matter how many ratings are provided by one advisor in a time window, we only keep the most recent one.

We then count the number of such pairs for P_i, N_{P_i}. The total number of rating pairs for all commonly rated providers, N_{all} will be calculated by summing up the number of rating pairs for each commonly rated provider as follows:

$$N_{all} = \sum_{i=1}^{m} N_{P_i}$$

The private reputation of the advisor is estimated by examining rating pairs for all commonly rated providers. We define a rating pair (r_{A,P_i}, r_{C,P_i}) as a positive pair if r_{A,P_i} is the same value as r_{C,P_i}. Otherwise, the pair is a negative pair. Suppose there are N_f number of positive pairs. The number of negative pairs will be $N_{all} - N_f$. The private reputation of the advisor A is estimated as the probability that A will provide reliable ratings to C. Because there is only incomplete information about the advisor, the best way of estimating the probability is to use the expected value of the probability. The expected value of a continuous random variable is dependent on a probability density function, which is used to model the probability that a variable will have a certain value. Because of its flexibility and the fact that it is the conjugate prior for distributions of binary events [12] and Norvig 2002), the beta family of probability density functions is commonly used to represent probability distributions of binary events (see, e.g. the generalized trust models BRS [5] and TRAVOS [13]). Therefore, the private reputation of A can be calculated as follows:

$$\alpha = N_f + 1, \ \beta = N_{all} - N_f + 1$$

$$R_{pri}(A) = E(Pr(A)) = \frac{\alpha}{\alpha + \beta},$$

where $Pr(A)$ is the probability that A will provide fair ratings to C, and $E(Pr(A))$ is the expected value of the probability.

3.2 Public Reputation

When there are not enough rating pairs, the consumer C will also consider A's public reputation. The public reputation of A is estimated based on its ratings and other ratings for the providers rated by A. Each time A provides a rating $r_{A,P}$, the rating will be judged centrally as a fair or unfair rating. We define a rating for a provider as a fair rating if it is consistent with the majority of ratings to the provider up to the moment when the rating is provided.[1] As before, we consider only the ratings within a time window prior to the moment when the rating $r_{A,P}$ is provided, and we only consider the most recent rating from each advisor. In so doing, as providers change their behavior and become more or less reputable to each advisor, the majority of ratings will be able to change.

Suppose that the advisor A totally provides N'_{all} ratings. If there are N'_f number of fair ratings, the number of unfair ratings provided by A will be $N'_{all} - N'_f$. In a similar way as estimating the private reputation, the public reputation of the advisor A is estimated as the probability that A will provide fair ratings. It can be calculated as follows:

$$\alpha' = N'_f + 1, \ \beta' = N'_{all} - N'_f + 1$$
$$R_{pub}(A) = \frac{\alpha'}{\alpha' + \beta'},$$

which also indicates that the more the percentage of fair ratings advisor A provides, the more reputable it will be.

3.3 Trustworthiness

To estimate the trustworthiness of advisor A, we combine the private reputation and public reputation values together. The private reputation and public reputation values are assigned different weights. The weights are determined by the reliability of the estimated private reputation value.

We first determine the minimum number of pairs needed for C to be confident about the private reputation value it has of A. The Chernoff Bound theo-

---

[1] Determining consistency with the majority of ratings can be achieved in a variety of ways, for instance averaging all the ratings and seeing if that is close to the advisor's rating.

rem [9] provides a bound for the probability that the estimation error of private reputation exceeds a threshold, given the number of pairs. Accordingly, the minimum number of pairs can be determined by an acceptable level of error and a confidence measurement as follows:

$$N_{min} = -\frac{1}{2\varepsilon^2}\ln\frac{1-\gamma}{2},$$

where ε is the maximal level of error that can be accepted by C, and γ is the confidence measure. If the total number of pairs N_{all} is larger than or equal to N_{min}, consumer C will be confident about the private reputation value estimated based on its ratings and the advisor A's ratings for all commonly rated providers. Otherwise, there are not enough rating pairs, the consumer will not be confident about the private reputation value, and it will then also consider public reputation. The reliability of the private reputation value can be measured as follows:

$$w = \begin{cases} \dfrac{N_{all}}{N_{min}} & \text{if } N_{all} < N_{min}; \\ 1 & otherwise. \end{cases}$$

The trust value of A will be calculated by combining the weighted private reputation and public reputation values as follows:

$$Tr(A) = wR_{pri}(A) + (1 - w)R_{pub}(A)$$

It is obvious that the consumer will consider less the public reputation value when the private reputation value is more reliable. Note that when $w = 1$, the consumer relies only on private reputation.

4 An Example

To illustrate how our approach models trustworthiness of advisors, this section provides an example that goes through each step of the approach.

In the setting of sharing information on the Semantic Web, a provider P_0, which is an information source, provides some statements. Whether a consumer C can trust these statements depends on how much C trusts P_0. To model the trustworthiness of the provider P_0, the consumer C seeks advice from two advisors A_x and A_y who have experience with P_0. The advice about P_0 from A_x and A_y are ratings representing the trustworthiness of P_0 in terms of providing reliable content. Before aggregating the ratings provided by A_x and A_y, the consumer C needs to evaluate the reliability of those ratings, which depends on the trustworthiness of the advisors A_x and A_y. Our approach effectively models the trustworthiness of advisors based on how reliable the previous ratings provided by them are.

To demonstrate what ratings provided by advisors may look like, we assume both the advisors A_x and A_y have rated one of the providers, P_i. We are in fact interested in all P_i's for which A_x or A_y has supplied ratings and C has had experience. Table 1 lists some of the ratings provided by A_x and A_y for P_i. The symbol "T" represents a sequence of time windows, in which T_1 is the most recent time window. To simplify the demonstration, we assume that each advisor provides at most one rating within each time window. Some advisors might have not provided any ratings for the provider within some time window. For example, the advisor A_y has not provided any ratings for P_i within the time window T_{n-1}. As can be seen from Table 1, the consumer C also provides some ratings for P_i; some of the ratings are within the same time windows as the ratings provided by A_x and A_y. We assume that the ratings provided by C are after those provided by A_x and A_y if they are within the same time window.

Table 1. Ratings Provided by A_x, A_y and C for P_i

T	T_1	T_2	...	T_j	...	T_{n-1}	T_n
				P_i			
A_x	1	1	...	1	...	1	1
A_y	1	0	...	1	...	-	0
C	1	-	...	0	...	1	1

Suppose that A_x and A_y each provides 40 ratings in total for providers. In this case, $N'_{all}(A_x) = N'_{all}(A_y) = 40$. The advisor A_x provides 35 fair ratings ($N'_f(A_x) = 35$), and A_y provides 20 fair ratings ($N'_f(A_y) = 20$). A rating here is considered as a fair rating when it is consistent with the majority of ratings for the provider within a same time window. Then the public reputation values of A_x and A_y are calculated as follows:

$$R_{pub}(A_x) = \frac{35+1}{35+1+(40-35)+1} = 0.86;$$

$$R_{pub}(A_y) = \frac{20+1}{20+1+(40-20)+1} = 0.5,$$

which means that A_x is more likely to provide fair ratings.

Suppose that the consumer C provides 30 ratings that are within the same time windows of the same providers with A_x and A_y. Therefore, $N_{all}(A_x) = N_{all}(A_y) = 30$. Within those 30 ratings pairs, 25 of ratings provided by A_x are same as the ratings provided by C ($N_f(A_x) = 25$), and A_y provides only 20 same ratings ($N_f(A_y) = 20$). Then the private reputation values of A_x and A_y are calculated as follows:

$$R_{pri}(A_x) = \frac{25+1}{25+1+(30-25)+1} = 0.81;$$

$$R_{pri}(A_y) = \frac{20+1}{20+1+(30-20)+1} = 0.66,$$

which means that A_x is more likely to provide fair ratings and have similar preferences with C.

To combine the private and public reputation values, the weight w should be determined. Suppose $\varepsilon = 0.1$ and $\gamma = 0.9$, then $N_{min} = -\frac{1}{2 \times 0.1^2} \ln \frac{1-0.9}{0.2} = 150$. Since N_{all} is less than N_{min}, $w = \frac{30}{150} = 0.2$. The trust values of A_x and A_y will be calculated as follows:

$$Tr(A_x) = 0.2 \times 0.81 + (1-0.2) \times 0.86 = 0.85;$$
$$Tr(A_y) = 0.2 \times 0.66 + (1-0.2) \times 0.5 = 0.53,$$

which clearly indicates that A_x is more trustworthy than A_y. As a result, the consumer C will place more trust in the advice provided by A_x. It will consider the advice provided by A_x more heavily when aggregating the advice provided by A_x and A_y for modeling the trustworthiness of the information provider P_0. Discussion of possible aggregation functions is necessary when employing our model to reach final decisions about which sources to trust. A brief summary

of some aggregation functions and references of some others can be found in
[11]. We leave the topic of selecting effective aggregation functions to future
work. Our framework serves the purpose of representing the trustworthiness of
advisors, so that this may be taken into account, when determining how heavily to rely on their advice.

5 Experimental Results

Our approach models the trustworthiness of advisors according to how reliable
the ratings provided by them are. To demonstrate the effectiveness of the approach, we carry out some modest preliminary experiments involving advisors
who provide different percentages of unfair ratings. The expectation is that
trustworthy advisors will be less likely to provide unfair ratings, and vice
versa. We also examine how large numbers of dishonest advisors (i.e. advisors
that provide unfair ratings) will affect the estimation of advisors' trustworthiness. Results indicate that our approach is still effective by making adjust-
ments to rely more heavily on private reputations of advisors, in this case.

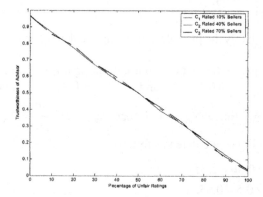

Fig. 1 Trustworthiness of Advisor

The first experiment involves 100 providers, 3 consumers, and one advisor.
The 3 consumers, C_1, C_2 and C_3, rate 10, 40 and 70 randomly selected provid-

ers, respectively. The advisor totally rates 40 randomly selected providers. [2] We examine how the trust values the consumers have of the advisor change when different percentages (from 0% to 100%) of its ratings are unfair. As illustrated in Figure 1, the trust values the consumers have of the advisor decrease when more percentages of the advisor's ratings are unfair. From this figure, we can also see that our approach is still effective when the consumer C_1 does not have much experience with providers, in the sense that C_1 can still reduce the reputation of the advisor when it provides more unfair ratings.

The second experiment involves 100 provides, 80 advisors, and one consumer. The consumer and each advisor rate 80 of the randomly selected providers. We model the trust value the consumer has of one of the advisors, A. The trustworthiness of the advisor will be modeled as the combination of its private and public reputations (referred to as the CR approach) and as only its public reputation (referred to as the PR approach), respectively. The advisor A will provide different percentages (from 10% to 100%) of unfair ratings. Figure 2 illustrates the trustworthiness of A when 24 (30% of all) advisors are dishonest. Those dishonest advisors provide the same percentage of unfair ratings as the advisor A does. Results indicate that the trustworthiness of A modeled

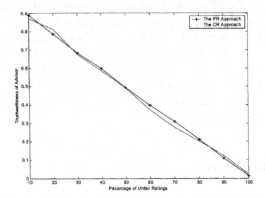

Fig. 2 Trustworthiness of A When Majority of Advisors are Honest

---

[2] Note that we simplify the experiments by limiting each consumer or advisor to provide at most one rating for each provider.

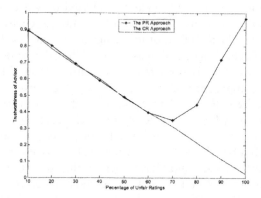

Fig. 3 Comparison of the CR and PR Approaches

by using the CR and PR approaches decreases when more percentages of ratings provided by A are unfair. Therefore, these two approaches are not affected when only a small number of advisors are dishonest. Figure 3 represents the trustworthiness of A when 40 (60% of all) advisors are dishonest. In this figure, the trustworthiness of A modeled by using the CR approach still decreases when more percentages of ratings provided by A are unfair, which indicates that our approach is still effective when the majority of advisors provide large numbers of unfair ratings. In contrast, the trustworthiness modeled by using the PR approach increases when more than 60% of ratings provided by the dishonest advisors are unfair, which indicates that the PR approach is only effective when the majority of ratings are fair.

6 Conclusions and Future Work

In this paper, we first introduce the Semantic Web setting for sharing information about sources. Due to the fact that any user on the Web can become an information source, there is a need to form a Web of Trust. Current research on modeling the trustworthiness of information sources on the Semantic Web relies on the unrealistic assumption that advice provided by advisors about an information source is truthful. A typical approach to address this problem is to critique advisors' advice based on their trustworthiness. We present an approach for modeling the trustworthiness of advisors. Our approach allows a consumer to estimate the trustworthiness of an advisor based on the advisor's ratings for providers with whom the consumer has already had some experience. It also models the trustworthiness of the advisor based on all its ratings and common knowledge of providers who might be totally unknown to the consumer. The above results are finally combined by our approach. The experiments are carried out in the setting where advisors might provide different numbers of unfair ratings. Experimental results indicate that our approach can effectively model the trustworthiness of advisors even when consumers do not have much experience with providers. Furthermore, our approach is still effective when the majority of advisors provide large numbers of unfair ratings.

Our approach of combining both private and public reputation values offers useful improvement for the modeling of the trustworthiness of advisors. A model such as BRS [5] that relies on public reputation has the problem that it is only effective when the majority of ratings are fair, whereas a model like TRAVOS [13] that uses private reputation has difficulty when a consumer is new to the system.

For the purpose of simplicity, the current approach limits ratings for providers to be binary. In future work, we will extend our approach to accept ratings in different ranges. Instead of using the numerical difference of two ratings, comparison of the two ratings could take into account the semantics of rating levels [1]. For example, although the numerical differences of the pairs are same, the difference between "5" (very trustworthy) and "3" (neutral) is smaller than that between "4" (trustworthy) and "2" (untrustworthy). In consequence, the similarity between "5" and "3", say 0.2, should be set to be larger than the similarity between "4" and "2", say 0. When these extensions are made, the Dirichlet family of probability density functions [3], which is the multivariate generalization of the beta family, can be used to represent probability distributions of discrete similarity values. Our model will evaluate private and public reputation values based on aggregation of those discrete similarity values

Our approach represents trustworthiness of providers using a single rating provided by consumers or advisors. For future work, as in the research of [11], we will also extend our approach to accept multiple ratings representing different dimensions of trustworthiness of providers. We could for example, examine credibility and reliability of providers as used by Gil and Ratnakar [4] and Ratnakar 2002) or a quality of service ontology used by Maximilien and Singh [7]. We would then need to explore methods to combine the different kinds of ratings provided by advisors, for example whether to weight one dimension more heavily than another.

Another valuable direction for future work is to go beyond a generalized reputation rating for an information source, to one that determines whether to trust a source on a particular topic or segment of its information. In this case, we would want to model the advisors' trustworthiness with respect to these segments of the provider, as well. This may result in the design of a more elaborate private reputation model or a method of determining what weight to place on this private reputation, when advisors have only currently rated different segments of the source. It would also be valuable to learn which advisors to rely on, for which different elements of a source.

For future work, we will also carry out further experiments to continue to compare our model with competing approaches. It is important to note that we are focused in this paper on the question of judging the trustworthiness of advisors, as part of the process of evaluating how much to trust the content of an information source. In fact, we would like to see our approach integrated into a full scale decision-theoretic framework for selecting reputable sources. The performance of the overall system would then need to be evaluated, as well.

References

1. Chen M, Singh JP (2001) Computing and using reputations for internet ratings.In: Proceedings of the 3nd ACM Conference on Electronic Commerce.
2. Dellarocas C (2000) Immunizing online reputation reporting systems against unfair ratings and discriminatory behavior. In: Proceedings of the 2nd ACM Conference on Electronic Commerce, Minneapolis, MN.
3. Gelman A, Carlin JB, Stern HS, Rubin DB (2004) Bayesian Data Analysis. Chapman & Hall/CRC, Boca Raton.
4. Gil Y, Ratnakar V (2002) Trusting information sources one citizen at a time. In Proceedings of the First International Semantic Web Conference (ISWC), Sardinia, Italy.
5. Jøsang A, Ismail R (2002) The beta reputation system. In: Proceedings of the 15th Bled Electronic Commerce Conference.
6. Kagal L, Finin T, Joshi A (2002) Developing secure agent systems using delegation based trust management. In: Proceedings of the First International Autonomous Agents and Multi Agent Systems (AAMAS), Bologna, Italy.

7. Maximilien EM, Singh MP (2004) Toward autonomic web services trust and selection. In: Proceedings of the 2th International Conference on Service Oriented Computing (ICSOC), pp 212–221.
8. Maximilien EM, Singh MP (2005) Agent-based trust model using multiple qualities. In: Proceedings of 4th International Autonomous Agents and Multi Agent Systems (AAMAS 2005).
9. Mui L, Mohtashemi M, Halberstadt A (2002) A computational model of trust and reputation. In: Proceedings of the 35th Hawaii International Conference on System Science (HICSS).
10. Paolucci M, Sycara K, Nishimura T, Srinivasan N (2003) Toward a semantic web ecommerce. In: Proceedings of 6th Conference on Business Information Systems (BIS2003), Colorado Springs, Co, USA, pp 153–161.
11. Richardson M, Agrawal R, Domingos P (2003) Trust management for the semantic web. In: Proceedings of the 2nd International Semantic Web Conference (ISWC).
12. Russell S, Norvig P (2002) Artificial Intelligence: A Modern Approach. Second Edition, Prentice Hall, Englewood Cliffs, New Jersey.
13. Teacy WTL, Patel J, Jennings NR, Luck M (2005) Coping with inaccurate reputation sources: Experimental analysis of a probabilistic trust model. In: Proceedings of 4th International Autonomous Agents and Multi Agent Systems (AAMAS 2005).
14. Zacharia G, Moukas A, Maes P (1999) Collaborative reputation mechanisms in electronic marketplaces. In: Proceedings of the 32nd Hawaii International Conference on System Sciences (HICSS-32), Maui, Hawaii.

A Distributed Agent System upon Semantic Web Technologies to Provide Biological Data

Farzad Kohantorabi, Gregory Butler, and Christopher J.O. Baker

Department of Computer Science and Software Engineering
Concordia University, Montréal, Canada

Abstract. Bioinformaticians are accustomed to going through analysis steps, in which they employ several data sources, like protein sequence and protein interaction databases, to carry out their study. However, the ever-growing size and the dynamic nature of the biological databases make it almost impossible to use the biological data without a sophisticated data-providing infrastructure. In this paper, we introduce a distributed data providing agent system that answers biological queries according to its ontology of biological entities.

1 Introduction

Computational data has become a primary source of new biological insights, and bioinformatic software now contributes significantly to biological initiatives.

Many widely used biology databases provide websites where researchers can submit their queries and construct the dataset they need for their research. For example, SwissProt [7] is accessible at http://ca.expasy.org/sprot/. There are even data warehouse systems that combine data from different sources and provide them in a single system, such as BioZon [8]. However, these databases do not provide convenient interfaces for software programs.

In the recent years, there has been some effort to fill this gap. For example, ToolBus [30], EBI web services [21], DDBJ web services [10], NCBI eFetch

[20], and BIND [5] offer services that computer programs can use to retrieve biological data and perform their computation. However, these services are tightly coupled to the definition of their data, and locating and using the right service is a problem.

In this paper, we introduce an agent system that provides access to biological data in a distributed environment. The novelty of this research is the use of ontologies for locating services according to their concept. This is done by using a service ontology and a data ontology that are both shared between service seekers and provider agents. In the context of a data warehouse, as an integrated database, the service ontology contains generic services such as retrieve. A parameter that is passed to the service is a query involving the data ontology. In this case there is a separation between the service ontology and the data ontology. Alternatively, specific services to retrieve genes or proteins could be available. In this case, the service ontology (below the generic retrieve service) mirrors a subset of the data ontology.

The agent system discussed in this paper is comprised of two different sets of agents. The first set of agents accesses and creates a data warehouse of biological data. This serves as instance data for the FungalWeb ontology [27]. The entities in the data warehouse match the foundational concepts in the ontology. The agents that create the data warehouse have explicit knowledge of a range of data resources: the agents know how to query the data resource, transform results, and load the data warehouse. The agents that access the data warehouse use the ontology query language, nRQL [17], for RACER [16]. One can also access the data warehouse through the native interface.

The second set of agents that is being developed is to create a distributed data space where agents can access the entities (matching the concepts in the ontology) either via the data warehouse or via the distributed data resources. This is transparent to the users.

2 Tools

This research depends upon the existence of specific tools. This section brings a brief introduction to those tools and to related research.

2.1 DECAF

DECAF (Distributed, Environment Centered Agent Framework) [15] is an agent development environment which facilitates rapid design and development of agents. Unlike other agent development environments that put their main focus on inter-agent communication protocols, DECAF provides a full cycle support for agent development.

In addition, DECAF resembles an operating systems' behavior toward user tasks. Specifically, each agent task is defined as a sequence of actions that should be done in a specific order, where DECAF provides the supporting environment to stipulate the actions and tasks. Moreover, using DECAF, it is possible to develop persistent, robust, and flexible agent systems.

2.2 Matchmaking Agent System

Matchmaking is a part of the DECAF framework that is responsible for connecting a service request to its appropriate server agent. When a request for a service is received the matchmaking component looks for an agent that can answer the service by using the service descriptions. The primary matching is done by string comparison, where the matchmaker matches the service description with the list of services available in the agent system. However, this kind of service matching is both performance inefficient and incomplete [2]. By incomplete, we mean that match making is highly dependent on the string that service provider agents declare, and how accurate the requester's service description is. To solve this problem, Al-Shaban et al. [2] proposed a matchmaking system that works using ontologies.

The matchmaking agent system replaces the standard matchmaking mechanism of DECAF. The matching process, then, works with the service ontology which contains all the possible predefined agent service domains in a hierarchical manner. After recognizing the service ontology, service provider agents should advertise their services in the system. This is done by adding a record in an internal database which contains the agent information and the place in the ontology where the agent service is defined. After that, the matchmaking mechanism receives a query from the service seeker and queries the service ontology using RACER [16] and the given query. The result of the query is matched against the internal database data and the suitable provider agent is found.

However, using ontologies for this reason raises two interesting issues that are worth discussing here. First, service seekers and service providers should have the same service ontology and data ontology so that they can work together otherwise there would need to be a matching mechanism to match concepts in one ontology to the other. However, this is not the case in the system we are designing because both sides are sharing the same service ontology for the matchmaking agent system, and for the data ontology, namely the FungalWeb ontology. As a result, it is always guaranteed that both sides are using the same set of concepts. Furthermore, biological ontologies are becoming results of community work, and they are maintained to be consistent in the future. Open Biomedical Ontologies (OBO) [23] is an example of such a community. As a result, individual groups that are building their own ontology can extend OBO's ontology and remain consistent with other ontologies in the domain.

The second interesting issue is how the service ontology and the data ontology can be employed together to locate a service. Currently what we do is that we define generic services in the service ontology, regardless of concepts in the data ontology. After that, generic services have parameters by which service concepts are linked with data concepts in the data ontology. For example, a retrieve service on the service ontology might have a class parameter, like gene, which comes from the data ontology. Essentially this parameter specifies the service. The advantage of this approach is that we don't need to worry about ontology maintenance, and the drawback is that services are not specific, therefore harder to implement and maintain. However, there is another approach that merges the data ontology into the service ontology, and the result is a third ontology that contains specialized versions of the generic services. For example, imagine that retrieve service is a generic service in the service ontology, and it operates on Gene and Protein concepts from the data ontology. After merging, the third ontology will have two versions of retrieve service: retrieve_gene and retrieve_protein. The benefit of this approach is that services are specific, but the drawback is that the third ontology should be maintained against the changes in either of the ontologies.

More details of Matchmaking Agent System can be found in [3]

2.3 BioXRT

Large volumes of biological data are being produced each day, and research teams need to publish their data both internally and publicly. BioXRT [31], previously known as XRT, aims to meet this need. BioXRT provides an easy way for biologists to publish their data on a simple web site. A significant advantage is that BioXRT does not need any database design knowledge, and it only needs a minimal knowledge of working with databases. BioXRT has a simple data structure, and it accepts simple data inputs.

BioXRT accepts a variety of input formats such as Microsoft Excel sheets, XML files, and flat BioXRT text files. These formats mostly represent data in a tabular manner; therefore, they are simple in structure. However, BioXRT inputs should comply with certain rules. For example, each input represents one class of data, which is the BioXRT's corresponding

ID	LongName	Order	Phylum	Kingdom
178477	Botryandromyces ornatus	Laboulbeniales	Ascomycota	Fungi
231773	Trichoderma sp. T-105	Hypocreales	Ascomycota	Fungi
205608	Buellia submuriformis	Lecanorales	Ascomycota	Fungi
193039	Patescospora separans	Jahnulales	Ascomycota	Fungi
4984	Bullera variabilis	Tremellales	Basidiomycota	Fungi
322976	fungal sp. 32.40	Unknown	Unknown	Fungi
307330	fungal sp. TRN236	Unknown	Unknown	Fungi
246499	Xylaria sp. F12	Xylariales	Ascomycota	Fungi
116810	Physcia albinea	Lecanorales	Ascomycota	Fungi

Fig. 1. A sample BioXRT input file from FungalWeb project. The file shows taxonomy information of fungi species

term for a table in relational databases. In addition, each file should start with an ID column which is the primary key of the class. Fig. 1 shows an example of a BioXRT input file, where columns are separated by the tab character, and the first row lists column names.

```
File: org_feature.xrt
ID   taxID    start   end    type    comment   source
1    162425   1213    1726   gene              MIT Broad Institute
2    162425   5806    3397   gene              MIT Broad Institute
3    162425   9062    6382   gene              MIT Broad Institute
4    162425   7822    1972   gene              MIT Broad Institute
File: gene.xrt
ID   P_ID/org_features   TaxID    GeneID     Name    ...
1    1                   162425   AN0001.2   protein ...
2    2                   162425   AN0002.2   protein ...
3    3                   162425   AN0003.2   protein ...
4    4                   162425   AN0004.2   protein ...
```

Fig. 2. These two classes of data show an example of BioXRT's parent and child relation in the FungalWeb data warehouse. org_feature is where we keep features of an organism, one of which is a gene feature. Details of a gene feature are kept in gene.xrt which is a child class of org feature.

Not only is BioXRT simple in terms of its input but also it is simple in the way it supports data relations. BioXRT supports only parent-child relations; that is, a BioXRT class can hold child data of another class. Fig. 2 shows an example of this relation, where gene.xrt is representing child data of org feature.xrt. The relation is defined by using a special naming convention on column names. The column that is keeping the parent id (foreign key) is named as P_ID/pc where pc is the name of the parent class, and it keeps the values of parent ID column.

Once the data is loaded in BioXRT, BioXRT provides online query, browsing, and viewing facilities for the data. The query tool is a powerful column based text search and full text search on each of the loaded classes. Fig. 3 shows a screen shot of BioXRT query page of the FungalWeb data warehouse.

Concordia FungalWeb Database

Table Browser

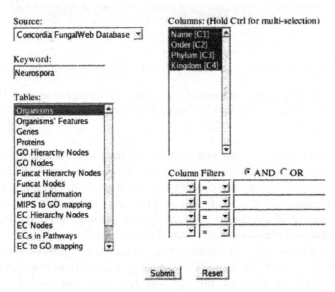

Fig. 3. FungalWeb's BioXRT web query interface. The screen shot shows a list of available classes of data. Users can select a class and query the selected class against any arbitrary set of columns. They can also do a keyword search. The example shows how the web interface can be used to find all *Neurospora* species.

Finally, TBrowse is the facility by which the result of the query page is shown. As shown in Fig. 4, TBrowse renders the results in a tabular fashion with controls to manipulate its view.

2.4 FungalWeb Ontology

Fungi are now increasingly used in industry. Baker et al. [6] mention that many decisions in R&D teams are made on the basis of incomplete knowledge. To fill this gap, they suggest that a range of interdisciplinary ontologies should be introduced. The suggested range covers taxonomy, gene discovery, protein family classification, enzyme characterization, enzyme improvement, enzyme production, enzyme substrates, enzyme performance benchmarking, and market niche [6].

The FungalWeb ontology [27] contains concepts and instances related

#	Name	Order	Phylum	Kingdom
1	Neurospora sublineolata	Sordariales	Ascomycota	Fungi
2	Neurospora calospora	Sordariales	Ascomycota	Fungi
3	Neurospora santi-florii	Sordariales	Ascomycota	Fungi

Fig. 4. The example shows the result of the search for *Neurospora* species. The results are rendered by BioXRT's TBrowse engine, which produces tabular data views in BioXRT.

to fungi, enzymes, substrates, and commercial enzyme products. The concepts and instances are divided into two groups of fungal organisms and fungal enzymes. Fungal organisms are classified by their phylum, class, order, family, genus and species. Moreover, fungal enzymes are classified based on International Union of Biochemistry and Molecular Biology's (IUBMB) recommended catalyzed reactions, the so-called EC numbers.

Fig. 5 illustrates different sources upon which the FungalWeb ontology has been built. In general, the FungalWeb ontology summarizes together different biological database schemes, biology web resources, knowledge of domain experts, and existing bio-ontologies. The FungalWeb ontology [27] is developed in OWL-DL, which features frame representation of OWL and expressiveness of Description Logics (DL).

3 Data Warehouse

As a part of FungalWeb project, this research aims to provide biological data as instances of the FungalWeb ontology. Therefore, we decided to load external data into an internal BioXRT database to create a data warehouse that agents can access instantaneously and reliably.

BioXRT is chosen for the backend because it has a flat data structure, and many existing biological data sources have flat structure [1]. Furthermore, it gives a web interface where online users can query and browse the data. In addition, BioXRT makes it easy to extend the data warehouse whenever new concepts are added to the ontology, and instance data is required.

We have gathered information on species such as *Aspergillus Nidulans, Aspergillus Niger, Neurospara Crassa, Coprinus Cinereus, Magnaporthe Grisea*, and *Saccharomyces Cerevisiae* from external sources like Broad Institute, NCBI, and Gene Ontology. Stored data is direct transformation of external sources into BioXRT's input structure and some computed data such as GO annotations. However, the internal data warehouse does not contain any mined data from the literature or other sources. Our data warehouse at this stage is intended to be an integrated database for data access, and it is not intended to support data mining in the sense of OLAP. In the future, we hope to perform visual data mining by using GraphLog [9].

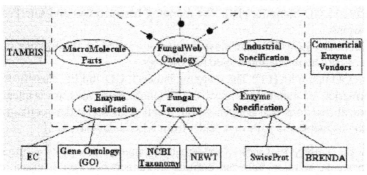

Fig. 5. FungalWeb ontology [27]

The internal data warehouse along with the agent system will help support a wide range of biological questions about Fungi. For example:

- "Give me all the instances of *Neolectaceae*" [26], which should answer: *Neolecta Irregularis, Neolecta Vitellina*, and . . .
- "All Enzymes that have been reported to be found in *Neurospora crassa*" [26], which should answer: *Xylanase, Cellulase, Pectinase, Lipase, Laccase*, and . . .

In order to facilitate answering these questions the internal data warehouse stores the following biological information:

- Fungi taxonomy [29]: That is where fungi are classified into a tree of life.
- Corresponding protein sequences of each fungi
- Corresponding gene sequences of each fungi
- FunCat hierarchy [25]: This is the hierarchy of FunCat classifications. This set of data describes each of the possible protein functions.

- FunCat [25] features of the corresponding proteins: That is, each protein for a given fungi can have different functions. This set of data contains the information that classifies these functions according to FunCat classification.
- Gene Ontology (GO) hierarchy [28]: Gene ontology is an effort to consistently describe gene products.
- GO annotations [14]: Genes and proteins annotated by GO
- MIPS to GO mapping [13]: The mapping between GO and FunCat classifications.
- InterPro scheme [4]: The scheme of InterPro database which provides views of commonly used databases.
- InterPro to GO mapping [18]: The mapping between GO and InterPro classifications.
- EC hierarchy [12]: Enzyme classification suggested by the International Union of Biochemistry and Molecular Biology.
- EC to GO mapping [11]: The mapping between GO and EC classifications.
- Information of metabolic pathways: Metabolic pathways are sequences of chemical reactions that happen within a cell. This set of data contain information of metabolic pathways taken from KEGG database [22].

Note the variety of types of information ranges from entities (organism, gene, protein), relation between entities (organism has gene), classification schemes (GO, EC, FunCat), links between entities and classification (protein has EC number), and mappings between classification schemes (EC to GO mapping).

The taxonomy class contains the fungi in a hierarchy according to their relation to each other. The other classes refer to this tree by the taxonomy id of each species. In addition, there are protein and gene classes which list the proteins and genes for each species.

We also store the FunCat information of proteins that are in the protein class. The FunCat information is a classification of functional categories for proteins. This kind of information is popular for finding the functional usage of unknown proteins by examining their sequence similarity against the proteins with known functional usage.

In addition, the data warehouse stores the Gene Ontology, by which we can unify the current available classification schemes such as FunCat, InterPro, and EC numbers. Consequently, the data warehouse stores the mapping between these classifications to GO. This way, it is possible to find how an entry in EC hierarchy is related to an entry in InterPro classification.

Although these different datasets are loaded separately into BioXRT, it stores the data inside its internal database in a flat format. That is, it stores all classes in a single table which keeps triples of (class, attribute, value). However, being internally related to each other, our data has the conceptual schema illustrated in Fig. 6.

Table 1 shows the current size of the data warehouse contents, though further development is ongoing.

Table 1. Contents of the internal data warehouse

Data	Size in Records
Genes	20161
Proteins	20161
Enzymes in Pathways	6680
FunCat Information	53045
Organism Features	40322
Taxonomy	21696
FunCat Hierarchy	4663
EC Hierarchy	14088
InterPro Nodes	11972
EC to GO mapping	3403
InterPro to GO mapping	15487
MIPS to GO mapping	482
GO Annotations	21553

4 The Agent System

The core component of this research is the agent system that is responsible for handling user requests and manipulating the internal data warehouse. The architecture of the agent system contains provider agents, updater agents, and ontologies, each of which plays a specific role in the system:

- Data provider agents get the request from the user and talk to either the internal data warehouse or to external data sources to retrieve answers.
- Updater agent maintains the internal data warehouse and updates it on a regular basis.
- A data ontology links concepts with data sources.
- A service ontology makes data provider agents locatable.

All the agents in the system are developed using the DECAF framework. Furthermore, we are using the matchmaking agent system to make our agents locatable across the system. Therefore, there are certain steps through which an agent registers itself in the system. The first step is that the agent should register with the matchmaking system and define its service using the service ontology. The next is for the agent to describe its service in OWL-S [24] so that seekers know how to communicate with the agent. After the agents register in the system, the seeker is able to find their services. Having the service ontology in hand, as illustrated in Fig. 7, a seeker sends a nRQL query to the matchmaking system. The nRQL query contains the information of the service that the seeker is looking for, and it is stated in terms of the service ontology concepts. For example, a

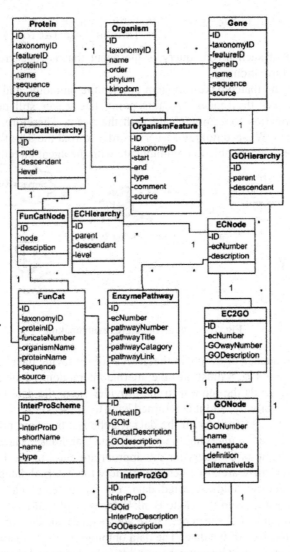

Fig. 6. Conceptual data schema of the FungalWeb data warehouse

seeker might be interested in finding the genes that regulate PYRUVATE KINASE. Then the nRQL query would look like:

```
(Retrieve (?x) (AND (?x |Agent|)
                    (?x |knows_regulation|)))
```

The result of such nRQL query is the agent that is registered to provide regulatory information.

After that, the matchmaking system queries the ontology, and it returns the agent that serves the request. At this point, the seeker still does not have enough information to communicate with the agent. Therefore, it communicates with the OWL-S ontology server in order to find the agent's parameters. After that the seeker is able to communicate with the agent directly.

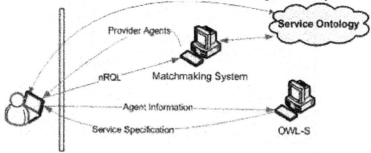

Fig. 7. Agent architecture: matchmaking

The next sequence of events in the process of retrieving data happens inside the agent system. Fig. 8 illustrates the internal interactions of the agent system. Once the user sends the request to the provider agent the data is taken either internally or externally, and it is returned back to the seeker.

Since certain data are kept in the data warehouse, there are provider agents that are specialized in querying the internal data warehouse. These agents handle the user requests by querying the appropriate class in the BioXRT database. However, there are also agents that query the external databases because the data warehouse holds selected data. For example, given a specific sequence, an agent goes to the Gene Bank database and returns the corresponding accession number of the gene. These agents query the data ontology to find the external location of the data. The data ontology is an extension of the FungalWeb ontology, in which we have added the location information of the concepts and the instances.

In addition to the data providing agents, there are agents in the system that are responsible for the maintenance of the internal data warehouse. These agents update the internal database by adding new datasets, and they update existing data when update is scheduled. The update process is intended to be automatic, but there are situations in which the update process fails. For example, in some cases, research groups change their file format for the same kind of results they are used to publish. We are still working on such situations, and we believe that using format templates and writing general updater agents is a good feasible solution to this problem.

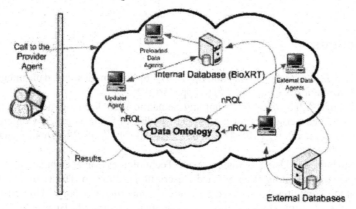

Fig. 8. Agent architecture: the data agents

5 Summary

Our research uses ontologies, the DECAF agent framework, improved matchmaking techniques, and the BioXRT database to construct an agent system that provides access to the biological data. The agent system aims to address the need of the programming interfaces for biology software. In addition, we envision that this agent system and others like it will motivate the development of other agent systems [19] that rely on data providing agents.

In addition, this research makes use of ontologies to enhance locating agent services and specializing their services. Based on our experience we feel that the use of ontologies has eased the development of the data warehouse and the agents. We aim to test the usage of this system with larger datasets and a larger user population.

6 Acknowledgement

This research is a part of *"Ontology, the Semantic Web and Intelligent Systems for Genomics"* project which is funded by Génome Québec.

More information about FungalWeb project is available online at http://www.cs.concordia.ca/FungalWeb/

References

1. Achard F, Vaysseix G, Barillot E, "XML, bioinformatics and data integration", Bioinformatics, Vol. 17 no. 2 2001, pp. 115–125.
2. Al Shaban A, Haarslev V, "Applying Semantic Web Technologies to Matchmaking and Web Service Descriptions", Proceedings of The Montreal Conference on eTechnologies 2005 (MCeTech2005), Jan. 20–21, 2005, Montreal, Canada, pp. 97–104.
3. Al-Shaban A, "Using Semantic Web Technologies for Matchmaking Software Agents Representing Web Service Description", 2005, A Thesis In The Department Of Computer Science and Software Engineering, Concordia Univeristy.
4. Apweiler R, Attwood TK, Bairoch A, Bateman A, Birney E, Biswas M, Bucher P, Cerutti L, Corpet F, Croning MD, Durbin R, Falquet L, Fleischmann W, Gouzy J, Hermjakob H, Hulo N, Jonassen I, Kahn D, Kanapin A, Karavidopoulou Y, Lopez R, Marx B, Mulder NJ, Oinn TM, Pagni M, Servant F, Sigrist CJ, Zdobnov EM, "The InterPro database, an integrated documentation resource for protein families, domains and functional sites.", Nucleic Acids Research, 2001, Vol. 29, No. 1 37–40
5. Bader GD, Betel D, Hogue CW, "BIND: the Biomolecular Interaction Network Database.", 2003, Nucleic Acids Res. 31(1):248–50 PMID: 12519993
6. Baker C J O, Witte Ren'e, Shaban-Nejad Arash, Butler Greg, Haarslev Volker, "The FungalWeb Ontology: Application Scenarios", Eighth Annual Bio- Ontologies Meeting,(Conf Pres) co-located with ISMB 2005, June 24, 2005, Detroit, Michigan, USA
7. Bairoch A, Apweiler R, "The SWISS-PROT protein sequence database and its supplement trEMBL in 2000.", Nucleic Acids Res., 28, 45–48.
8. Birkland A, Yona G, "The BIOZON Database: a Hub of Heterogeneous Biological Data.", 2005, Nucl. Acids Res. 2006 34: D235–D242; doi:10.1093/nar/gkj153
9. Butler G, Wang G, Wang Y, Zou L, "A graph database with visual queries for genomics", 2005, The Asia Pacific Bioinformatics Conference 2005, 31-40
10. DDBJ: http://xml.ddbj.nig.ac.jp/wsdl/index.jsp, Last accessed on 20 Mar 2006.

11. EC to GO: http://www.geneontology.org/external2go/ec2go, Last accessed on 20 Mar 2006.
12. EC: http://www.chem.qmul.ac.uk/iubmb/enzyme/, Last accessed on 20 Mar 2006.
13. FunCat to GO: http://www.geneontology.org/external2go/mips2go, Last accessed on 20 Mar 2006.
14. Gene Ontology: http://www.geneontology.org, Last accessed on 20 Mar 2006.
15. Graham J R, Decker K S, Mersic M, "DECAF—A Flexible Multi Agent System Architecture", Autonomous Agents and Multi-Agent Systems. 2003.
16. Haarslev V, Möller R, "Description of the RACER System and its Applications", Proceedings of the International Workshop on Description Logics (DL—2001), Stanford, USA, 1.–3. August 2001, pp. 132–141.
17. Haarslev V, Möller R, Wessel M, "Querying the Semantic Web with Racer + nRQL", Proceedings of the KI-2004 International Workshop on Applications of Description Logics (ADL'04), Ulm, Germany, September 24, 2004.
18. InterPro to GO: http://www.geneontology.org/external2go/interpro2go, Last accessed on 20 Mar 2006.
19. Keele J W, Wray J E, "Software agents in molecular computational biology", 2005, Briefings in Bioinformatics 2005 6(4):370-379; doi:10.1093/bib/6.4.370
20. NCBI eFetch: http://www.ncbi.nlm.nih.gov/entrez/query/static/eutils_help.html, Last accessed on 20 Mar 2006.
21. Pillai S, Silventoinen V, Kallio K, Senger M, Sobhany S, Tate J, Velankar S, Golovin A, Henrick K, Rice P, Stoehr P, Lopez R, "SOAP-based services provided by the European Bioinformatics Institute", Nucl. Acids Res. 2005 33: W25–W28; doi:10.1093/nar/gki491
22. Ogata H, Goto S, Sato K, Fujibuchi W, Bono H, Kanehisa M, "KEGG: Kyoto Encyclopedia of Genes and Genomes." 1999, Nucleic Acids Research, 27(1), 29–34.
23. Open Biomedical Ontologies: http://obo.sourceforge.net/, Last accessed on 20 Mar 2006.
24. OWL-S website: http://www.daml.org/services/owl-s/, Last accessed on 20 Mar 2006.
25. Ruepp A, Zollner A, Maier D, Albermann K, Hani J, Mokrejs M, Tetko I, G"'uldener U, Mannhaupt G, Münsterkötter, Mewes H W, "The FunCat, a functional annotation scheme for systematic classification of proteins from whole genomes", Nucleic Acids Research, 2004, Vol. 32, No. 18 5539-5545, doi:10.1093/nar/gkh894.
26. Shaban-Nejad A, Baker C J O, Butler G, Haarslev V, "The FungalWeb Ontology, The Core of a Semantic Web Application for Fungal Genomics", 2004, Canadian Semantic Web Interest Group in conjunction with LORNET, Universit de Quebec a Montreal, Friday afternoon 19 November 2004
27. Shaban-Nejad A, Baker C J O, Haarslev V, Butler G, "The FungalWeb Ontology : Semantic Web Challenges in Bioinformatics and Genomics.", Semantic Web

Challenge — Proceedings of the 4th International Semantic Web Conference ISWC 2005, Nov. 6–10, Galway, Ireland, Volume 3729 / 2005

28. Stevens R, Goble CA, Bechhofer S, "Ontology-based knowledge representation for bioinformatics.", Brief Bioinform. 2000 ; 1: 398–414.

29. Wheeler DL, Chappey C, Lash AE, Leipe DD, Madden TL, Schuler GD, Tatusova TA, Rapp BA, "Database resources of the National Center for Biotechnology Information.", 2000 Nucleic Acids Res 2000 Jan 1;28(1):10–4

30. Yang B, Nordberg E K, Eckart J D, Sobral B W S, "ToolBus — An Interoperable Environment for Biological Researchers", 2005 International Conference on Mathematics and Engineering Techniques in Medicine and Biological Sciences (METMBS '05), June 2005, Las Vegas, NV.

31. Zhang J, Duggan G E, Khaja R, Scherer S W, "Generalized biological database platform based on cross-referenced tables (XRT)"

Fulfilling the Needs of a Metadata Creator and Analyst- An Investigation of RDF Browsing and Visualization Tools

Shah Kushro and A. Min Tjoa

Institute for Software Technology and Interactive Systems
Vienna University of Technology, Vienna, Austria
{khusro, tjoa,}@ifs.tuwien.ac.at

Abstract. The realization of Semantic Web vision is based on the creation and use of semantic web content which needs software tools both for semantic web developers and end users. Over the past few years, semantic web software tools like ontology editors and triple storage systems have emerged and are growing in maturity with time. While working on a large triple dataset during the course of a research aiming at a life-long "semantic" repository of personal information, besides other semantic web tools, we used several RDF browsing and visualization tools for analyzing our data. This analysis included ensuring the correctness of the data, conformance of instance data to the ontology, finding patterns and trails in the data, cross-checking and evaluating inferred data, etc. We found that many of the features needed by a metadata creator and analyst are missing from these tools. This paper presents an investigation of the tools that are used for browsing and visualizing the datasets. It first identifies the browsing and visualization features required by a semantic web developer and a metadata creator and analyst and then based on these features evaluates the most common RDF browsing and visualization tools available till date. We conclude this paper with recommendations for requirements to be fulfilled for future semantic web browsing and visualization.

1 Introduction and background

The current web despite all its benefits assumes human presence for the inter-pretation of its content. The Semantic Web [3] is an extension of the current web, based on the idea of exchanging information with explicit, formal and machine-accessible description of meaning. Semantic Web technologies like RDF [29], Topic Maps [4,17], and Ontologies are used for making the seman-tics of information explicit and thus machine-processable.

At the Institute of Software Technology and Interactive Systems, Vienna University of Technology, Vienna, Austria, we are working on a research pro-ject called SemanticLife [1] which aims at a life-long "semantic" repository of personal information. Our system is based on semantic web technologies like OWL and RDF. For proof-of-concept, we implemented the first prototype us-ing both RDF and Topic Maps. Though Topic Maps are a very promising technology but since RDF is more mature, is supported by many tools espe-cially the open source, is better for resource centric paradigms, and most of the existing ontologies on the web are RDF and OWL based so we implemented the second prototype using RDF. In SemanticLife several datafeeds are re-sponsible for collecting and uploading user's information to a central triple store. These datafeeds monitor users' emails, browsing sessions, chat sessions, program execution, and filesystem operations. A user can upload his/her files and can manually annotate items in the repository. These feeds collect user in-formation in different formats which is ultimately converted into RDF. A GUI is provided for user interaction with the SemanticLife system. It provides user control over the information upload process e.g. which programs should be monitored, which emails shouldn't be uploaded, etc. Moreover, the user can select and annotate information in the repository and can visualize it on a timescale. The system is based on a plugin mechanism and all these features are provided by separate plugins.

In our research we have been using several semantic web tools for different tasks. These include Protégé [11] and SWOOP [14] for ontology development and Jena2 [31] and Kowari [15] as triple stores. We are making use of several ontologies, some existing like FOAF [10] and others developed for our own domain. We also used several RDF browsing and visualization tools which are briefly introduced in section 4. Though we see a considerable growth in the development and maturity of semantic web tools but still there is a long way to achieve a position that the relational database theory and tools enjoy. While working with these tools and several ontologies and instance data from different sources with sometime unknown structure, we strongly felt the need for a better RDF browsing and visualization tool.

Currently, SemanticLife collects most of the user's personal information, stores it in a repository, and allows the user to manually annotate it. Our next step is the automatic and semi-automatic analysis of this information. By analysis we mean that the system should automatically identify pieces of information and, either automatically or with the intervention of the user, should link those pieces with other related items in the store. Browsing and visualization tools are also needed to support the research and development activity in this area.

As mentioned earlier, user information in our system is ultimately stored in the form of RDF triples. Though, RDF makes the semantics of information explicit, but this machine-oriented content representation does not lend itself for presentation in a human-readable way. Over the past few years several applications have attempted to solve this problem by using different representation paradigms. These tools attempt to provide support to Semantic Web users, developers and metadata analysts with varying degrees of abstraction and usability [21].

This paper gives a survey of existing RDF browsing and visualization tools and concludes with recommendations for a tool which could prove more useful and effective for a metadata creator and analyst. Section 2 identifies the needs of a metadata creator and analyst. Section 3 presents the evaluation framework that we have employed for our comparison. Section 4 gives a brief description of RDF browsing and visualization tools selected for our survey and those used in SemanticLife. Section 5 provides the comparison of the basic and more technical features of the tools. Section 6 lists some recommendations for a future tool and Sections 7 finally concludes this paper.

2   The Needs of a Metadata Creator and Analyst

Producer and Consumer of semantic web data are the two important roles of people and most of the research and development emphasis is on their support. The aim of this paper is to identify another role related to the Producer and his/her needs; that of a metadata creator and analyst. Semantic web developers and people working with metadata always need to have their data visualized in different ways. Their browsing and visualization needs are different from those of the end users; some are listed below [25]:

- To produce good-quality RDF and to cover the limited expertise in defining ontologies, creating RDF, and converting existing XML-based metadata into RDF.
- To have a way to rapidly test and visualize a dataset and to understand if there are mistakes in the model as well as spelling mistakes in the name-spaces and URIs.
- To get a mental model of an unfamiliar dataset (including the ontologies used to describe it)
- To have a sense of the density of connectivity of a particular dataset or data-set fragment.
- To identify potential mappings between resources and ontologies.
- To discover the parts of a dataset having special graph-theoretical properties and therefore might 'stand out' as having some latent meaning that might get otherwise unnoticed.
- To have the ability to drill down from global view to local information at the resource level.
- To use as few tools as possible for carrying out the analysis and visualization tasks.
- And at the same time to have the simplicity and the ease of use that an end user enjoys.

Semantic web development tools like ontology editors, triple storage systems, and semantic web toolkits seldom address these needs. Tools targeted towards the end user allow browsing the semantic web content if available and otherwise extract it from existing documents. Triple storage systems also provide some browsing and visualization features like Sesame Explore Mode and Kowari web interface, but do not show more than a list of triples. Moreover, ontology editors also provide some browsing and visualization features but they mostly show and edit the ontology structure rather than intelligent browsing of the ontology instances [2].

3 Evaluation Framework of RDF Browsing and Visualization Tools

A general evaluation framework used to compare RDF browsing and visualization tools comprises of the following four criteria:

3.1 Supported RDF Representation Formats

Import/Export Formats: An RDF graph can be serialized in several different formats including RDF/XML, Notation-3, N-Triples, and TriX. The most known serialization format is RDF/XML which is an XML representation of RDF graph in terms of XML Information Set and Namespaces. Notation 3 or N3 is a shorthand non-XML serialization of RDF, designed with human-readability in mind. N-Triples is a line-based, plain text format and was designed to be a fixed subset of N3, hence all tools which currently work with N3 can seamlessly work with it too. Each triple is written on a separate line, and consists of a subject specifier, a predicate specifier, then an object specifier, followed by a period. TriX (Triples in XML) is a serialization for named graphs. It is an attempt to provide a highly normalized and consistent XML representation of RDF model, which allows the effective use of generic XML tools as XSLT, XQuery and others [30].

For an RDF tool to be effective and useful it should support as many of these formats as possible. As "common understanding" and "shared knowledge" lie at the heart of semantic web, this enables a metadata creator and analyst to use existing ontologies and data encoded in any format and also to map between different formats.

Accessing Data in a Triple Store: In the previous years, several RDF storage systems have emerged and continue in growth and use. Besides local and remote files, the metadata may exist in these triple stores. For local and remote access these systems define interfaces mainly based on RMI, HTTP, and SOAP. Like any other RDF tool, a browsing and visualization tool having the facility of accessing local and remote triple store data will make it more flexible and useful.

Integration of Inference Capabilities: Ideally, an RDF visualization tool should allow a range of inference engines or reasoners to be plugged into it which allow additional facts to be inferred from instance data and class descriptions. Such engines are used to derive additional RDF assertions which are entailed from some base RDF together with any optional ontology information and the axioms and rules associated with the reasoner.

This inferred data may be utilized by the visualization tool for providing an integrated interface for browsing the data. The global part of this integrated interface may group resources based on their type and the class hierarchies. The local interface may utilize inferred information such as resource and class labels and comments for a more user friendly view of the data. Ideally, an RDF visualization tool should allow the use of a range of inference engines or reasoners suitable for different datasets.

Merging Input Files: RDF data is usually dispersed across different files and data sources, and instance data is usually created separate from the ontology. A tool is more useful and effective if it can read data from several data sources to merge and show a unified display.

3.2 Display Features

Display Interface: Browsing a document repository is simple as it usually consists of a small number of large chunks of information, with few explicit relationships. The situation is exactly opposite with RDF data which consists of many small chunks of information with many explicit relationships among them. An RDF browsing tool may provide a *Global* view of these many relationships, or a *Local* view to concentrate on a single piece of information, or an *Integrated* view to combine these two [22].

An analyst usually needs to identify emerging structures within the relationships in an RDF dataset. This is achieved by a Global interfaces which emphasizes global structure by providing large scale views of RDF data. An RDF browser that generates graph-based views of RDF statements gives some information about the underlying structure, in particular with some grouping performed by its layout algorithm. More advance interfaces may use grouping, ordering, or prioritizing information to provide global views. Data in global interfaces may be grouped based on the user search or resource types and concept hierarchies obtained through inference.

In contrast to global interfaces, a Local view provides richer details for a particular information item. Users and analysts usually need information at this level of specificity. Local interfaces can have hyperlinks to each other, providing users with navigation through the entire repository. Sesame's Explore Mode [6] and Kowari's 15] Web Interface provide a browser like interface to RDF. Kowari provides a query web interface to its metadata store and the result is displayed in the form of triples. Selecting a URI in this list or in Sesame's Explore Mode shows all RDF statements with that URI as subject, predicate, or object, thus making RDF browsable. But the current view is always limited to the immediate vicinity of the current resource and no underlying structure is visible [22].

A more useful approach is the Integrated view in which these two approaches are combined. Usually a global view is presented at the beginning from where the data can be explored at different levels of detail. Automation of this view is quite difficult and a general technique for this is a question that needs to be answered.

Sharing Presentation Knowledge: The two major issues in displaying RDF data is the specification of content selection and content formatting and styling which are addressed by each tool in a different and ad hoc way. This makes it difficult to share and reuse this presentation knowledge across applications. The need to use a shared display vocabulary for presenting RDF content and sharing presentation knowledge has been recognized in the Semantic Web community. Fresnel [5] is an attempt to address this issue. It is a browser-independent, extensible vocabulary for modeling Semantic Web content presentation knowledge. Its selection, manipulation and styling concepts are applicable across representation paradigms, layout methods, and output formats. Its core modules are currently implemented in various types of applications [9, 26, 28].

Presentation Paradigm: Displaying RDF data in a user-friendly manner is a problem addressed by various types of applications using different representation paradigms. Some tools represent RDF models as node-link diagrams explicitly showing their graph structure [12, 28]. Other tools use nested box layouts or table-like layouts for displaying properties of RDF resources with varying levels of details [26]. Another approach combines these paradigms and extends them with specialized user interface widgets [20, 23].

Editing Features: These may vary from simple triple editing to more advanced features like resource linking and annotation. Usually other systems like ontology editors are used for this purpose but the tool proves more effective if these features are also available.

Graph Statistics: This is an important feature always needed by metadata analysts and needs to be implemented by a browsing tool. These vary from general graph statistics to more advanced features like in-degree, out-degree, clustering coefficient and other graph theoretical properties.

3.3 Scalability Issues

Maximum Dataset Size: One of the most import features to measure the scalability of a tool is the size of input RDF file or the maximum number of statements in a model or nodes in a graph. For demonstration purposes the size of input data is usually very small (within a megabyte or a graph with less than a thousand nodes). But a working RDF dataset may be in hundreds of megabytes with millions of statements which, if a tool is not unable to load, will compel the analyst to split it up and thus lose its global view. Hence a more effective tool should allow a user to work with much bigger models.

Visual Scalability: Sometime a tool can load a very large dataset but is unable to render it in a way that a user can make sense out of it. Tools that provide a graph based view usually have limited visual scalability but the inclusion of visual cues and search and query options make the situation better. A text-based tool is usually better in visual scalability and heavily depends on grouping and ordering of data to produce the global interface. Visual scalability is lost if a text-based tool cannot visualize global structures and there is little difference between global and local views.

Extension Mechanism: A static tool with no extension mechanism may be useful for sometime but becomes useless as the changing trends and emerging technologies are not accommodated. Plugins are a general concept that allows extra functionally to be dropped into a tool, usually by simply adding files to a directory. Plugins are very loosely coupled to the base tool, and can thus be added very easily without modifying the tool itself. Plugin architecture provides an organized way for independent groups of people to add new behavior to an application without having to modify it.

3.4 Search, Query and Filtering

Selection and Filtering: This gives a user the ability to select sections of an RDF graph based on some criteria. This selection may be based on global or local filters. Global filters like *rdf:type*, *rdfs:domain*, and *rdfs:range* are applied to the whole graph independent of its domain. Local filters are domain-specific and include namespaces, specific properties and classes, and generally resources and URIs. Selection and Filtering allows the not-so-technical user to browse and analyze the model. Furthermore, the user can also perform selection by hand, possibly in conjunction with automated search.

Support for RDF Query Language: Usually more fine-grained control over data selection and filtering is needed which is provided by an RDF query language. Several RDF query languages have been developed each with its own features and expressiveness but SPARQL [19] has been recently adopted as the standard RDF query language. To use this feature, though the analyst should be aware of the query language syntax but it also gives him a total control over his data.

Full Text Graph Search: Sometime the exact name of a resource or the exact contents of a literal are not known in advance or resources or literals with a common text pattern need to be filtered out. Full text graph search if available enables a user to search for keywords and text patterns inside resource names and literals contents.

Full Text Document Search: Sometime the URI references in an RDF model point to text-based documents stored locally or available on remote systems. Such a search, if available, checks the contents of these documents for matches.

4 Description of RDF Browsing and Visualization Tools

Here we briefly present each tool in terms of general descriptive criteria. In particular, we present a brief general description, and information about its current release, its software development platform/ implementation language, the software execution platform of the tool, the application type i.e., desktop or web-based, as well as the pricing policy followed by the tool developers. Then it is followed by a brief introduction to end-user Semantic Web browsing tools. In this section we introduce these tools as they are closely related to and share many features with the RDF browsing and visualization tools.

4.1   RDF Browsing and Visualization Tools

Following is a brief description of the tools that we used during our research for analyzing our datasets. This subsection is only a brief introduction to these tools and their detailed investigation is presented in the next section.

4.1.1   Drive RDF Browser and W3C's RDF Validation Service

Though a very simple and primitive tool, Drive RDF Browser [27] is an effective tool for validating and browsing small RDF datasets. It is developed in C# for the .NET platform and is available as open source under the terms of the GNU LGPL license. On one page in the form of HTML, Drive displays separately all nodes, edges, literals, namespaces, triples, graph summary, and errors and warnings, if any. Similar to Drive is the W3C RDF Validation Service [7] which provides a hyperlinked list of triples with errors and warnings, if any, and optionally a graph-based view of the validated statements.

4.1.2   Ontopia Omnigator

Omnigator [16] is a generic application built on top of the Ontopia Navigator Framework that allows users to load and browse any conforming topic map. Designed primarily as a teaching aid to help newcomers understand the topic map concepts, it is now an extremely useful tool for debugging topic maps and for building demo applications. Some of the features in the Omnigator 8 include plug-ins for performing querying, filtering, full text search, the ability to display class hierarchies (in both text and graphics modes), better stylesheets, RDF to Topic Map mapping, and an improved statistics printer.

4.1.3   SIMILE RDF Browsing Tools (Welkin, Longwell, Knowle)

The SIMILE project, jointly developed by the W3C, HP, and MIT, is working to make it easier to browse diverse collections of metadata and, more generally, to find the way around in the Semantic Web. SIMILE's domain specific and end-user friendly Longwell [26] and domain independent and RDF-savvy friendly Welkin [25] and Knowle [26] are proving very useful in different application areas. Suitable for end-users, Longwell is a faceted browser that displays only the metadata fields that are configured to be 'facets' and hides the presence of the underlying RDF model. Knowle which is shipped as part of the

Longwell distribution is a node-focused graph navigation browser that is targeted at people who want to see or debug the underlying RDF model. Longwell and Knowle work together to provide a user-friendly Web-based front-end to RDF. As Longwell requires a thorough understanding of the structure of the data being examined and it is hard to get a global overview of an RDF model, thus Welkin was created by the SIMILE team to summarize and to give a quick mental model of the data being manipulated. Designed for metadata analysts, Welkin is a graph based tool that provides global view and cluster characteristics of its data. According to the SIMILE team "Welkin is not meant to be a tool to discover a single RDF statement out of thousands, but it's meant as a "telescope" for your RDF data, a tool that lets you understand its global *shape* and cluster characteristics rather than the individual item".

4.1.4 IsaViz

IsaViz [28] is a visual environment for browsing and authoring RDF models represented as graphs. It allows smooth zooming and navigation in the graph; creation and editing of graphs by drawing ellipses, boxes, and arcs, and has support for several import and export RDF formats. Since version 2.0, IsaViz can render RDF graphs using GSS (Graph Stylesheets), a stylesheet language derived from CSS and SVG for styling RDF models represented as node-link diagrams and version 3 will have support for Fresnel display vocabulary.

4.1.5 RDF Gravity

Based on JUNG Graph API and Jena2, RDF Gravity [12] from Salzburg Research is a graph visualization tool for RDF/OWL datasets of moderate sizes. Though only a graph visualization tool, RDF Gravity has a rich set of features that can satisfy several of the needs of a metadata creator and analyst. These include graph visualization and navigation features, local, global and custom filters, full text search, RDQL [24] queries, and multiple RDF file visualization. Because of these features we have been using RDF Gravity during the course of our project for visualization of our data.

4.1.6 SWOOP and Protégé

SWOOP [14] and Protégé [11] are ontology development toolkits that provide an integrated environment to build and edit ontologies, check for errors and

	Drive RDF	RDF Gravity	Longwell	Welkin	Omni-gator	IsaViz
Current Release	Version 1.0	Version 1.0	Version 1.1 Dev. Rel. 2.0	Version 1.1	Version 8	Stable: 2.1 Dev. Rel. 3.0
Implement. Language	C#	Java	Java	Java	Java	Java
Platform	Any .NET Platform	Any (Java)	Any (Java)	Any (Java)	Any (Java)	Any (Java)
Software Availability	Available for Download	Available for Download	Available for Download	Available for Download	Trial Version Available	Available for Download
Application Type	Desktop Application	Desktop Application	Web Application	Desktop	Web Application	Desktop Application
Pricing Policy	Open Source GNU LGPL	Freeware, Not Open Source	Open Source BSD License	Open Source BSD License	Copy Righted	Open Source W3C License

Table 1. Overview of RDF browsing and visualization tools

inconsistencies, browse multiple ontologies, and share and reuse existing data by establishing mappings among different ontological entities. Protégé is a desktop application based on a plugin design. Different plugins are available for Protégé which drop different functionalities in it. SWOOP on the other hand is hypermedia inspired, is a web based tool, and is more light weight than Protégé. SWOOP is also based on plugin architecture with some very useful plugins like Annotea that provides collaborative annotation support. SWOOP and Protégé though basically ontology development tools can be used for visualizing small RDF datasets but their visualization capabilities are limited and we are not including them in our survey.

4.1.7 *Fresnel Display Vocabulary*

Fresnel [5] is an RDF vocabulary which aims to model information about how to present Semantic Web content (i.e., what content to show, and how to show it) as presentation knowledge that can be exchanged and reused between browsers and other applications. Fresnel presentation knowledge is based on two fundamental concepts: *lenses* which specify the properties and ordering of RDF resources to be displayed, and *formats* which indicate how to format the content selected by lenses. Content is selection is supported by using URIs, SPARQL, or its own language called Fresnel Selector Language [18]. The upcoming versions of Longwell and IsaViz will support Fresnel and some other tools like Horus[9] and Arago claim to support its core features.

4.2 End User Semantic Web Browsing Tools

The Semantic Web vision is based on laying information bare so that it can be collected, manipulated, and annotated independent of its location or presentation formatting. Tools specifically designed for working with this information are required but without substantial quantities of semantic web data available users cannot benefit from such tools. Moreover, the semantic web is not an alternate web but will coexist with the current web. Hence, most of the tools for browsing and working with semantic web take a different approach, i.e. they work with the current web, if semantic web content is available can process it, and if not available can extract from the current pages. They provide browsing and visualization of different levels of metadata detail and allows for the integration of multiple information sources to provide a more complete view of information about web resources. Though our survey does not include these end-user tools but being the most relevant tools and sharing several ideas with RDF browsing and visualization tools, this subsection gives a brief introduction to these tools.

Piggy Bank [13] from SIMILE is an extension of the Firefox web browser that lets web users extract individual information items from within web pages and save them in semantic web format. If the HTML of a web page or site is linked to the same information in RDF, Piggy Bank retrieves that RDF. Otherwise, Piggy Bank can employ screen scrappers that attempt to extract and re-structure information encoded in the served HTML. These items, collected from different sites, can now be browsed, searched, sorted, and organized together, regardless of their origin and types. The user can also subscribe to a Semantic Bank in order to publish and thus share his information on the web.

Haystack [20] is the most impressive client-side application built on a Semantic Web framework. It is an environment that allows users to easily manage their documents, e-mail, appointments, tasks, and other information. It is called "universal information client" that seeks to link together different kinds of user data with a consistent interface. Haystack uses the concept of the "collection" as an organizing principle. A collection might be a list of bookmarks or a set of email messages, which can then be displayed in different "views" or through different "lenses." Haystack is, ultimately, a tool for managing collections of these collections, all interlinked.

Magpie [8] also extends a standard web browser and automatically associates a semantic layer with web pages using a user-selected ontology. It has the ability to identify and filter out the concepts-of-interest from any webpage it is given. The current set of concepts can be influenced by a selection of a particular ontology of concepts and relations. In addition, each such concept may provide an applicable set of relations or commands that can be executed. Another feature that improves the user's experience is the ability to turn the semantic menus ON or OFF, to highlight all instances belonging to a particular ontological class, to follow and semantically process the links embedded in the document. Another interesting feature available in the non-public release of Magpie is its Collectors which is a trigger service that collects items of interest as they are browsed.

Similarly, other semantic web browsing tools for the end user are available each provide access to the user with different layers of abstraction.

5   Comparison of RDF Browsing and Visualization Tools

Following is a comparison of the tools against the evaluation framework adopted in section 3. These tools were briefly introduced in section 4 and here their more technical features are evaluated from the view point of a metadata creator and analyst.

RDF is an abstract model and it can be realized in several concrete serializations like RDF/XML, N3, and N-Triple. RDF data may also reside in in-memory databases and remote triple stores. During our investigation we found that all of the tools have support for RDF/XML as its import/export format and most of the tools also support other common formats like N3 and N-Triples. Originally a Topic Map browser, Omnigator has import/export support only for RDF/XML which provides the facility of mapping between RDF and Topic Maps, though the results are not always promising. Longwell can access data in several triple storage systems but needs several configurations steps. Omnigator can also access data available on its native Ontopia Knowledge Server. IsaViz can browse and edit data in a Sesame triple store by using a plugin. All of the tools support reading data from several RDF files, merge the resulting graphs, and provide a unified display. Longwell utilizes its built-in inference mechanism for providing a more friendly display but none of the tools have the option of integrating an external inference engine. Longwell is not domain independent and the dataset needs to be prepared before browsing. Table 2 provides a summary of these features.

Table 2. Triple data format related features of RDF browsing and visualization tools

	Import Format	Export Format	Triple Store Access	File Merging	Inference Support
RDF Gravity	RDF/XML	RDF/XML	No	Yes	No
Drive RDF	RDF/XML	RDF/XML, HTML output	No	Yes	No
Longwell	RDF/XML, N3, N-Triple	RDF/XML, N3, N-Triple	Jena, Joseki, 3Store, Kowari, Sesame	Yes	Built-in
Welkin	Turtle/N3, RDF/XML	RDF/XML,	No	Yes	No
IsaViz	RDF/XML, N3, N-Triple	RDF/XML, N3, N-Triple, SVG, PNG	Through Plugin for Sesame	Yes	No
Omnigator	XTM, LTM, HyTM, RDF	XTM, HTM, HyTM, CXTM, RDF	OKS only	Yes	No

Table 3 shows an overview of the display features of the RDF browsing and visualization tools. Text-based representation, in general, cannot nicely depict the structure of a large amount of data but is very effective for data mining, i.e., posing targeted queries once the required structure is known. Moreover, text-based displays are not effective for data "understanding", i.e., making sense of a large dataset of unknown global structure. Gravity, Welkin, and Is-aViz provide graph-based displays consisting of node-link diagrams whereas Drive, Longwell, and Omnigator are text-based. Omnigator can also display a graph output by using its Vizigator plugin. Only Longwell and Omnigator provide an integrated interface consisting of a global view and the details of a selected item. All of the graphical browsers provide a general global view of the data with no grouping and clustering of similar items. Gravity and IsaViz use several visual cues (shape, color, size, and shading) together to visualize similar items. The development releases (alpha versions) of Longwell and Is-aViz have support for Fresnel Display Vocabulary. Graph statistics are not available in Gravity, IsaViz and Longwell; Omnigator provides some useful statistics on the graph, whereas Welkin is capable of showing more advanced graph-theoretical properties. Graph editing features are only available in Is-aViz which is basically an RDF graphical editor and browser. Other editors like Protégé can also be used for browsing RDF datasets but these display information in a hierarchical way which makes it difficult to grasp the inherent graph structure.

Table 3. Display features of RDF browsing and visualization tools

	Display Interface	Presentation Paradigm	Graph Editing	Support for Fresnel Voc.	Graph Statistics
RDF Gravity	Global	Graph	No	No	No
Drive RDF	Local	HTML	Very Poor	No	Simple
Longwell	Integrated	HTML	No	Yes (2.0)	No
Welkin	Global	Graph	No	No	More Advanced
IsaViz	Global	Graph	Yes	Yes (3.0)	No
Omnigator	Integrated	HTML, Graphical support (Vizigator Plugin)	Yes	No	Advanced

For scalability tests, besides our own datasets we used data from SIMILE project and Open Directory Project. Table 4 lists our results. We found that most of the tools can work only with a few megabytes of RDF data or a model consisting of a thousand statements at the most. Longwell and Omnigator can work with larger datasets scaling up to several thousand statements. A graphical tool may load a larger file but its visual scalability is very limited as compared to a text-based tool. Graph display in Gravity is improved by visual cues and by selection and filtering. The output of IsaViz, though not better than Gravity, is much better than Welkin mainly because of its zoomable user interface. Omnigator has plugin architecture and can be extended very easily. Longwell also provides the facility of extension.

Table 4. RDF browsing tools' scalability factors

	Max. Dataset Size	Visual Scalability	Extension Mechanism
RDF Gravity	Limited (<1000 statements or Approx. 1 MB of RDF)	Limited	No
Drive RDF	Limited (<1000 statements or Approx. 2 MB of RDF)	Poor for relatively large graphs	No. Tool is not in active development
Longwell	High (>500,000 statements)	High	Yes
Welkin	Limited (<1000 statements or Approx. 1 MB of RDF)	Limited	No
IsaViz	Limited (<1000 statements or Approx. 1 MB of RDF)	Limited	No
Omnigator	High (up to 100,000 TAOs)	Fairly high in text mode	Plugins

Table 5 is a listing of searching, querying, and filtering facilities available in the RDF visualization tools that we investigated. Selection and filtering features available in Longwell and Omnigator are based on ontological concepts like classes, properties, resource types, etc. A Gravity user can apply local and global filters and can hide selected graph elements. Similarly, IsaViz also provides simple selection and activation/deactivation of nodes, links, and regions.

For fine-grained control RDF gravity provides support for RDQL and Omnigator supports its own topic map query language, tolog. Full text search of graph elements is available in almost all of the tools and none can create full text indexes of the documents annotated by the underlying RDF model.

Table 5. Search, query, and filtering facilities in RDF browsing and visualization tools

	Selection & Filtering	RDF Query Language	Full Text Graph Search	Full Text Document Search
RDF Gravity	Yes	Yes (RDQL)	Yes	No
Drive RDF	No	No	No	No
Longwell	Yes	No	Yes	No
Welkin	Yes	No	Yes	No
IsaViz	Simple	No	Yes	No
Omnigator	Yes	Yes (tolog)	Yes	No

6 Recommendations

The following recommendations for future effective and useful tools can be deduced from our investigation:

- Import/export support for common RDF serialization formats like RDF/XML, N3, N-Triple, TriX, etc. and extendable to other upcoming formats
- Support for reading from multiple data sources and providing a unified display
- Possibility of connecting to a triple store over common protocols
- Support for graphical and textual display of information
- The option of simple and more advanced graph statistics
- An integrated display interface consisting of both local and global views of RDF data
- Built-in support for basic reasoning and possibility of plugging in different inference engines

- Global and local filters for simple selection and browsing
- Support for SPARQL RDF query language
- Full text graph and annotated documents search
- Use of visual cues for highlighting similar items
- Support for Fresnel Display Vocabulary
- Support for data in the range of millions of triples
- Tool extension by a plugin mechanism

The maximum support for the features in the future releases of semantic web browsers or development toolkits will enable metadata creators and analysts to better perform their tasks.

7 Conclusions

In this paper we presented and compared a set of tools for the browsing and visualization of Semantic Web data expressed in RDF from the point of view of a metadata creator and analyst. All of tools that we investigated provide source validation, have support for RDF/XML as its import/export format, have the facility of merging different RDF files, and have limited scalability in terms of maximum number of triples that could be loaded.

All graphical tools have very limited visual scalability and most of them use a single display representation, and very few have promised to provide support in their coming releases for Fresnel display vocabulary. Moreover, most of the tools have searching and filtering facilities but at different levels of granularity, few have the option of Full text search, none has support for SPARQL, and none can build full text indexes for RDF annotated documents. Few tools provide the facility of accessing data in triple stores. None of the tools allows the integration of external inference engines and only Omnigator can be extended by using plugins.

Like in other semantic web tools, we found Java as the pre-dominant implementation language, Jena as semantic web development toolkit, Lucene as full text search engine, and Velocity as template engine.

References

1. Ahmed, M., et al: SemanticLife – A Framework for Managing Information of a Human Lifetime, in *The Sixth International Conference on Information Integration and Web-based Applications and Services*, 27-29th September, 2004

2. Albertoni, R., Bertone, A., De Martino, M.,: Semantic Web and Information Visualization. *1st Italian Semantic Web Workshop*, 10th December 2004, Ancona, Italy

3. Berners-Lee, T., Hendler, J., Lassila, O. The Semantic Web, *Scientific American*, May, 2001.

4. Biezunski, M., Newcomb, S. (Editors): ISO/IEC 13250 Topic Maps.1999. See http://www.y12.doe.gov/sgml/sc34/document/0129.pdf

5. Bizer, C., Lee, R., Pietriga, E.: Fresnel - Display Vocabulary for RDF (2005) http://www.w3.org/2005/04/fresnel-info/manual-20050726/

6. Broekstra, J., Kampman, A., Harmelen, F.: Sesame: A Generic Architecture for Storing and Querying RDF and RDF Schema, in *International Semantic Web Conference 2002*: 54-68

7. E. Prud'hommeaux and R. Lee. W3C RDF Validation Service. http://www.w3.org/RDF/Validator/

8. Dzbor, M., Domingue, J. and Motta, E.: Magpie - towards a semantic web browser. Proceedings of the *2nd International Semantic Web Conference 2003* (ISWC 2003), 20-23 October 2003, Florida, USA.

9. Erdmann, T.I.: Horus RDF Browser (2005) http://www.wiwiss.fuberlin.de/suhl/bizer/rdfapi/tutorial/horus/.

10. Friend-of-a-Friend (FOAF) (2001) http://www.foaf-project.org/.

11. Gennari, J., et al: The evolution of Protégé-2000: An environment for knowledge-based systems development. *International Journal of Human-Computer Studies*, 58(1):89–123, 2003.

12. Goyal, S., Westenthaler, Rupert.: RDF Gravity (RDF Graph Visualization Tool). Salzburg Research, Austria. http://semweb.salzburgresearch.at/apps/rdf-gravity/

13. Huynh, D., Mazzocchi, S., Karger. D. Piggy Bank: Experience the Semantic Web Inside Your Web Browser. *4th International Semantic Web Conference* (ISWC 2005)

14. Kalyanpur, A., Parsia, B., Hendler, J.: A Tool for Working with Web Ontologies. In: Proceedings of *Extreme Markup Languages*. (2004)

15. Kowari Metastore: http://www.kowari.org/

16. Ontopia Omnigator: http:///www.ontopia.net/omnigator/

17. Pepper, S. and Moore, G. (2001). XML topic maps (XTM) 1.0. Xtm speci-

fication. http://www.topicmaps.org/xtm/1.0/.

18. Pietriga, E.: Fresnel Selector Language for RDF (2005) http://www.w3.org/2005/04/fresnel-info/fsl-20050726/.

19. Prud'hommeaux, E., Seaborne, A.: SPARQL Query Language for RDF (2005) http://www.w3.org/TR/rdf-sparql-query/.

20. Quan, D., Huynh, D., Karger, D.: Haystack: A platform for authoring end user semantic web applications. In *The SemanticWeb . ISWC 2003*, LNCS 2870, pages 738.753, Heidelberg, 2003. Springer-Verlag.

21. Quan, D., Karger, D.: How to Make a Semantic Web Browser. In: Proceedings of the *13th International Conference on World Wide Web. (2004)* 255–265

22. Rutledge, L., van Ossenbruggen, J., Hardman, L.: Making RDF Presentable: Selection, Structure and Surfability for the Semantic Web. In: Proceedings of the *14th international conference on World Wide Web. (2005)*

23. Schraefel, Mc., Smith, D.: The Evolving mSpace Plateform: Leveraging the Semantic Web on the Trail of the Memex. In: *16th ACM Conference on Hypertext and Hypermedia. (2005)*

24. Seaborne, A. RDQL – RDF Data Query Language, part of the Jena RDF Toolkit, HPLabs Semantic Web activity, http://hpl.hp.com/semweb/, W3C Working Draft 23 November 2005, http://www.w3.org/Submission/2004/SUBM-RDQL-20040109

25. SIMILE: Welkin (2004-2005) http://simile.mit.edu/welkin/

26. SIMILE: Longwell RDF Browser (2003-2005) http://simile.mit.edu/longwell/

27. Singh, R.: Drive: An RDF Parser for .NET (2002), http://www.driverdf.org/

28. W3C: IsaViz: A Visual Authoring Tool for RDF (2001-2005) http://www.w3.org/2001/11/IsaViz/

29. W3C: Resource description framework (RDF): Concepts and Abstract Syntax (2004), http://www.w3.org/TR/rdf-concepts/

30. W3C: RDF Test Cases: W3C Recommendation 10 February 2004, http://www.w3.org/TR/rdf-testcases/

31. Wilkinson, K., Sayers, C., Kuno, H., and Reynolds, D.: Efficient RDF storage and retrieval inJena2. In *First International Workshop on Semantic Web and Databases* (SWDB'03, with VLDB03), Berlin, September 2003.

A Rule-based Approach for Semantic Annotation Evolution in the CoSWEM System

Phuc-Hiep Luong and Rose Dieng-Kuntz

INRIA Sophia Antipolis, 2004 route des Lucioles, BP 93
06902 Sophia Antipolis, France
{Phuc-Hiep.Luong, Rose.Dieng}@sophia.inria.fr
http://www-sop.inria.fr/acacia/

Abstract. An approach for managing knowledge in an organisation in the new infrastructure of Semantic Web consists of building a Corporate Semantic Web (CSW). The main components of a CSW are (i) evolving resources distributed over an intranet and indexed using (ii) semantic annotations expressed with the vocabulary provided by (iii) shared ontology. However, changes in the operating environment may lead to some inconsistencies in the system and they result in need of modifications of the CSW components. These changes need to be evolved and well managed. In this paper we present a rule-based approach allowing to detect and correct semantic annotation inconsistencies. This rule-based approach is implemented in the CoSWEM system enabling to manage the evolution of such a CSW, especially to address the evolution of semantic annotations when its underlying ontologies change.

1 Introduction

Organisational knowledge is considered as one of the most important assets of organisations, which decisively influences its competitiveness. More and more organisations set up a Knowledge Management (KM) system in order to better facilitate the access, sharing, and reuse of that knowledge as well as creation of new organisational knowledge [6]. One approach for managing knowledge in an organisation consists of capturing organisational knowledge and building an Organisational memory or Corporate memory [17]. In the next generation of Semantic Web aiming at a better cooperation among humans and machines [1], organisational memories can be materialised as a Corporate Semantic Web (CSW), which are composed of heterogeneous, evolving resources distributed over an intranet and indexed using semantic annotations expressed with the vocabulary provided by a shared ontology [5,18].

However, organisations live in dynamic and changing environments because of the changes in their business, technologies and processes. These changes often lead to continuous changes in the organisation's KM system in which ontologies are the evolving factor since they are used as a backbone for providing and accessing knowledge sources in ontology-based KM systems [23]. Ontological changes in underlying ontologies then need to be propagated to all semantic annotations that are created based on the shared vocabulary of these ontologies. Consequently, such modifications influence activities and performance of the KM system and they are still not well addressed [11].

In this paper, we introduce the Corporate Semantic Web as a particular approach to KM and analyse its evolution problem. We present the CoSWEM[1] system enabling to manage the evolution of such an CSW and we focus particularly on the evolution of semantic annotations when their underlying ontologies change. In this system, a rule-based approach is implemented in order to detect inconsistent annotations and to guide the process of solving these inconsistencies by applying correction rules and resolution procedures. First of all, we introduce our CSW approach and its evolution problems in Sect. 2. We describe the CoSWEM system architecture and its main functions. In Sect. 3, we propose a rule-based approach including inconsistency detection rules and correction rules. Then, we summarize briefly in Sect. 4 a survey of current researches on the evolution of ontology and ontology-based KM systems, the impacts of theirs changes on components of the system. Before giving a conclusion and further work in the last section, we will also discuss on the similarity between our work and several existing studies.

2 Evolution Management for a Corporate Semantic Web

2.1 Corporate Semantic Web approach

With the purpose of deployment organisational knowledge using Internet and web technologies for an organisation, many researches have been carried out

---

[1] Corporate Semantic Web Evolution Management

to study the integration of a corporate memory [6] in a new Semantic Web environment. Semantic Web aims at making the semantic contents of Web resources understandable not only by human but also by programs, for a better cooperation among humans and machines [1]. The ACACIA[2] research team has been studying the materialization of a corporate memory as a Corporate Semantic Web (CSW) [5] [6] using ontologies to formalize the vocabulary shared by a community, and semantic annotations based on these ontologies to describe heterogeneous knowledge sources and facilitate their access via intranet/internet (as Fig.1). Considering our illustrating example in biomedical domain, this CSW consists of:

- Resources: they can be documents, databases that store biomedical information. These resources also correspond to people, services, software or programs.
- Ontologies: they describe the conceptual vocabulary in biomedical domain (i.e UMLS[3] metathesaurus and ontology).
- Ontology-based semantic annotations: they use the conceptual vocabulary defined in ontologies to describe resources, for example biomedical information, symptoms and experiments stored in the databases...

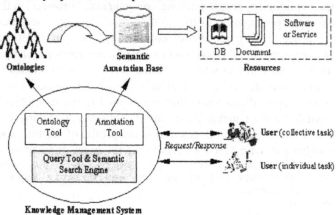

Fig. 1 - Architecture of a Corporate Semantic Web

---

[2] http://www-sop.inria.fr/acacia/
[3] Unified Medical Language System.

2.2 Evolution problems in a Corporate Semantic Web

When one of three main components of a CSW is changed, it might have an impact on the consistency of the overall system. In this case, other related parts may need to evolve as well to reflect the changes. Among these three components, ontologies are the evolving factor since their domains are changing fast (new concepts may appear, concepts are removed, concept hierarchy is reorganized... etc). The authors of [7] have proposed three types of changes in ontology evolution: changes in domain, changes in conceptualisation and changes in specification. A modification in one part of the ontology may generate inconsistencies in other parts of the same ontology, in the ontology-based instances as well as in depending ontologies and in the applications using this modified ontology [22]. Moreover, changes in ontology may impact to the semantic annotations that use concepts or properties defined in this ontology. Like the ontologies, resources also influence on the semantic annotations in case of change since the latter describe the content of knowledge sources. In order to manage changes in a CSW, we have proposed an evolution management system CoSWEM that aims at managing the evolution of each component and the evolutionary relation among components. However, in this paper we emphasize the propagation of the ontological changes to the semantic annotations in order to keep an overall consistency. This change propagation phase can be considered in the process of semantic annotation evolution.

We examine a scenario in which a biologist (or a doctor) needs to create semantic annotations describing a patient's profile. These semantic annotations use several specialized terms that are defined in the biomedical UMLS ontology containing the concept Fever and its subconcept Malaria Fever. For instance, s/he describes some information in the profile of her/his patient John Beeman who has a disease Malaria Fever in the following annotation:

```
<ev:Person rdf:about="http://persinfo.com/John.Beeman">
    <ev:hasDisease rdf:resource='&ev;Malaria_Fever'>
    </ev:hasDisease>
</ev:Person>
```

Annotation before updating statement

After some executed changes in the biomedical UMLS ontology (e.g. the concept Malaria Fever is deleted), this existing statement of annotation will be inconsistent with respect to the ontology because of lack of the reference to the deleted concept Malaria Fever. One possible solution in this case is to replace the deleted concept name Malaria Fever in annotation by its parent's name Fever.

```
<ev:Person rdf:about="http://persinfo.com/John.Beeman">
    <ev:hasDisease rdf:resource='&ev;Fever'>
    </ev:hasDisease>
</ev:Person>
```

Annotation after updating statement

In order to describe the inconsistency of semantic annotation, we define what is a consistency constraint and what is an inconsistent semantic annotation. We also give a definition of an annotation model that is based on the data model RDF presented in [24].

Definition 1: *A **consistency constraint** ensures a consistent agreement among semantic annotations entities with respect to their underlying ontology.*

Definition 2: *A semantic annotation is defined to be **inconsistent** with respect to its ontology model if it violates the consistency constraints defined for annotation model.*

Definition 3: *An **annotation model** is a tuple $SA:=(R_A, C_A, P_A, L, T_A)$ where:*

- R_A : *set of resources*
- C_A : *set of concept names defined in ontology ($C_A \subset R_A$)*
- P_A : *set of property names defined in ontology ($P_A \subset R_A$)*
- L : *set of literal values*
- T_A : *set of triples (s, p, v .) where $s \in R_A$, $p \in P_A$ and $v \in (R_A \cup L)$*

2.3 Process of semantic annotation evolution in the CoSWEM system

As we mentioned in previous sections, semantic annotations might be inconsistent after having applied some ontological changes. We present in this section a process of the CoSWEM system enabling to address the inconsistency of semantic annotations. In our system, we choose RDF(S) languages [24], which are recommended by W3C, to formalize our ontologies and annotations. RDF uses a triple model and an XML syntax to represent properties of Web resources and their relationships in what we call RDF annotations. The system process includes the following main steps:

Step 1 : convert UMLS metathesaurus and semantic type into a RDF(S) ontology

The UMLS metathesaurus and semantic types are represented in structured textual files, so they need to be converted into a suitable format of an ontology in RDF(S) for later processing. We also convert the log file capturing realised changes between two UMLS metathesaurus versions to appropriate format (e.g. this change log format can include some information related to the author of change, type of change, the old/new value...). This converted log file allows to determine quickly the annotations related to ontology changes.

Step 2 : query semantic annotations, using Corese
Corese, a semantic search engine developed by the Acacia team [4] (see below), allows to query the annotation bases taking into account the concept hierarchy and the relation hierarchy defined in the ontologies. It makes inferences on the whole annotation according to user's queries. In this step, Corese especially can be used to retrieve from existing annotation bases:
- annotations related to modified ontology by using their reference link to this ontology.
- potential inconsistent annotations (they may include both related consistent and inconsistent annotations) by using a set of ontology changes. A potential inconsistent annotation means that it relates to the ontological change but its consistency constraint has not been verified.

Step 3 : apply inconsistency detection rules
We apply inconsistency detection rules in this step in order to detect the real inconsistent annotations from a set of potential inconsistent annotations. A real inconsistent annotation means that it violates the consistency constraint defined for the annotation. These detection rules are formulated from a set of constraints and are expressed in the syntax of Corese rule language.

Step 4 : apply inconsistency correction rules and resolution procedures
After having determined real inconsistent annotations from a set of potential inconsistent annotations, these annotations will be repaired by applying correction rules. We have established all possible solutions that solve the propagation of ontological changes to their semantic annotations in order to keep consistency status.

Step 5 : versioning management
This step enables us to manage versions of the ontology and its semantic annotation in case of storing different versions.

In this system process, we focus on the Step 3 which is responsible for checking the consistency of an semantic annotation with respect to its underlying ontology. This step also enables to find "parts" in the semantic annotation that violate consistency constraints. The Step 4 is responsible for ensuring the consistency of the semantic annotation by applying the correction rules and the resolution procedures that resolve the detected inconsistencies.

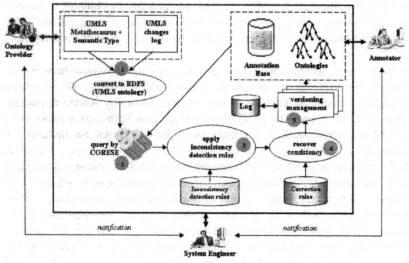

Fig. 2 - Process of semantic annotation evolution

The actors involved in this system (as Fig.2) are the System Engineer who manages the overall system, the Annotator who creates annotations based on existing ontology, the Ontology Provider who provides changing ontology source (e.g. UMLS project offering biomedical information from a variety of different sources). UMLS metathesaurus[4] contains information about biomedical concepts and terms from many controlled vocabularies and classifications used in patient records, full-text databases and expert systems. All concepts in metathesaurus are assigned to at least one semantic type from the semantic network. This provides consistent categorization of all concepts in metathesaurus at the relatively general level represented in semantic network. Currently, the structure of semantic network is quite stable while the metathesaurus is updated at least three times a year, some concepts in metathesaurus are inserted, deleted or renamed after each released version. Changes between two consecutive released versions are captured in a log file that allows us to watch for which type of changes and how these changes were executed. This is a

---

[4] http://www.nlm.nih.gov/research/umls/meta2.html

good example for illustrating the influence of a frequent changing domain source to its metadata sources. The Acacia team has generated we have built an ontology represented in RDFS in order to describe the biological domain (drugs, cells, genes, processes). This ontology consists of concepts and relations extracted from UMLS semantic type network and a part of metathesaurus [13].

We use Corese[5], an ontology-based search engine for the semantic web: it is dedicated to the retrieval of web resources annotated in RDF(S) [4] by using a query language based on RDF(S). Corese engine internally works on conceptual graphs (CG). It enables an RDFS ontology and RDF annotations to be loaded and translated into CG, and then, using the CG projection operator, allows the base of annotations to be queried. Corese proposes a query language for RDF very similar to SPARQL[6]; for each query, an RDF graph is generated, related to the same RDF Schema as the one of the annotations to which it is to be matched. When matching a query with an annotation, according to their common ontology, both RDF graphs and their schemas are translated in the CG model [9]. Besides, Corese provides a rule language enabling us to deduce new knowledge from existing one [3]. For example, when we modify the underlying ontology (e.g. deletion of concept Malaria Fever), annotations based on this ontology may be in inconsistent status. Corese enables us to retrieve all annotations related to this ontology change by applying query to the annotation base (as Fig.3).

---

[5] COnceptual REsource Search Engine (http://www-sop.inria.fr/acacia/soft/corese/)
[6] http://www.w3.org/TR/rdf-sparql-query/

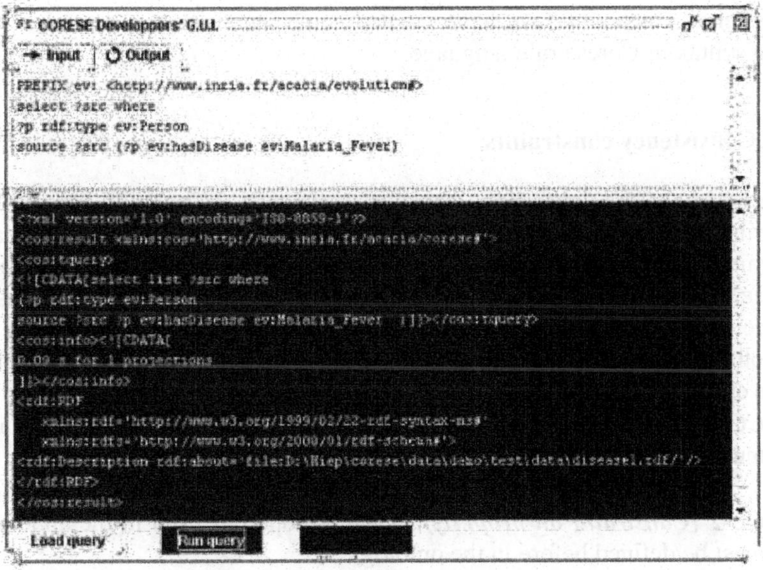

Fig. 3 - A query example using Corese

The following query determines Person (?p) who has a disease called Malaria Fever. This query also indicates the affected statement and the source location of the annotation containing this statement (e.g. this statement is located in an RDF annotation file *disease1.rdf*).

```
PREFIX ev: <http://www.inria.fr/acacia/evolution#>
select ?src where
?p rdf:type ev:Person
source ?src (?p ev:hasDisease ev:Malaria_Fever)
```

3 Rule-based approach for solving inconsistencies of semantic annotation

Our rule-based approach is constructed from some consistency constraints that must be satisfied for any annotation model. Consistency is an attribute of a (logical) system that is so constituted that none of the facts deducible from the model contradicts an other [21]. Therefore, we have proposed some consistency constraints that can be considered as an agreement among semantic annotations entities with respect to their underlying ontology. Based on thes consistency constraints, we have created some inconsistency detection rules using syntax of Corese rule language.

3.1 Consistency constraints

In order to express consistency constraints, we take the notation from [24] to describe an RDF triple in annotation as a triple *(s p v .)*. This triple makes statement about resource and it can be expressed as a subject *s* has a property *p* whose value is *v*. We use the primitive *rdf:type* to indicate a resource as instance of specific types or classes (e.g. resource has type Class or Property), and other primitives with prefix *rdfs:* to describe classes or relationship among these classes in the ontology.

- **CC-1 (Constraint on concept):** All the concepts used in the annotation must be defined before in the ontology.

    (s rdf:type c) $\Rightarrow$ *(c rdf:type rdfs:Class)*

- **CC-2 (Constraint on property):** All the properties used in the annotation must be defined before in the ontology.

    (s p v.) $\Rightarrow$ *(p rdf:type rdf:Property)*

- **CC-3 (Constraint on property domain):** The resource which is the domain of a property in the annotation must be compatible with the domain of the corresponding property defined in the ontology.

    (p rdf:type rdf:Property) $\wedge$ *(p rdfs:domain d)* $\wedge$ *(d_1 p v .)*
    $\Rightarrow$ *(d_1 rdf:type d)*

- **CC-4 (Constraint on property range):** The resource which is the range of a property in the annotation must be compatible with the range of the corresponding property defined in the ontology.

    (p rdf:type rdf:Property) $\wedge$ *(p rdfs:range r)* $\wedge$ *(s p r_1 .)*
    $\Rightarrow$ *(r_1 rdf:type r)*

- **CC-5 (Constraint on datatype):** The datatype of a value of property in the annotation must be compatible with the value of the corresponding property defined in the ontology.

    (p rdf:type rdf:Property) $\wedge$ *(p rdfs:range r)* $\wedge$
    (r rdf:type rdfs:Datatype) $\wedge$ *(s p r_1 .)* $\Rightarrow$ *(r_1 rdf:type r)*

3.2 Inconsistency detection rules

We have established several inconsistency detection rules enabling us to find inconsistent annotations that are obsolete related to a modified ontology considered as a reference. These rules are based on consistency constraints and are represented in syntax of Corese rule language. We have implemented these detection rules in Corese in order to make use of its queries for the task of inconsistency detection. Below is an example of a rule that detects inconsistent annotations whose concept has not been defined before in the ontology.

Detection rule for concept resource: If a concept is used in an annotation but it has not been defined in the ontology, then this annotation leads to inconsistent status.

This detection rule can be expressed as following:

```
IF
    ?x rdf:type ?c
    not(?c rdf:type rdfs:Class)
THEN
    error("inconsistent")
```

We use the syntax of Corese rule language (including some primitives in SPARQL) to represent this detection rule as below:

```
<cos:rule>
    <cos:if>
        ?x rdf:type ?c
        option( ?c rdf:type ?class
        ?class = rdfs:Class
        )
        filter ! bound(?class)
    </cos:if>
    <cos:then>
        ?x rdf:type cos:Error
    </cos:then>
</cos:rule>
```

3.3 Inconsistency correction rules and resolution procedures

After having collected all inconsistent annotations from a set of potential inconsistent annotations, we need to correct these inconsistencies by applying some correction rules on these annotations (e.g. what should the system do if a leaf concept is deleted?). We have established several resolution procedures for each ontological change (e.g. how to solve an inconsistent annotation if it relates to a deleted leaf concept in ontology?) and specified how to propagate the change resolution to inconsistent annotations in order to keep an overall consistency. We examine an example of the deletion of a leaf concept in the ontology. Suppose we have a leaf concept Malaria_Fever *(Malaria_Fever rdf:type rdfs:Class)* which is the child of an unique super-concept Fever *(Fever rdf:type rdfs:Class, Malaria_Fever rdfs:subClassOf Fever)*, a property *p* *(p rdf:type rdf:Property)* that may receive Fever as its domain/range. Now we make a change in the ontology by removing the leaf concept Malaria_Fever. After having deleted this leaf concept in the ontology, several statements in annotations related to this concept Malaria_Fever may be in inconsistent status with respect to this modified ontology. To solve this problem, there are several possible solutions (see table below) that can be applied to obsolete annotations depending on each ontological change resolution.

Inconsistency correction rules	*Resolution Procedure*
If the Fever concept is the domain of *p* in the ontology, and the evolution strategy consists of changing the instances of the deleted concept Malaria_Fever into instances of its unique super-concept Fever, **Then** the system will transform a resource instance of the Malaria_Fever concept into an instance of the Fever concept, it will keep unchanged the annotations concerning the property *p* on this resource.	The instance of the concept Malaria_Fever will become instance of its super-concept Fever, but the RDF triple involving the property *p* on this instance will remain the same. *Replace* *(inst_disease rdf:type Malaria_Fever .)* *(inst_disease p v .)* *By* *(inst_disease rdf:type Fever .)* *(inst_disease p v .)* with *v* can be a literal value or an instance of concept;
If the Fever concept is the range of *p* in the ontology, and the evolution strategy consists of changing the instances of the deleted concept Malaria_Fever into instances of its unique super-concept Fever, **Then** the system will transform a resource instance of the Malaria_Fever concept into an instance of the Fever concept, it will keep unchanged the annotations expressing the value of the property *p* for this resource.	The instance of the concept Malaria_Fever will become instance of its super-concept Fever, but the RDF triple involving this instance as value of the property *p*. *Replace* *(inst_disease rdf:type Malaria_Fever .)* *(s p inst_disease .)* *By* *(inst_disease rdf:type Fever .)* *(s p inst_disease .)* with *s* is the instance of a concept;

If the Malaria_Fever concept is the unique domain/range of p in the ontology, **Then** system will delete all statements including the instance of concept Malaria_Fever in annotation.	All obsolete statements including the instance of concept Malaria_Fever will be removed. ***Remove*** *(inst_disease rdf:type Malaria_Fever .)* *(inst_disease p v.)* *(s p inst_disease .)* with v can be a literal value or a concept; s is the instance of a concept;

In addition, for each change in ontology that may affect a semantic annotation, we have different strategies to restore the consistency of this annotation. For instance, an obsolete statement can be totally removed or it can be modified according to the new update of corresponding part (concept/property) in ontology.

4 Related Work and Discussion

The majority of researches in the field of KM system, ontology or semantic annotation are focused mainly on construction issues. There are few studies coping with the changes and providing maintenance facilities in KM system. In this section, we make a survey on these existing studies and we try to give an comparison between our work and some other related researches.

4.1 Related Work

An interesting research on the evolution of KM system is presented in [11]. This paper analyses two types of changes: (i) functional changes and (ii) structural changes that can appear in KM systems. The authors in [12] point out that ontologies on the Web will need to evolve. They provide a new formal definition of ontologies for the use in dynamic, distributed environments and also present SHOE, a Web-based knowledge representation language. [12] mentions to the support of multiple versions of ontologies and ontology reuse but it does not process the change propagation between distributed and dependent ontologies. There are also some studies of managing changes in ontologies [7] [21] that take ideas from research on database schema evolution [8]. [14] describes an ontology versioning system that allows access to data through different versions of the ontology. This approach is based on the comparison of two ontology versions in order to detect changes. But the change detection phase is a complicated and time-consuming process. It is impossible to determine the cause and the consequences of a change, which is a crucial requirement for the consistency of the dependent ontologies [22]. Moreover, the authors of [7] [15] have proposed a framework for ontology evolution but their approach lacks a detailed analysis of the effect of specific changes on the interpretation data. In contrast to that approach of versioning, which detects changes by comparing ontologies, Stojanovic et al. present their ontology evolution approach that allows access to all data only through the newest ontology. In their paper [10], the authors have summarized briefly these two main approaches of ontology evolution and versioning. The authors have presented in [22] a process of six-phases for ontology evolution with some procedures of change resolution. They have focused on the two important phases (i) semantic of change that enables the resolution of ontology changes in a systematic manner by ensuring the consistency of the whole ontology and (ii) change propagation that brings automatically dependent artefacts (ontology based instances, applications and dependent ontologies) into a consistent state after an ontology update has been performed. [19] has also presented an integrated framework for managing multiple and distributed ontologies. This paper presents a conceptual modeling approach along with its mathematical definition and formal semantics in order to solve the change propagation of distributed ontologies. However, both [22] [19] have not mentioned about the change propagation to the related annotations in case of related changes in ontologies. In [20], the authors have introduced a combined approach that supports the process of ontology evolution and ontology versioning by managing the history of ontology changes.

There are very few approaches investigating the problems of propagation of the ontological changes to semantic annotations. In [23], the authors proposed a framework CREAM to solve the evolution of metadata based on their existing research on the ontology evolution. Nevertheless this approach only presented their proposition of a framework for enabling consistency of the descriptions of the knowledge sources in case of changes in the domain ontology but they do not specify techniques to solve it. Another study of ontology evolution influence on metadata via relational constraints of a database system is also given in [2]. According to this approach, the knowledge-based environments rely on a relational database to store the RDF and RDFS used for representing respectively ontology-based assertions and the ontology structure itself. Ontology maintenance events can be managed using database triggers for automatically modifying property ranges or domains in the stored assertions.

4.2 Discussion

Our work presented in this paper can be compared with some similar existing studies. Regarding to the resolution of inconsistencies in semantic annotations in the context of modifications in ontology, [23] has presented the framework CREAM enabling the consistency of semantic annotations when ontologies changes but has not specified a particular technique to solve it. In [2], a technique of using triggers in relational database for automatically modifying property ranges or domains in the stored assertions has been introduced but it has not mentioned the inconsistency resolution process. Our evolution management system CoSWEM not only proposes the propagation process of the ontological changes to semantic annotations but also specifies a rule-based approach to detect inconsistent annotations and the correction procedures to solve these inconsistencies. Relying on rule-based approach, our work differs from the rules for change in [15] for finding complex ontology changes. In contrast to this method which is based on a set of rules and heuristics to generate a complex change from a set of elementary changes, our approach relies on the executed ontological changes stored in the evolution log. Our detection rules deal with the semantic annotations only related to these changes instead of examining all annotation base.

We have also suggested a solution to manage several different versions of ontology and semantic annotations for a CSW after some changes. This version management can be related to some previous works [15] [16] [20]. We are carrying out several studies on methodologies and techniques for this issue.

5 Conclusion

We have presented in this paper the Corporate Semantic Web as one particular approach for managing knowledge for an organisation in the new infrastructure of Semantic Web. However, such a CSW system needs the ability to adapt efficiently to the changes from its components such as ontologies, annotations or resources. For this reason, we have proposed the CoSWEM system enabling us to manage its evolution, especially to manage effects on annotations when the ontologies change. In this system, we have implemented a rule-based approach for solving inconsistencies in semantic annotations. This approach enables to find inconsistent annotations through inconsistency detection rules and then to repair these inconsistencies by using correction rules and resolution procedures.

As further work, we will refine this rule-based approach and study some effective algorithms on the process of correction and validation for semantic annotations changes. We will also focus on the problem of versioning management allowing to use different versions of semantic annotations and ontologies.

References

1. Berners-Lee, T. , Hendler, J. and O. Lassila (2001). The Semantic Web, In Scientific American, May 2001, p35-43
2. Ceravolo, P. A. Corallo, G. Elia and A. Zilli (2004). Managing Ontology Evolution Via Relational Constraints. Knowledge-Based Intelligent Information and Engineering Sys-tems, 8th International Conference, KES 2004, Wellington, New Zealand. Lecture Notes in Computer Science 3215, Springer 2004
3. Corby, O. (2005). Corese RDF Query and Rule language. INRIA Research Report 2005
4. Corby, O., R.Dieng-Kuntz, C.Faron-Zucker (2004).Querying the Semantic Web with the CORESE search engine. In R. Lopez de Mantaras and L. Saitta eds, Proc. of the 16th European Conference on Artificial Intelligence (ECAI'2004), Valencia, 22-27 August 2004, IOS Press, p. 705-709
5. Dieng-Kuntz, R. (2005). Corporate Semantic Webs. In Encyclopaedia of Knowledge Management, D. Schwartz ed, Idea Publishing Group, September 2005.
6. Dieng-Kuntz, R., O. Corby, F. Gandon, A. Giboin, J. Golebiowska, N. Matta and M. Ribire. (2005). Knowledge Management-Methodes et outils pour la gestion des connaissances; une approche pluridisciplinaire du Knowledge Management. 2e dition, Dunod, Paris, 2005.
7. Noy, N.F. and Klein, M.. Ontology evolution: Not the same as schema evolution. Knowledge and Information Systems, 6(4):428-440.

8. Roddick, J.F. (1996). A Survey of Schema Versioning Issues for Database Systems, Information and Software Technology, 37(7):383-393, 1996.
9. Gandon, F. (2002). Distributed Artificial Intelligence and Knowledge Management: Ontologies and Multi-Agent System for a Corporate Semantic Web. PhD Thesis at INRIA Sophia Antipolis, ACACIA team.
10. Haase, P. and Sure Y. (2004). D3.1.1.b State-of-the-Art on Ontology Evolution. SEKT/2004/D.3.1.1.b/v0.5. Institute AIFB, University of Karlsruhe.
11. Hardless, C. Lindgren, R. U. Nulden and K. Pessi (2000). The Evolution of knowledge management system need to be managed, http://www.viktoria.informatik.gu.se/groups/ KnowledgeManagement/Documents/kmman.pdf, 2000.
12. Heflin, J. Hendler, J. (2000). Dynamic Ontologies on theWeb. Proceedings of the 7th National Conference on Artificial Intelligence AAAI-2000, Menlo Park, CA, August 2000, pp 443-449. AAAI/MIT Press, Cambridge, MA
13. Khelif, K. Dieng-Kuntz, R., and P. Barbry (2005). Semantic Web Technologies for Interpreting DNA microarray analyses: the MEAT system. Proc. of the 6th International Conference on Web Information Systems Engineering WISE'05, New York, novembre 2005.
14. Klein, M. Kiryakov, A. Ognyanov, D. D. Fensel (2002). Ontology versioning and change detection on the Web. Proceedings of the 13th European Conference on Knowledge Engineering and Knowledge Management (EKAW-2002), Siguenza, Spain, October 2002, pp 197-212
15. Klein, M. (2004). Change Management for Distributed Ontologies. PhD thesis, Vrije Universiteit Amsterdam, Aug. 2004.
16. Klein, M., Noy, N.F. (2003). A component-based framework for ontology evolution. Proceedings of Workshop IJCAI'2003 on Ontologies and Distributed Systems, Acapulco, Mexico, CEUR-WS Volume 71, available as Technical Report IR-504, Vrije Universiteit Amsterdam, 2003.
17. Kuhn, O. and Abecker, A. (1997) Corporate memories for Knowledge Management in Industrial Practice: Prospects and Challenges, Journal of Universal Computer Science, vol. 3, no. 8.
18. Luong, P-H. Dieng, R. (2005). Evolution Management System for a Corporate SemanticWeb, Conference YVSM 2005 (Young Vietnamese Scientists Meeting 2005), June 12-16, 2005 in Nha Trang, Vietnam.
19. Maedche, A. Motik, B. and L. Stojanovic. (2003). Managing multiple and distributed ontologies on the semantic web. The VLDB Journal, 12:286-302.

20. Rogozan, D. and G. Paquette (2005). Managing Ontology Changes on the Semantic Web. Proceedings of the 2005 IEEE/WIC/ACM International Conference on Web Intelligence (WI'05)
21. Stojanovic, L. (2004). Methods and Tools for Ontology Evolution. PhD thesis, University of Karlsruhe, 2004.
22. Stojanovic, L. A. Maedche, N. Stojanovic and B. Motik (2002). User-driven ontology evolution management. Proceedings of the 13th European Conference on Knowledge Engineering and Knowledge Management (EKAW-2002), Siguenza, Spain, October 2002, pages 285-300. Springer-Verlag, 2002.
23. Stojanovic, L., Stojanovic, N., and S. Handschuh (2002). Evolution of the Metadata in the Ontology-based Knowledge Management Systems, The 1st German Workshop on Experience Management: Sharing Experiences about the Sharing of Experience, 2002.
24. W3C Resource Description Framework, http://www.w3.org/RDF.

Integrating Ontologies by means of Semantic Partitioning

Gizem OLGU[1] and Atilla ELÇİ[2]

[1]Department of Computer Engineering,
Cyprus International University (CIU),
Nicosia, TRNC, via Mersin 10, Turkey,

[2]Department of Computer Engineering,
Eastern Mediterranean University (EMU),
Famagusta, TRNC, via Mersin 10, Turkey.

Abstract. The growth of interest in Semantic Web has increased the number of ontologies. Necessity of dealing with different ontologies at the same time has enhanced the research on ontology integration. This paper is focused on integrating ontologies covering the same domain. In particular, a novel approach of semantically parsing multiword elements (SPME) is presented in this paper. What is more, paper exemplifies the approach on ontology examples from e-learning domain and confirms the approach with existing ontologies. In addition, paper shows that it produces results with respect to information retrieval techniques.

1 Introduction

An ontology is an explicit specification of a conceptualization [15]. Ontologies are widely used in Semantic Web [14], where they provide the base for semantic annotation to web pages. The wide usage of Semantic Web and the number of people contributing to the web increase numbers of ontologies.

One of the basic problems in the development of the Semantic Web is the integration of ontologies. Due to the creation of ontologies by different people, there have been large numbers of disparate ontologies covering the same domain, therefore, in order to extract information from web, semantic integration of these ontologies is required.

Ontologies tend to differ from each other in syntax, logical representations, language expressivity, scope, model coverage, and concept description [8]. These differences in ontologies are called mismatches and they are explained in [12] detail. Also there are synonym terms (naming differences) and homonym terms (subjective meaning) problems between ontologies [3]. In literature, several approaches have been proposed and they are explained in detail in Sect. 2.

This paper deals with the problem of integrating independently created ontologies of a specific domain. First existing methods are reviewed. Proposed approach is semantically parsing multiword elements (SPME) into single word elements and then using them to create relations between ontologies.

The case study concerns an e-learning scenario. First, the approach is tested on sample ontologies in e-learning domain that are represented in OWL [7]; then followed its application to existing ontologies. Finally, using the existing ontologies so integrated, utility of our approach is exemplified in information retrieval for novel searches. It is shown that the new approach of SPME helps to improve integration process, especially in the case of data mining using ontologies.

The remainder part of the paper is organized as follows. In Sect. 2, the problems arising while integrating ontologies and known solutions are explained. Sect. 3 describes a problem in using e-learning scenarios. In Sect. 4 SPME approach is described. Sect. 5 displays the utility of this approach with information retrieval. Sect. 6 concludes the paper

2 Reconciliation of Ontology Mismatches

2.1 Mismatches

Differences in ontologies are referred to as mismatch by Klein [8]. Due to the fact that the universe, which is the domain part of ontologies, can be specified in many different ways, the problem of mismatch in ontologies arises. Detection of mismatches and resolving them has an important role in integration.

Visser et al. [12] propose a classification of ontology mismatches to explain semantic heterogeneity in systems. They follow Gruber's [15] original definition of an ontology which includes conceptualizing of domain and explicating of domain. Mismatches are classified into two categories as Conceptualization and Explication mismatches.

Conceptualization mismatches are those between two or more conceptualization instances of the same domain; they come as class mismatches and relation mismatches. Class mismatches concern classes and their subclasses. Relation mismatches concern hierarchical relations between classes or, the assignment of attributes to classes.

Explication mismatches are those that relate to the way the conceptualization is specified. For that purpose, 3-tuple Def=<T, D, C> is defined where T is a term (class name), D is a definiens and C is an ontological concept (meaning of classes) that is explicated. Explication mismatches are grouped into six categories. First one is CT (concept and term) mismatch that occurs when two ontologies use the same definiens D, but differ in both concept C they define and term T linked to definiens. Second one is CD (concept and definiens) mismatch that occurs when two ontologies use the same term T but differ in both concept C they define and definiens D used for definition. Note that CD mismatch implies that the term T is a homonym. Third one is C (concept) mismatch that occurs when two ontologies use the same term T and the definiens D but differ in concept C they define. Like the CD mismatch, the C mismatch implies that T is a homonym. Forth one is TD (term and definiens) mismatch that occurs when two ontologies define the same concept C but differ in both term T and definiens D. Note that TD mismatch implies that two terms T are synonym. Fifth one is T (term) mismatch that occurs when two ontologies define the same concept C using same definiens D but with different terms T. Note that like TD mismatch, T mismatch implies that two terms T are synonym. Last one is D (definiens) mismatch that occurs when two ontologies define the same concept C and use the same term T but with different definiens D. Solutions have already been proposed for these mismatches. For example, the CD (concept and definiens) mismatch can be resolved by renaming the terms T. The C (concept) mismatch can be resolved by renaming expressions as in the CD mismatch. The D (definiens) mismatch can be resolved by either renaming terms or mapping link terms. These are utilized in our integration process to start with.

In addition to these, Klein [8] determines further kinds of mismatches. Language level mismatches relate to syntax, logical representation semantics of primitives and language expressivity. And encoding differences, where values in ontologies may be encoded in different formats, for example, date with fo mats dd-mm-yy and dd/mm/yyyy.

2.2 Mapping and Similarity Approaches

There are mapping algorithms developed through some similarity approaches that propose specific formulas and matching schemes. These approaches are also used to solve the above-mentioned mismatches.

Many matching algorithms, like Su's [16 & 17], calculate similarities with linguistic information, that is by examining the structure of word, such as, its prefix, suffix, and root. Maedche et al. [2] propose another structural way, the lexical comparison, for example, two lexical entities "TopHotel" and "Top_Hotel" are similar to each other. Also in schema matching algorithm with Cupid approach [4], Jayant et al. propose structure matching in addition to linguistic approach. Structure matching looks for hierarchical schemas of ontologies. Another one, the similarity flooding algorithm [13] is based on a fix point computation. In this algorithm, the model is first converted into directed labeled graph, and then algorithm takes two graphs as input and produces mapping between corresponding nodes of graphs as output. For computing similarities, two distinct nodes can be similar when their adjacent elements are similar. In Rodriguez et al. [6] present a semantic similarity model where they detect similar entity classes based on synonym set, distinguishing features and semantic neighborhoods that are classified into parts, functions and attributes.

One of the existing tools used for ontology mapping is PROMPT [10]. PROMPT algorithm provides semi-automatic approach to ontology merging and alignment. PROMPT starts with linguistic-similarity matches initially, but concentrates on finding clues based on the structure of the ontology and user's actions. When user invokes an operation, PROMPT creates members of these three sets based on the arguments to specific invocation of the operation. The set of ontology-merging operations that is identified includes both the operations that are normally performed during traditional ontology editing and operations specific to merging and alignment, such as: merge classes, merge slots, merge bindings between a slot and a class.

In this work, we have seen that there are semantically near ontologies not integrated even after detection of above-mentioned mismatches and employing corresponding solutions. In the following we will show how integration of such cases may be possible.

The next section introduces a problem in ontology integration that manifests itself in information retrieval during finding of suitable material in e-learning.

3   Problem in Hand with E-Learning Scenario

One of the basic problems of the Semantic Web is the integration of ontologies. Indeed, the web includes variety of information however in order to extract and combine information, say in a summary document, semantic integration is required. This section introduces a similar situation, where e-learning material in the form of Semantic Web pages has been developed by parties independently from each other. Let's suppose that we are aiming to generate a composite e-learning material using existing modules or generating an extended summary for reclamation purposes.

As mentioned earlier, there are several problems arising while trying to integrate ontologies.

For solving integration problems and creating better integration, a scenario related to e-learning is used as illustrated in Fig. 1. Consider web pages that include information about e-learning each of which has its own implicit ontology. In order to extract information from these pages, it is necessary to review each of the independently created ontologies, which is a tedious process. However if the ontologies of the web pages can be integrated into a virtual ontology (V.O.), then only that would be searched; doing so would increase the performance of a semantic search. Moreover, while a new web page is created with its ontology, this new ontology is added into integrated virtual ontology as shown in the bottom left corner of Fig. 1.

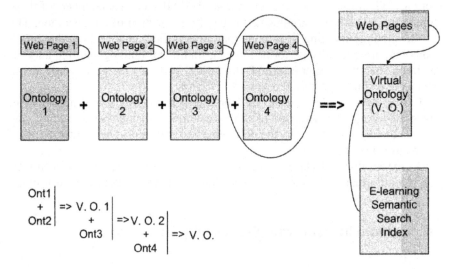

Fig. 1. The scenario illustrates web pages, their ontologies, and all web pages with one Virtual Ontology (V.O.), which is created by integrating all of them. Note that, if new ontology (such as ontology 4) is added, it is compared with V.O and then it is appended to V.O., like shown on the left bottom corner of the figure.

The sample ontologies on e-learning domain are manually generated from papers chosen from several proceedings on educational technology conference. For ontology extraction only the abstracts of these papers are considered in order to reduce the amount of work required, to simplify ontologies and the protocol coding schema, described in [1], is used to identify concepts and relationships from a paragraph. After that, these concepts and relationships are used to construct RDF statements as directed labeled graphs and then ontologies are created. For convenience, Protégé 3.0 [11] ontology editor tool with OWL plug-in is used in engineering ontologies.

By taking nouns from abstract part of papers, class names are formed with meaningful words (dictionary meanings). This is important point in approach of semantically parsing multiword elements that is explained in the following section.

4   Proposed Solution

For solution of ontology mismatches, known methods of integration are initially applied for integration of ontologies. In this respect, firstly mismatches are found and then solved with proposed solutions as in [12 & 8], which are explained in Sect. 2.1. Then, mismatches due to synonym terms, such as *instructor* and *teacher*, are solved using OWL mapping methods [9] that is owl:equivalentClass property. Then, similarities between ontologies are recognized using similarity approaches as mentioned in Sect. 2.2. We have concentrated on similarity approach of Su in [16] that calculates the similarities with linguistic information, such as looking into structure of word, its prefix, suffix and root. We used only exactly similar classes for our similarity inspection.

Even after applying these methods, ontologies that are not integrated still remain. For such cases we created the SPME approach introduced below.

4.1   Approach of Semantically Parsing Multiword Elements

In this approach, we assert that if some multiword class elements in ontologies are parsed into significant words that make them up then integration process can be continued.

In order to test it, following SPME algorithm is proposed. In this algorithm MW stands for a multiword element and W_1 is the 1st word in a multiword element, W_2: 2nd,... W_n: n^{th}. Therefore multiword element MW is a combination of $W_1, W_2, ... W_n$ like $MW = W_1 + W_2 + ... + W_n$. In such cases, $W_1, W_2 ... W_n$ are super classes of MW.

SPME takes ontologies as input and creates an integrated ontology as output. First SPME selects multiword elements (elements as classes) and creates a list of them. Then the following cycle takes place: (1) Parse MW elements into words $W_1, W_2,...$ (2) Check if these words already exist in one of the ontologies and eliminate the duplicate if any. (3) Insert the subclass relations MW has with words $W_1, W_2....$ This cycle continues until all ontologies have interconnected or some ontologies still remain isolated but there are no MWs left in any ontology in the set.

The SPME algorithm is as follows:

in Ontologies:
> *select* all multiword elements *MWs*.
> *for each* *MW*
>> *try* all paths from any source to any target element
>>> *make sure that* all ontologies are interconnected *then* *exit*
>>> *else*
>>>> *parse* *MW* *into* W$_i$, i=1..n where n= # of words in *MW*;
>>>> *for each* W$_i$ *if* W$_i$ *exists* in any ontology
>>>>> *then* eliminate newly created duplicate W$_i$;
>>>> *connect* *MW* with W$_i$ as subclass.
> *continue*.

To test the above algorithm, ontologies from e-learning scenario, which is introduced in Sect. 3, are used. Multiword class names are detected that can be parsed into single words. Thus, some class names have a few similarities. For example, consider the "LearningApproach", which can be parsed as "Learning" and "Approach", and "LearningSystems", which can be parsed as "Learning" and "Systems", also "OnlineLearning", it can be parsed as "Online" and "Learning". Subsequently these can be integrated around the common term "Learning" (see Fig. 2). Consequently, if multiword class names are parsed, there can be some other meaningful single word class names, that are considered as implicit classes. This is illustrated in Fig. 2, therefore "Learning" is an implicit class and it can be an individual class. Also other parts of classes (Approach, Online, and System) become other individual classes. Furthermore, classes, which are not parsed, and new individual classes are combined with subclass property thus having integrated otherwise disparate ontologies.

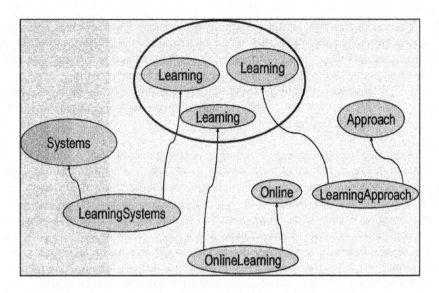

Fig. 2. Parsing the multiword class names and creating new individual classes.

There may be three concerns developing while applying this approach. The first is: until when to continue parsing multiword elements? Do all or do just enough of them? The answer is: until reaching a significant integration point, that is, all ontologies being interconnected by at least a single link. Doing more than sufficient or all of them creates problems as the integrated ontology becomes very large and complex. The second one: is it feasible to parse all multiword elements? Of course not, we should be careful not to break elements like "connectionless" into "connection" and "-less" as the suffix is not useable as a class name. Finally, in parsing multiword class names we look out for words that have semantics, such as meaningful nouns.

5 sUtility of Semantically Parsing Multiword Elements

To verify SPME approach, it is applied to existing (previously independently published) ontologies. Then the integrated ontology is used for information retrieval.

The various ontologies on e-learning domain are selected using ontology search engine Swoogle [5], and SPME approach is applied on these selected ontologies. Because these ontologies are huge, here we are able to display only small parts that are considered in this paper. These ontologies are:

[i]   Research.owl: http://ebiquity.umbc.edu/ontology/research.owl, and
[ii] Ka.owl: http://protege.semanticweb.org/plugins/owl/owl-library/ka.owl

A portion of Research.owl ontology is illustrated in Fig. 3, and that of Ka.owl in Fig. 4. Note that these ontologies do not have common terms. Consider the Research class in Fig. 3 and ResearchTopic class in Fig. 4, which have similarities. The SPME approach proposes that ResearchTopic class can be parsed as Research and Topic (see Fig. 4), and the new Research class can be considered as same with Research class in Fig. 3; then ResearchTopic class becomes subclass of Research class. In addition, in this example "Topic" class is eliminated to prevent confusion in figure. Fig. 5 shows the integrated ontology after using the approach of semantically parsing multiword elements.

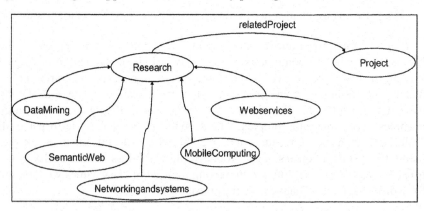

Fig. 3 Portion of Research.owl [i] ontology.

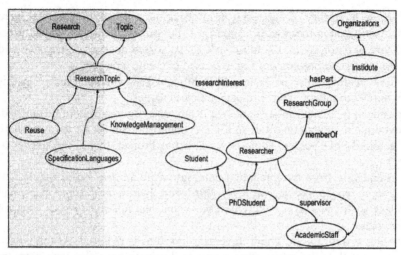

Fig. 4 Portion of Ka.owl [ii] ontology, after using SPME approach.

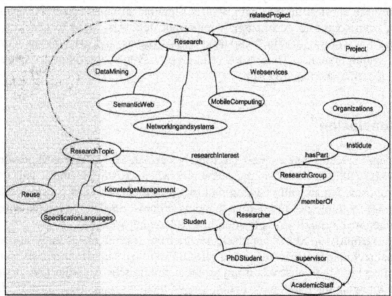

Fig. 5 Integrated portion of Research.owl [i] and Ka.owl [ii] ontologies, after using SPME approach.

To show the utility of this result in information retrieval, assume that there is a semantic search index (SSI, as in Fig. 1, bottom right corner), which refers to the virtual ontology. In the following, first a search query is determined and then the integrated ontology of Fig. 5 is used to create a response.

Sample search query is: Which PhD Student has which Projects? In this query the "PhdStudent" and "Project" are class names.

Consider Fig. 3 and Fig. 4, an answer from these figures can not be reached, however the integrated ontology in Fig. 5, contains a path for an answer. There can be found PhD Student some how related to Project, that is the answer of query.

Consequently from the integrated ontology, *PhD Student* is the subclass of *Researcher*, whose has *Research Interest* listed in *Research Topic* class, and this class is the subclass of *Research* class that has *Related Project* listed in *Project* class.

For this search a good graph traversal algorithm is required. At the outset, the answer, path to the query, from source to destination is unknown, therefore at that point the reachability is important; similarly it is important to obtain possibly the shortest answer path, that is semantic distance (ontological distance) from source to destination is important, too. Also need to generate a strategy for avoiding deadlock and dead-end situations, and reducing the number of search branches. Thus, a powerful graph traversal algorithm is required that can extract the required path.

6 Conclusion

This paper presents a new approach, namely "Semantically Parsing Multiword Elements" (SPME) in integrating ontologies where existing methods fail. Paper proposes, semantically parsing multiword elements (classes considered as elements) in ontologies to improve mapping process. SPME was implemented and illustrated through an application in an e-learning scenario.

For exemplifying SPME approach, papers from several proceedings on educational technology conference were selected and then sample ontologies were generated from their abstracts using protocol coding schema. After that, in order to integrate the ontologies, firstly, known methods were used; then SPME approach was applied if all ontologies were still not interconnected. The

SPME approach was further demonstrated with existing ontologies for information retrieval to carry out novel searches.

To conclude, we reiterate that the integration of ontologies where other known methods fail may still be possible using the approach of semantically parsing multiword elements introduced in this paper.

References

1. A. Hameed, D. Sleeman, A. Preece, "Detecting Mismatches Among Experts' Ontologies Acquired Through Knowledge Elicitation", In Proceedings of 21st SGES International Conference on Knowledge Based Systems and Applied Artificial Intelligence, Vol. 15, No.5-6, pp. 265-273, June 2002.

2. A. Maedche and S. Staab. "Measuring Similarity between Ontologies." In Proceedings of the European Knowledge Acquisition and Management (EKAW 2002), pp. 251-263, October 2002.

3. G. Wiederhold, "An Algebra for Ontology Composition", In Proceedings of 1994 Monterey Workshop on Formal Methods, pp. 56-61, Monterey CA, 1994.

4. J. Madhavan, P. A. Bernstein, and E. Rahm. "Generic Schema Matching with Cupid." In Proceedings of the 27th International Conferences on Very Large Databases, pp. 49-58, August 2001.

5. L. Ding, T. Finin, A. Joshi, R. Pan, R. S. Cost, Y. Peng, P. Reddivari, V. Doshi, J. Sachs, "Swoogle: a search and metadata engine for the semantic web", In Proceedings of the 13th ACM International Conference on Information and Knowledge Management, pp. 652 – 659, 2004.   URL: http://swoogle.umbc.edu/, last visited: March, 2006.

6. M. A. Rodriguez and M. J. Egenhofer, "Determining Semantic Similarity Among Entity Classes from Different Ontologies", IEEE Transactions on Knowledge and Data Engineering, Vol. 15, No. 2, pp. 442-456, 2003.

7. M. Dean, G. Schreiber, (eds.), "OWL Web Ontology Language Reference", W3C Recommendation, February 2004.

8. M. Klein, "Combining and Relating Ontologies: an Analysis of Problems and Solutions." In Proceedings of the 17th International Joint Conference on Artificial Intelligence (IJCAI-01), Workshop on Ontologies and Information Sharing, Vol. 47, pp. 53-62, Seattle, USA, August 2001.

9. M. K. Smith, C. Welty, D. L. McGuinness, (eds.), "OWL Web Ontology Language Guide", W3C Recommendation, February 2004.
10. N. F. Noy, M. A. Musen, "PROMPT: Algorithm and tool for automated ontology merging and alignment", In Proceedings of the 17th National Conference on Artificial Intelligent (AAAI-2000), pp.450-455, Austin, TX, 2000.
11. Protégé. Project at Stanford University. http://protege.stanford.edu/, last visited: March 2006.
12. P. R. S. Visser, D. M. Jones, T. J. M. Bench-Capon, M. J. R. Shave, "An Analysis of Ontology Mismatches; Heterogeneity versus Interoperability", American Association for Artificial Intelligence (AAAI 1997) Spring Symposium on Ontological Engineering, pp. 164-172, Stanford University, California, USA. 1997.
13. S. Melnik, H. Garcia-Molina, E. Rahm, "Similarity Flooding: A Versatile Graph Matching Algorithm and its Application to Schema Matching." In Proceedings of the 18th International Conference on Data Engineering (ICDE'02), pp.117-128, San Jose CA, 2002.
14. T. Berners-Lee, J. Hendler, and O. Lassila., "The Semantic Web", Scientific American, Vol. 284, No. 5, pp. 34-43, May 2001.
15. T. R. Gruber, "A Translation Approach to Portable Ontology Specifications", Knowledge Acquisition, Vol. 5, pp.199-220, June 1993.
16. X. Su, "A Text Categorization Perspective for Ontology Mapping." Technical report, Department of Computer and Information Science, Norwegian University of Science and Technology, Norway, 2002.
17. X. Su, S. Hakkarainen, T. Brasethvik, "Semantic Enrichment for Improving Systems Interoperability.", In Proceedings of the 19th ACM Symposium on Applied Computing (SAC 2004), pp.1634-1641, 2004.

Toward the Identification and Elimination of Semantic Conflicts for the Integration of RuleML-based Ontologies

Yevgen Biletskiy[1], David Hirtle[2], and Olga Vorochek[3]

[1]Department of Electrical and Computer Engineering, University of New Brunswick. P.O. Box 4400, 15 Dineen Dr., D41 Head Hall, Fredericton, NB, E3B 5A3, Canada, biletski@unb.ca
[2]Faculty of Computer Science, University of New Brunswick, P.O. Box 4400, 540 Windsor Street, Gillin Hall, Fredericton, NB, E3B 5A3, Canada, david.hirtle@unb.ca
[3]Department of Software Engineering, Kharkiv National University of Radio-Electronics, 14 Lenin av., Kharkiv, 61166, Ukraine, relf@kture.kharkov.ua

Abstract. Integration of ontologies of information sources and consumers is important for achieving web-based interoperability and thus for the success of the Semantic Web as a whole. The present work describes an approach for eliminating semantic conflicts with the purpose of integrating ontologies of heterogeneous information sources. The paper is focused on elimination of homonymy and finding synonymy in ontologies of learning objects (namely course outlines) and identification of (in)compatibilities between course descriptions. As a proof of concept, ontologies are implemented using the XML-based Rule Markup Language (RuleML), which has been combined with the Web Ontology Language (OWL), a W3C standard, to form the Semantic Web Rule Language (SWRL). This representation in RuleML allows the ontology to be executable, flexibly extensible and platform-independent. The RuleML source representation can also easily be converted to other XML-based languages (such as RDF, OWL and SWRL) as well as incorporated into existing XML-based repositories (such as IEEE LOM and CanLOM) using XSL Transformations (XSLT). The facts and rules of the RuleML-based ontology are used by the OO jDREW reasoning engine to identify semantic homonymy and synonymy between components of course descriptions.

1 Introduction

Interoperability is key to the Semantic Web and e-Activities. The most important effort in order to achieve interoperability between information sources and consumers on the Web is building source, consumer and domain ontologies [2]. An essential step of building ontologies for interoperability is their integration [9] with the purpose of building a domain of common ontology [7, 8] for all information sources and consumers participating in particular scenarios of data exchange (for example, delivery of learning objects to learners' contexts) [4]. This common ontology must explicitly specify the information sources' basic ontologies, relationships between sources, and also relationships between concepts found within sources' metadata and consumers' profile models for further conversion of such information to the consumer's context [3]. Such integration of ontologies often causes semantic conflicts between ontologies of information sources. The majority of conflicts belong to the class of naming conflicts: homonymy, which occurs when ontological objects with the same name specify different conceptualizations, and synonymy, which involves different ontological objects specifying the same conceptualization. The present work is devoted to eliminating homonymy with the purpose of excluding invalid links of interoperability between ontological objects, and finding synonymy to install links of interoperability between ontologies to be integrated. In particular, this paper is focused on the elimination of naming conflicts between *specifying* learning objects (such as university curricula, course outlines, etc.) that specify the use of other learning objects in a particular course context and scenario [4]. Section 2 of the paper describes an approach to finding homonymy and synonymy between such kinds of information sources. Section 3 describes an application of this approach to RuleML-based ontologies of specifying learning objects (in particular, course outlines) and finding interoperability between them.

2 A formal approach to identification of homonymy and synonymy

This section of the paper describes a formal rule-based approach for the identification of semantic homonyms and synonyms. This approach is implemented using RuleML in section 3. Let us consider a fragment of a course outline (Fig. 2.1). From the ontological perspective, course outlines and other learning objects consist of learning object metadata (LOM) and content. Name and author are attributes of LOM. Assume we have two course outlines with the same title (Fig. 2.1) where: LOM – learning object metadata; title, author – LOM attributes; structure – structure of course topics, resources, and other content; SWE – Software Engineering; YB – author of Course1; OV – author of Course2.

The same title means that these two ontological fragments are potentially homonymous:

Potential_Homonymy (CourseX, CourseY) ⇐ *D (title(CourseX), title(CourseY)),*	(2.1)

where D is the predicate of semantic identity: $D(x, y) \Leftarrow (x=y)$; the objects x and y are not exactly the same, but have the same meaning.

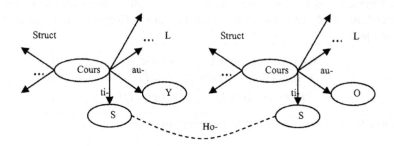

Fig. 2.1 Homonymy of learning objects

Potential homonymy becomes true homonymy if other attributes of LOM are not identical:

$$Homonymy\ (CourseX,\ CourseY)\ \Leftarrow Potential\_Homonymy \qquad (2.2)$$
$$(CourseX,\ CourseY)\ \wedge\neg\ (\ \underset{i}{\wedge}\ D\ (LOM_i(CourseX),LOM_i(CourseY)),$$

where LOM_i is the ith attribute of learning object metadata.

Thus, homonymy has been identified; one of the objects must be renamed in order to eliminate this semantic conflict, e.g., from SWE to SWE_1.

Analysis of synonymy is more complicated because synonymy of two objects in different ontologies assumes full compatibility of links from these objects to other objects; therefore, the analysis of synonymy can be performed through comparison of links to other objects and/or comparison of metadata attributes. Let us consider two other fragments of course outline ontologies (Fig. 2.2), where: ADS – Advanced Digital Systems; VLSI – VLSI Systems Design; Intro – Introduction to FPGA-based Systems and VLSI Technology; C&S – Combinational and Sequential Circuits; FPGA – FPGA Fabrics; LSIS – Large Scale Integration Systems. In the proposed approach the analysis of synonymy is performed in the following order:

1. Extraction of an object of the first ontology to be potentially integrated (Course1);
2. Forming a set of links from this object (Course1) to other objects (mask of potential interoperability) [5];
3. Comparing objects of this mask (Intro, C&S, FPGA, LSIS) with every object of the second ontology.

If these objects are semantically identical to the corresponding objects of the second ontology, then coincidence is found. Coincidence means that the objects Course1 and Course2 are synonymous; in this case interoperability is achieved, or steady association between the objects Course1 and Course2 can be installed:

$$Synonymy\ (CourseX,\ CourseY)\ \Leftarrow \qquad (2.3)$$
$$\neg\,D\ (title(CourseX)\ title(CourseY)\ \wedge$$
$$(\underset{i}{\wedge}\ D\ (topic_i(CourseX),\ topic_i(CourseY)),$$

where $topic_i$ is the ith topic of a course outline.

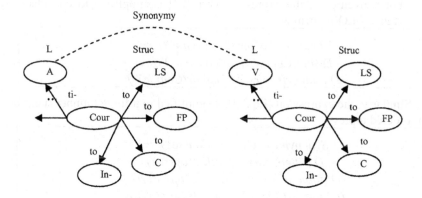

Fig.2.2 Synonymy between learning objects

3 Identification of semantic conflicts in RuleML-based ontologies

The Rule Markup Language (RuleML) is an XML-based markup language for publishing and sharing rules used for derivation, query, transformation, integrity checking and reactive behavior. Rules play an important role in the Semantic Web and Web Services [5]. They are being used in many application domains such as Engineering, e-Business, Law, and Artificial Intelligence. RuleML consists of a hierarchy of sublanguages to maximize interoperability by accommodating related technologies such as RDF and OWL; it is the most appropriate knowledge representation for this work because it is a neutral interchange format allowing rules, the representation of concepts and the relationships between them all in one document.

RuleML is used in the present work for ontology coding and the elimination of semantic conflicts with the purpose of further integration of the information sources' and consumers' ontologies and building a common ontology. The resulting ontology consists of facts extracted from the course outline documents and rules to be applied to these facts in order to find homonymy and synonymy.

For convenience, the expression (Eq. 2.2) is simplified to consider only the "author" LOM attribute:

$$Homonymy\ (CourseX,\ CourseY) \Leftarrow$$
$$D(title(CourseX),\ title(CourseY)) \wedge$$
$$\neg D\ (author(CourseX),\ author(CourseY)).$$

(3.1)

Similarly, the expression (Eq 2.3) is simplified to a finite number (i.e., four) of ordered topics:

$$Synonymy\ (CourseX,\ CourseY) \Leftarrow$$
$$\neg D\ (title(CourseX),\ title(CourseY) \wedge$$
$$(D\ (topic_1(CourseX),\ topic_1(CourseY)) \wedge$$
$$(D\ (topic_2(CourseX),\ topic_2(CourseY)) \wedge$$
$$(D\ (topic_3(CourseX),\ topic_3(CourseY)) \wedge$$
$$(D\ (topic_4(CourseX),\ topic_4(CourseY)).$$

(3.2)

The RuleML representation of the rules (Eq 3.1, Eq. 3.2) in the more compact Positional Slotted Language (POSL) [6] syntax is as follows:

```
Homonymy(?CourseX,?CourseY):-
Title(?CourseX,?TitleX),Title(?CourseY,?TitleY),equal(?TitleX,?TitleY),
Author(?CourseX,?AuthorX),Author(?CourseY,?AuthorY),
notEqual(?AuthorX,?AuthorY).
Synonymy(?CourseX,?CourseY):-
Title(?CourseX,?TitleX),Title(?CourseY,?TitleY),

notEqual(?TitleX,?TitleY),

Topic1(?CourseX,?Topic1X),Topic1(?CourseY,?Topic1Y),
equal(?Topic1X,?Topic1Y),
Topic2(?CourseX,?Topic2X),Topic2(?CourseY,?Topic2Y),
equal(?Topic2X, ?Topic2Y),
Topic3(?CourseX,?Topic3X),Topic3(?CourseY,?Topic3Y),
equal(?Topic3X,?Topic3Y),
Topic4(?CourseX,?Topic4X),Topic4(?CourseY,?Topic4Y),
equal(?Topic4X,?Topic4Y).
```

These rules as well as facts (Fig. 2.1, Fig. 2.2) can be easily converted to the RuleML syntax. For example:

```
<Atom>
    <Rel>Title</Rel>
    <Ind>Course1</Ind>
    <Ind>Software Engineering</Ind>
</Atom>
```

Querying the RuleML-based ontology about the semantic conflicts between course outlines has been successfully performed using the OO jDREW reasoning engine [1].

The domain of RuleML-based ontologies is extensible. In order to add a new solution to identify more complicated cases of homonymy and synonymy, another piece of RuleML description would be added to the document. The RuleML representation is thus shown to be flexible, extensible and platform-independent.

4 Conclusion

This paper presented an approach for identifying the semantic conflicts of homonymy and synonymy and an application of this approach to RuleML-based ontologies of learning objects on the Semantic Web. The theoretical foundation and methodology were first presented, followed by examples of RuleML ontologies of course outlines. These learning objects were selected because they, in turn, specify others. It is important to identify semantic conflicts between such specifying learning objects because the same technique can be partially applied to attain interoperability between other resources referenced from them. The RuleML ontology built was then manipulated by the OO jDREW reasoning engine.

This work identified some important tasks for further research:
1. Enumeration of learning object metadata (LOM) attributes in RuleML.
2. Identification and enumeration of course topics.
3. Identification of partial synonymy.
4. Order of relationships to other objects (in RuleML) for analysis of synonymy.
5. Identification of semantic (but not exact) identity.

References

1. Ball M (2004) Object-Oriented Java Deductive Reasoning Engine for the Web, Available: http://www.jdrew.org/oojdrew

2. Biletskiy Y, Hirtle D (2006) Conceptualization of Specifying Learning Objects. WSEAS Transaction on Computers 1/5: 177-185

3. Biletskiy Y, Boley H, Zhu L (2006) A RuleML-Based Ontology for Interoperation between Learning Objects and Learners. UCFV Research Review 1/2006, Available: http://journals.ucfv.ca/ojs/rr/article-PDFs/biletskiy-boley-zhu.pdf

4. Biletskiy Y, Vorochek O, Medovoy O (2004) Building Ontologies for Interoperability among Learning Objects and Learners. Lecture Notes in Computer Science, Springer-Verlag, vol. 3029/2004, pp. 977-986

5. Boley H (2003) Object-Oriented RuleML: User-Level Roles, URI-Grounded Clauses and Order-Sorted Terms. In Schroeder, M. Wagner, G. (Eds.): Rules and Rule Markup Languages for the Semantic Web, Springer-Verlag, Heidelberg, LNCS-2876: 1-16.

6. Boley H (2004) POSL: An Integrated Positional-Slotted Language for Semantic Web Knowledge, Available: http://www.ruleml.org/submission/ruleml-shortation.html

7. Firat A, Madnick S, Grosof B (2002) Financial Information Integration in the Presence of Equational Ontological Conflicts. Proceedings of the Workshopon Information Technology and Systems (WITS), Barcelona, Spain, pp 211-216

8. Goh CH, Madnick SE, Siegel MD (1994) Context interchange: overcoming the challenges of large scale interoperable database systems in a dynamic environment. Proceedings of the Third International Conference on Information and Knowledge Management, Gaithersburg, Maryland, USA, pp 337-346

9. Uschold M, Gruninger M (1996) Ontologies: principles, methods and applications. The Knowledge Engineering Review Research 11/2: 93-136.

Incorporating Multiple Ontologies into the IEEE Learning Object Metadata Standard

Phaedra Mohammed and Permanand Mohan

Department of Mathematics and Computer Science, The University of the West Indies, St. Augustine, Trinidad and Tobago.
{fedre@lycos.com, pmohan@tstt.net.tt}

Abstract: Learning objects are the currency for Educational Information Systems which support learning on the Educational Semantic Web. As such, proper metadata infrastructure must be set up around learning objects so that they are described in a way that agents can understand and also in a way that allows re-use. There are numerous problems with the LOM specification to date, but many research attempts advocate the use of various ontologies in alleviating some of the problems faced with the learning object metadata standards. However, there is a lack of practical examples describing exactly how these ontologies can be attached to a learning object. In light of this, our paper describes a practical approach that makes use of the IEEE LOM standard and which allows multiple ontologies to be included in the markup of learning objects.

1 Introduction

Learning objects are the currency for Educational Information Systems which support learning on the Educational Semantic Web. As such, a proper metadata infrastructure must be set up around learning objects so that they are described in a way that agents can understand and also in a way that allows reuse. This is done through the use of standardized information about the learning object called metadata which allows learning systems, learners or instructors to understand the purpose of a learning object as well as to discover, manage and use the learning material appropriately.

Several cataloguing schemes exist for marking-up learning objects. However the IEEE 1484.12.1-2002 Standard for Learning Object Metadata (LOM) is the recognized standard which consists of nine categories of data elements which define a structure for describing learning objects [9]. In addition, the Instructional Management System (IMS) has developed the IMS Content Packaging Specification [7] which encapsulates the learning material and all associated metadata into a single file or content package. Essentially, one or more learning objects and the associated metadata can be neatly wrapped up in a content package which conforms to an international standard for learning technologies.

Nonetheless, the IEEE Learning Object Metadata (LOM) Specification in handling the reusability of learning objects, is deficient in many ways. The very nature of the language in which it is described together with the organization, design and scope are problematic in capturing the various facets of learning that a learning object is meant to represent. Mohan and Brooks [3] suggest that ontologies are needed for describing the structure, content, teaching and learning strategies of learning objects. Various research efforts support this idea and this can be seen with the advent of numerous types of ontologies describing these facets of a learning object. However, the question remains as to exactly how these ontologies can be attached to a learning object and whether it is possible to distinguish between the types of ontologies.

In light of these questions, this paper examines the importance of using multiple ontologies for describing learning objects. These descriptions improve the usability of educational resources and they promote better search and discovery of appropriate learning material. As a result, the reusability of learning objects is enhanced since semantic information would enrich the descriptive nature of the metadata.

This paper is organised as follows. Section 2 outlines the various research threads that use ontologies for describing learning objects. Several approaches to alleviating the problem of the LOM's lack of semantic expressiveness are discussed in Section 3 with a particular focus on the use ontologies. Section 4 describes the practical approach taken by the authors in extending the LOM with domain ontologies in order to increase the reusability of learning objects. A prototype system which makes use of our approach in making learning object recommendations is described in Section 5. Finally, Section 6 concludes the paper with the usefulness of this approach and future research directions.

2   Multiple Ontologies Describing a Learning Object

All of the arguments about the size and usability of the LOM are trivial compared to the complaints about the actual elements in the LOM. The most important problem concerning the specification is its lack of expressiveness. However, there are no sufficient provisions for describing the content of the learning object other than a cursory account in the *Description* element that uses a string that is under two thousand characters in length [9]. Such a description is by no means adequate and certainly does not position learning objects for the emerging Educational Semantic Web [4] where ontologies quickly take the place of simple string descriptions of resources. This has given rise to the idea of using ontologies instead of the *Description* element since they are used on the Semantic Web for representing rich descriptive knowledge.

Researchers have proposed various types of ontologies for describing aspects of a learning object. For instance, learning design ontologies have been created by both Knight et al [7] and Lama et al [8] which map out the entire IMD Learning Design Specification in relation to a learning object. Verbert et al. [7] fashioned the ALOCOM ontology that describes the physical structure of a learning object. Wang and Kim [8] produced a teaching strategy ontology and Kasai et al. [8] developed an ontology that captures the goal of IT education in relation to learning. Moreover, numerous other research groups have created domain ontologies describing the learning content itself such as in the Database domain [10] for example.

All of these claims for using ontologies are justified but there is a lack of practical examples describing exactly how these ontologies can be attached to a learning object. Simple explanations can be found in the research literature as to which categories of the LOM can be used for this attachment but these are limited to attaching only one ontology per learning object. While these examples may have been sufficient a few years ago, the true Semantic Web vision requires multiple ontologies to be attached to resources. This implies that on the Educational Semantic Web, all of the ontologies described earlier can be attached to a learning object since they all contribute meaningful information about the learning object. A single ontology describing a learning object is no longer sufficient for supporting the tasks envisioned on the Educational Semantic Web [4].

3   Incorporating Semantics into the LOM

Techniques ranging from metadata extension, modification and in one case, entire replacement of the LOM have been used in increasing the semantic meaning of the LOM. Metadata extension is the simplest method since the existing elements in the LOM are not changed but enhanced by new elements such as the proposed additional metadata structure in [10] that describes information about context, the learning object itself and the object's usage history. Another LOM extension was implemented in the MD2 platform which facilitates the creation and annotation of learning objects [12]. The researchers clearly state that in order to increase a learning object's reusability, more specialized metadata than that provided by the IEEE LOM must be used. In particular, they declare that ontologies are an appropriate starting point for annotating learning objects.

Brooks et al [2] go even further and argue that instead of the IEEE LOM, a more flexible approach is needed. They explain that three types of ontologies about the learning object's domain and pedagogy and learner's characteristics can be used to link to content as a form of dynamic evolutionary metadata. These would contribute to the gradual accumulation of information about a learning object that would determine whether the material is obsolete or useful. But such an approach calls for the discontinuation of a standard way of describing learning material. This paper opts for a more gentle progression by using the existing LOM, since, although it is insufficient in many ways, it is still an approved IEEE standard and is widely used. Consequently, existing learning objects can be simply improved by following our approach rather than needing an entire redesign as is advocated by Brooks et al [2].

In addition, Semantic Web languages [3] have also been used to update the LOM specification which is presently expressed in XML. The LOM to RDF binding [15] is one conversion attempt that translates LOM elements written in XML into an equivalent representation written in RDF. Again, this requires that the current learning objects be reworked from having metadata in XML to having the same metadata in RDF. Our approach updates the LOM in an unobtrusive way and gives the flexibility of using any Semantic Web language for describing the learning object.

Most of these attempts advocate the use of ontologies in alleviating some of the problems faced with the learning object metadata standards. However, the process of actually connecting one or even more than one ontology to a learning object has not been extensively discussed. This first step is important before ontologies can be used for widespread metadata improvement. The authors concur with the notion of using ontologies and propose a practical way of integrating one or more ontologies into the LOM metadata of learning objects.

4   Integration of Domain Ontologies into the LOM

An ontology is perceived to be the chief medium by which meaningful data will be associated with services and resources in general [1]. This is because of the ontology's potential for describing meaning and also for its characteristic ability of being linked to one or more resources. In light of this, a simple approach that makes use of the LOM standard and which allows ontologies to be included in the markup of learning objects is described in this section. The motivation and background for this approach follows from the prototype implementation proposed by Sicilia et al. [17] which is based on the concept of a *learning link* where learning resources are made reusable through link ontologies. Further support is provided by the work of Zarraonandía et al. [12] where a similar approach is used. However, our approach differs in that not only one, but multiple ontologies can be attached to a learning object through the LOM. Furthermore, provisions are made for classifying the multiple ontologies under categories such as those related to the domain, or the learner or the pedagogy or the physical structure of the learning object.

This connection can be realised by modifying the use of the IEEE LOM specification within the *Classification* metadata element. Since this element is used to describe the *Classification* of the learning object, it seems fitting to place the ontological information within here as an ontology does essentially the same thing, that is, it organises the concepts related to the learning material. The works of both Zarraoanadía et al. [12] and Sicilia et al. [17] follow this reasoning.

Within the *Classification* metadata element, several tags are available for filling in important information regarding the ontology. According to the LOM specification, the *taxonpath* element represents specific classification paths so that there may be more than one path within the element. Similarly, each type of ontology can be considered to be a path for classifying a learning object thus the *taxonpath* element is suitable for containing and grouping the information about the ontologies that relate to a particular facet of a learning object, such as its domain or its pedagogy.

Two elements exist within the *taxonpath* element, the *source* and the *taxon* elements. The *source* element is used specify the name of the classification. An example is given in the LOM specification where the Dewey Decimal System classification is used to specify the organization of books in a library. The type of classification in this case would be best referred to as the type of ontology such as "DOMAIN ONTOLOGY" or "PEDAGOGICAL ONTOLOGY" since several different types of ontologies can be used to classify the learning object's material. The *taxon* element is taken to represent the actual ontology where the *id* element can identify an ontology in terms of best relevance to the learning material. The *entry* element contains the textual label of the *taxon* which would be the identifier of the *taxon* in the metadata. This element is suitable for citing the location of the ontology since this location is unique and there is only one *entry* per *taxon*. When all this information is filled in, the metadata now incorporates the ontological information.

Sicilia et al. however, differed from our approach at this point by specifying the location of their ontology under the *source* element [17]. This approach can be considered valid under the LOM specification's definition of the *source* element but this practice does not allow more than one ontology to describe a resource. In the following sample code, two domain ontologies are used to describe a learning object's domain. Our approach is also valid under the LOM specification's description of the *taxon* element and it goes further by allowing up to fifteen ontologies to be included under the fifteen *taxon* elements that are permitted in the specification. Furthermore, by using the *source* element to identify the type of ontology contained by a particular *taxonpath* element, other types of ontologies such as instructional ontologies that relate to the teaching style can be included as a separate classification system as shown in the code snippet below.

In this example, three different ontologies are used to describe a learning object with material about Wireless Local Area Networks: two domain ontologies and one pedagogical ontology. Each ontology is written in a different language and each ontology can be identified according to which aspect of a learning object it describes such as the domain or the pedagogy. So, by investigating the two domain ontologies under the first *taxonpath* element, the abstract representation of the context of this educational resource's domain can be examined.

```
<classification>
    <taxonpath>
        <source>
            <langstring       xml:lang="en">       DOMAIN       ONTOLOGY
</langstring>
        <source>
        <taxon>
            <id>DOMAIN 1</id>
            <entry>
                <langstring xml:lang="en"> Networking.owl
</langstring>
            </entry>
        </taxon>
        <taxon>
            <id>DOMAIN 2</id>
            <entry>
                <langstring xml:lang="en"> WirelessTransmission.daml
</langstring>
            </entry>
        </taxon>
    </taxonpath>
    <taxonpath>
        <source>
            <langstring xml:lang="en"> PEDAGOGICAL ONTOLOGY
            </langstring>
        </source>
        <taxon>
            <id>PEDAGOGY 1</id>
            <entry>
                <langstring xml:lang="en"> ProblemBasedLearning.rdf
                </langstring>
            </entry>
        </taxon>
    </taxonpath>
</classification>
```

By using multiple ontologies to describe a learning object, the context of a learning object can be modelled. A learning object's context refers to the frame of reference under which the learning material is used. It represents the overall theme of the learning material, the topics covered, and the relationships between those topics. A learning object's context then, clarifies the meaning of the learning material by describing the circumstances relevant to it such as the intended learners, the learning style(s) used, and the desired learning outcomes. This is information disambiguates the purpose of a learning object and promotes greater learning object reuse.

5   The Practicality of Our Approach

In our research, we have developed a preliminary prototype system which considers thematic learning object context information. This system is a multi-agent recommendation system called MARS which recommends learning objects to users based on their search criteria. MARS was built using the Java Agent DEvelopment Framework (JADE) and performed recommendations by analyzing the domain ontologies of the learning objects. The analysis of the learning objects' relevance to user requests was performed by inference rules written in Jess. These rules encoded recommendation criteria which considered the topics covered by learning material, and the relationships that connect these topics in the domain ontologies.

Six learning objects were built, annotated with domain ontologies, and wrapped in content packages created using Reload [18]. The domain ontologies were created in OWL using the Protégé Ontology Editor and described the concepts, their hierarchical classification and the relationships present in the respective learning material. These learning objects were then placed in the care of several agents residing on an agent network. In order to make recommendations, the metadata of each learning object was retrieved from the content package and the LOM was parsed by a MARS agent. The respective XML elements were checked and the uniform resource identifier (URI) of the domain ontology was extracted. The ontologies were not stored in the same location as the learning objects, so URIs were used instead of the filenames as shown in the code snippet above. The system successfully used these URIs to locate the ontology files which were used to create a knowledge base for the inference rules to operate on.

The inference rules used in MARS examined several ontological constructs in the domain ontologies in order to assess the appropriateness of a learning object for a request. In particular, these rules examined the relationships between the topics or concepts in an ontology. For example, Fig. 1 illustrates the design of two rules which detect *superclass-of* and *subclass-of* relationships between two concepts A and B irrespective of the number of intermediate concepts between them as indicated by the dotted lines. These rules searched the contextual model of learning objects for meaningful relationships between the topics which a user was interested and those covered by the learning objects. Whenever a link was found, the strength of the association determined the strength of the recommendation.

Valuable recommendations were made that allowed the learning objects to be ranked according to their appropriateness to a request in a given context of use. For example, learning objects which contained material about Queues and Stacks in Computer Science in the form of Java programs were recommended to a user searching for learning material on Integers and Java. Although the programs were not meant for a lesson on how to use integers in Java, they were still useful to the user because they illustrated how to declare, instantiate, and use integers in the Java language. Another recommendation was made to a user searching for material on Animals and Nuts whereby a learning object that described a Macaw was suggested. This learning object was also reused in a different context because it described an animal (a Macaw) that had nuts (Brazilian nuts) in its diet. Hence, these recommendations show that our approach incorporates ontologies into the LOM metadata in way that is practical, useful and effective.

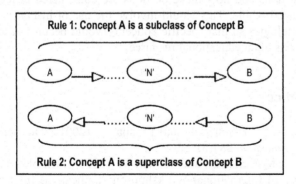

Fig.1 Diagram showing subsumption rule configurations

6   Conclusion and Future Work

The approach described is a practical one that makes use of the LOM specifications in its current state. It gives a simple yet effective method for describing any facet of a learning object, be it about the domain, the instructional style, and the organization of the learning object's structure or even about the learners that used the learning object. The learning objects that are described using this approach to metadata enhancement can be used by any system that already works with the LOM standards since no new elements were added.

Because of this new approach on how the *Classification* element should be interpreted given the advances in ontologies and Semantic Web research, these learning objects are automatically placed in a position to be understood by software agents [4] as shown by its use in the MARS system. Furthermore, the partitioning of the semantic information is easily achieved by simply using multiple *taxonpath* elements. This allows harvesting semantic information in an efficient manner and prevents the problem of reducing the reusability of the ontologies through too much specificity.

Future work that is to be undertaken is the use of multiple ontologies in describing not only the entire learning object material but rather in relating specific portions of the learning material to the exact domain information that the portions concern, the necessary pedagogical constraints that apply to the individualized portions and how those portions are constructed in relation to the entire aggregated whole. This would involve the use of instances and classes of various ontologies so that specific concepts would become associated with specific portions of an educational resource.

7   References

1.   Berners-Lee, T., Hendler, J., and Lassila, O. (2001). The Semantic Web. *Scientific American* 284(5): 33-43.
2.   Brooks, C., McCalla, G., and Winter, M. (2005). Flexible learning object metadata. 3rd International Workshop on Applications of Semantic Web

Technologies for E-Learning (SW-EL 05) at the 12th International Conference on Artificial Intelligence in Education (AIED 2005), July 18 – 22, 2005. Amsterdam, The Netherlands.1-9. Amsterdam: IOS Press.

3. Gómez-Pérez, A., and Corcho, O. (2002). Ontology languages for the Semantic Web. *IEEE Intelligent Systems* 14(2): 45-53.

4. Hendler, J. (2001). Agents and the Semantic Web. IEEE Intelligent Systems 16(2):30-37.

5. Instructional Management System Content Packaging Overview. (2005). Available   online   from: http://www.imsglobal.org/content/packaging/cpv1p2pd/imscp_oviewv1p2 pd.html .

6. Kasai, T., Yamaguchi, H., Nagano, K., and Mizoguchi, R. (2005). A Semantic Web system for helping teachers plan lessons using ontology alignment. In Proc. Semantic Web for E-Learning Workshop at the 12th International Conference on Artificial Intelligence in Education, Amsterdam, the Netherlands. 9-18. Amsterdam: IOS Press.

7. Knight, C., Gašević, D., and Richards, G. (2005). Ontologies for context-dependent reuse of learning designs and learning content. In Proc. Second Annual Lornet Conference, Vancouver, Canada, 15-18 November, 2005.

8. Lama, M., Sanchez, E., Amorim, R.R., and Vila, X.A. (2005). Semantic description of the IMS Learning Design specification. In Proc. Semantic Web for E-Learning Workshop at the 12th International Conference on Artificial Intelligence in Education, Amsterdam, the Netherlands. Amsterdam: IOS Press.

9. Learning Object Metadata Draft Standard. (2002). Available online from: http://ltsc.ieee.org/wg12/files/LOM_1484_12_1_v1_Final_Draft.pdf

10. [Lui, J., and Greer, J. (2004). Individualized selection of learning objects. In Proc. International Workshop on Applications of Semantic Web Technologies for E-Learning at the International Conference on Intelligent Tutoring Systems, Maceios-Alagoas, Brazil, 30 August- 3 September 2004. 29-34.

11. McCalla, G. (2004). The ecological approach to the design of e-learning environments: Purpose-based capture and use of information about learners. *Journal of Interactive Media   in Education*, 2004 (7). Special Issue on the Educational Semantic Web. ISSN:1365-893X [online] Available from:< www-jime.open.ac.uk/2004/7>.

12. Mitrovich, A., and Devedžić, V. (2002). A model of Multitutor ontology-based learning   environment. In Proc. ICCE Workshop on Concepts

and Ontologies in Web-Based Educational Sys   tems   3   December, 2002, Auckland, New Zealand. Edited by L. Aroyo, and D. Dicheva, 17-24. Eindhoven: Computer Science Reports 02/15.

13. [13]   Mohan, P., and Brooks, C. (2003). Learning objects on the Semantic Web. In Proc. Inter   national Conference on Advanced Learning Technologies 7-14 July, 2003. Athens,   Greece. 195-199. Los Alamitos, California: IEEE Computer Society Press.

14. Nilsson, M., Palmer, M., and Brase, J. (2003). The LOM RDF binding – principles and implementation. Paper presented at the 3rd Annual Ariadne Conference, Belgium, 20-21 November 2003

15. RELOAD   Project.   (2006).   Available   online   from: http://www.reload.ac.uk/

16. Sicilia, M.A., García, E., Díaz, P., and Aedo, I. (2002). LEARNING LINKS: Reusable assets with support for vagueness and ontology-based typing. In Proc. ICCE Workshop on Concepts and Ontologies in Web-Based Educational Systems 3 December 2002, Auckland, New Zealand. Edited by L. Aroyo and D. Dicheva, 11-16. Eindhoven: Computer Science Reports 02/15.

17. Verbert, K., Gašević, D., Jovanović, J., and Duval, E. (2005). Ontology-based learning   content repurposing. In Proceedings of the 14th International World Wide Web Confer   ence, Chiba, Japan, 10-14 May, 2005. 1140-1141. Seattle, Washington: ACM Press.

18. Wang, E., and Kim, Y.S. (2005). Ontological support for teaching strategy in intelligent   visual reasoning tutor. In Proc. Semantic Web for E-Learning Workshop at the 12th Inter   national Conference on Artificial Intelligence in Education, 18 July, 2005, Amsterdam, the   Netherlands. 77-78. Amsterdam: IOS Press.

19. Zarraonandía, T., Dodero, J.M., Díaz, P., and Sarasa, A. (2004). Domain ontologies inte gration into the learning objects annotation process. In Proc. International Workshop on Applications of Semantic Web Technologies for E-Learning at the International Confer ence on Intelligent Tutoring Systems, Maceios-Alagoas, Brazil, 30 August- 3 September 2004. 35-40.

Ontoligent Interactive Query Tool

Christopher J. O. Baker, Xiao Su, Greg Butler, and Volker Haarslev

Department of Computer Science & Software Engineering, Concordia University, Montreal, Quebec, Canada. http://www.cs.concordia.ca/FungalWeb/
baker@cs.concordia.cax_su@cs.concordia.ca, gregb@cs.concordia.ca,
haarslev@cs.concordia.ca

Abstract. Recognizing the complexity of the Description Logic-based query of OWL-DL ontologies for the non-specialist, we introduce a query tool called Ontoligent Interactive Query (OntoIQ). This tool provides a well-organized user interface for a variety of users, from the beginner to the professional. Users can browse ontologies and build queries using query patterns and ontology content. OntoIQ translates queries automatically into the new RACER Query language (nRQL) syntax and presents them to description logic automated reasoner RACER which returns the query results. The tool includes import and export functions so that queries can be stored, shared, and re-imported by other users. Users are not required to learn the nRQL syntax. OntoIQ software is available for download at The FungalWeb website.

1 Introduction

Ontologies are now cornerstones of many knowledge discovery platforms and are integrated within information systems. In recent years much effort has been focused on the development of ontologies and the tools for their creation / edit. Despite this increase in the abundance of freely accessible ontologies a number of additional challenges remain. These include ontology visualization, for which some tools now exist. Tools such as the Protégé [8] plug-in TGViz-

Tab [1], and Growl [4] are critical tools in the iterative development lifecycle of ontologies involving the ontology engineer, the domain expert and end user. The full value of OWL ontologies can only however be realized through the Description Logic (DL) paradigm and associated tools [6, 7, 3] which support reasoning over the ontological conceptualization to derive implicit knowledge. Appropriately, a plug-in for Protégé makes it possible to for users to pose DL-queries from the ontology editor [9]. Although DL-query languages facilitate the interrogation of ontologies, the Lisp based syntaxes such as that of nRQL [7] and RACER [6] are difficult for domain experts to master [11] particularly when seeking to evaluate ontologies for use in their own contexts. For this reason we sought to develop an interactive query tool called the Ontoligent Interactive Query tool (OntoIQ) which mirrors the basic query functionalities provided by nRQL used with RACER but with the advantage of browse and click operability.

1.1 nRQL as a Knowledge Representation Query Language

The query of knowledge representation formalisms such as ontologies is a central requirement of the Semantic Web. Since the recent establishment of the Ontology Web Language (OWL), design specifications for DL-based query languages have been proposed and existing languages contrasted, highlighting their advantages and limitations [2].

nRQL emerges as a prominent and highly expressive DL-query language. It extends the existing capabilities of the RACER with a series of query atoms, namely Unary concept query atoms, Binary role query atoms, Binary constraint query atoms, Binary same-as atoms, Unary has-known-successor atoms, and Negation atoms. nRQL uses a Lisp based syntax and the general structure of a query is composed of a query head i.e. Retrieve (?x) upon which variables used in the body are projected e.g. (?x Fungi), where (retrieve (?x) (?xFungi)), queries for instances of the concept Fungi. In this paper we illustrate conjunctive queries where the atoms are simple concept or role assertions where the variables in the body of the query match the corresponding individuals in the ontology that satisfy all query conditions. For some elements/operations of nRQL queries a closed world assumption is assumed, referred to also as 'active domain semantics' where only named individuals from the Abox will be considered as matches for query variables. A detailed description of nRQL is given in [7] and verbose examples outlined in [12].

2   The Ontoligent Interactive Query Tool

OntoIQ was designed to give domain experts the opportunity to interface with OWL conceptualizations and interrogate them to assess their content using semantic web technology. In the next sections we introduce OntoIQ system architecture, query patterns and features of the query interface.

2.1   System Architecture

We developed OntoIQ using a multi-tiered architecture shown in Fig. 1. This comprises of the following; an Ontology Download Manager, a RACER Server Connection Interface, an Ontology File Manager, and a Query Interface. Screenshots of these interfaces are shown in Fig 2. The Ontology Download Manager allows for specification of server settings for the download of knowledge representation resources hosted locally on a user's machine or available elsewhere on the World Wide Web. The RACER Server Connection interface allows specification of a remote connection to the RACER Server or to a local executable file of the reasoning engine. Where a remote connection with a RACER server is established the ontology file (OWL file) must be transported from the OntoIQ client. OntoIQ uses a socket on the TCP/IP protocol requiring the specification of the IP address of the remote RACER server. The remote RACER server must be running in the unsafe mode to permit upload and storage of the OWL file. Large ontology files greater than 5Mb have slower transfer speeds.

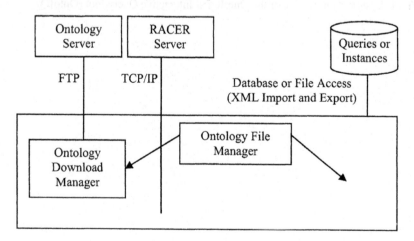

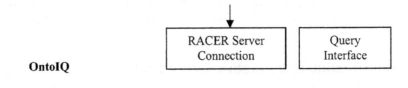

OntoIQ

RACER Server
Connection

Query
Interface

Fig. 1. System Architecture of the Ontoligent Interactive Query tool (OntoIQ).

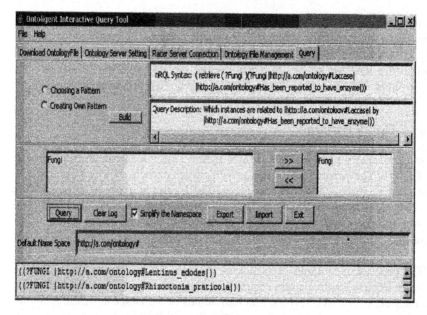

Fig. 2 Screenshots of OntoIO User Interaction Panels

The Ontology File Manager serves to load local ontology files to the RACER Server and to invoke the checking of the consistency and classification of the loaded ontology. It further permits the selection of six nRQL running modes [12]. The Query Interface provides the gateway to a series of query options. Direct access to the command line of the RACER reasoning engine is provided for advanced users wishing to pose queries using RACER syntax not supported by OntoIQ.

2.2   User Overview

To illustrate the interaction of the user with OntoIQ, we describe a typical workflow for a new user. The user downloads the OntoIQ tool and runs it from the local machine. An IP address for the remote Ontology Server is provided by the user to the Ontology Download Manager and an ontology file is downloaded. A connection is established between OntoIQ and a RACER server. An ontology file is loaded and a consistency and classification check on the ontology is run. The user then builds queries using the query interface selecting a query pattern and ontology specific content by browsing the ontology with OntoIQ. Queries are subsequently translated to nRQL syntax and sent to the RACER server. RACER returns the query results which can be saved along with the query syntax for export and reuse at a later time.

2.3   Query Patterns

A range of query patterns are available within OntoIQ. These are summarized in Table 1. The capabilities of the query patterns and the required information that must be provided by the user are outlined. Simple query patterns such as the *concept* pattern, the *role* pattern, and more complex patterns such as *intersect-conjunction, union-disjunction* and *combination* patterns can also be constructed.

   The process of building such queries through a browser requires a user to identify in advance the pattern required for their intended query. Thereafter the user selects the concepts, roles, and individuals of the concepts or the relationships among these individuals from within the ontology.

Table 1 Query patters available in OntoIQ

Pattern	Syntax	Query
Concept	A concept and a variable	Is there any instance (not) belonging to the concept Enzyme? What individuals (do not) belong to the concept Enzyme? Does the instance Laccase (not) belong to the concept Enzyme?
Role	A role and the role's domain and range.	What pairs of individuals are (not) related by role *has_been_reported_to_have_enzyme*? Is there any instance (not) related by the role *has_been_reported_to_have_enzyme*? To what individuals is the instance Laccase related by the role *has_been_reported_to_have_enzyme*?
Intersect / Conjunction	Simple concept or role patterns in combination	What pairs of individuals are (not) related by role *has_been_reported_to_have_enzyme* and are related to the concept 'Substrate' by the role *has_activity_towards_substrate*

		Simple concept or role patterns in combination	Retrieve individuals that belong to concept Hydrolase or individuals that belong to concept Lyase
Union / Disjunction			
Combo (And / Union)		Combines any combination of patterns.	Find individuals of the concept Commercial_Enzyme_Product that are related by the role *contains* where the instance is xylanase.

2.4   Query Interface

The Query panel (Fig. 2) provides access to a cascade of windows, the first of which allows for the selection of query patterns using the 'build' button to access the Pattern Selection pane (Fig. 3). The 'Pattern List' menu of the Pattern Selection pane permits the selection of five pattern templates. Depending on the pattern selected a series of additional information must be provided. The Concept Pattern template shown requires a variable, i.e. a symbol or name representing the concept, or instance of the concept in the query syntax, along with the description of the concept or instance in the ontology i.e. its name obtained from browsing the ontology file. In Fig. 3 the OntoIQ query pattern templates are illustrated using the OWL file of the FungalWeb Ontology [9]. The Concept Pattern built selects for instances of the concept *Enzyme*. Each query pattern template can be built to specify affirmation or negation, i.e. presence or absence of instances using a drop box menu.

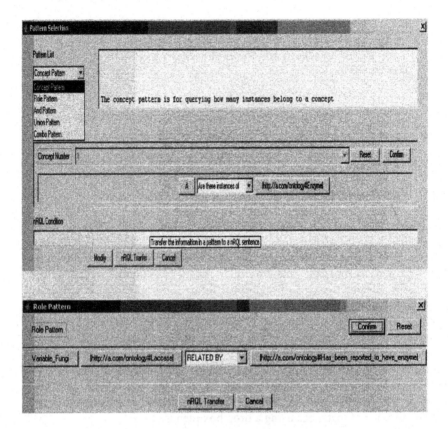

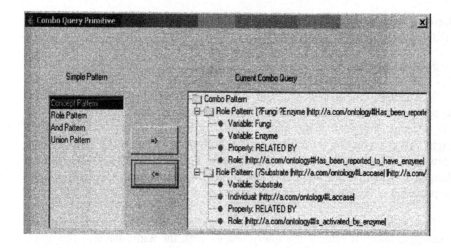

Fig. 3. Pattern Selection panels of OntoIQ: concept query panel, role pattern query panel and a combo query panel. Screenshots shown in Fig. 2 illustrate OntoIQ query pattern functionality using the OWL file of the FungalWeb Ontology [9].

In the case of the role pattern template the role with its domain and range must be selected from the ontology and variable names supplied. The role pattern template is displayed after the user selects the role pattern. Three buttons are displayed. The user must first select the role by browsing the ontology. OntoIQ will then lookup in the ontology the selectable domain and range associated with the role chosen by the user. Domain and range buttons can then be used to browse and select the appropriate variable, concept or instance. In the Role Pattern example the role *has_been_reported_to_have_enzyme* with the domain *Fungi* as a variable and the range *Laccase* as an instance, is selected. In the case of the COMBO pattern, a pattern manager, the Combo Query Primitive, is provided where different combinations of nested patterns can be built from the simpler patterns. This interface links to each of the query pattern templates for the input of variables and parameters from the ontology.

After providing the ontology specific information in the pattern the user must declare completion of the user input and invoke its conversion to nRQL syntax using the 'Confirm' and 'nRQL Transfer' buttons. The pattern is translated into nRQL according to the syntax of the selected pattern. In the role pattern the user defined the role, with its domain and range, is matched to the nRQL syntax of a role pattern:

Retrieve (?x) (AND (?xFungi) (?xLaccase *has_been_reported_to_have_enzyme*))))

Subsequently the user is returned to the main Query panel (Fig. 2) with the specified variable, Fungi, in the left variable window. Any or all variables can be selected to appear in the query results by transferring the variable to the right variable window with the direction buttons '>>'. The nRQL Syntax window then displays the corresponding syntax. For elementary queries a natural language description of the query, including the ontology specific information is provided in the Query Description panel.

The Query button submits the syntax to the RACER server loaded with the ontology. RACER returns the query results with the namespace of the ontology elements, which can be removed by specifying the check box 'Simplify the Namespace'. Using the 'Export' button query results can be exported in XML format along with the syntax used to retrieve them.

2.5   Import and Export

We envision the need for researchers using the ontology for data mining of its instances to share query syntaxes. Both for the sake of speed and simplicity we have developed import and export facilities to enable the sharing of syntax between users. Fig. 4 shows the exported query syntax and query results in XML format. The <OWL> tag contains the description of the ontology to which queries were made. The <Pattern> tag describes the type of query pattern and its components as defined by the user. In the example below a concept pattern that selects instances of the concept 'Enzyme' is shown. The corresponding nRQL syntax is described in the similarly named tag, <nRQLSyntax>. The natural language description of the query is in the <Description> tag and the instances returned by the query are in the multiple instance tags.

```
<?xml version="1.0" encoding="UTF-8" standalone="yes" ?>
- <rdf:RDF xmlns:daml="http://www.daml.org/2001/03/daml+oil#"
    xmlns:dc="http://purl.org/dc/elements/1.1/" xmlns:jms="http://jena.hpl.hp.com/2003/08/jms#"
    xmlns:owl="http://www.w3.org/2002/07/owl#" xmlns:rdf="http://www.w3.org/1999/02/22-rdf-syntax-
    ns#" xmlns:rdfs="http://www.w3.org/2000/01/rdf-schema#" xmlns:rss="http://purl.org/rss/1.0/"
    xmlns:vcard="http://www.w3.org/2001/vcard-rdf/3.0#"
    xmlns:xsd="http://www.w3.org/2001/XMLSchema#">
  - <owl:Ontology rdf:about="fungalwebontology.owl">
    - <Pattern>
      - <ConceptPattern>
        <Variable>a</Variable>
        <Concept>|http://a.com/ontology#Enzyme|</Concept>
        <Property>Are there instances of</Property>
      </ConceptPattern>
      <nRQLSyntax>( retrieve ( ?a )(?a |http://a.com/ontology#Enzyme|))</nRQLSyntax>
      <Description>What instances belong to the concept |http://a.com/ontology#Enzyme|</Description>
      <Instances>((?A |http://a.com/ontology#mannan_1_4-mannobiosidase|))</Instances>
      <Instances>((?A |http://a.com/ontology#alkaline_phosphatase|))</Instances>
      <Instances>((?A |http://a.com/ontology#beta-glucuronidase|))</Instances>
      <Instances>((?A |http://a.com/ontology#Fluorothreonine_transaldolase|))</Instances>
      <Instances>((?A |http://a.com/ontology#galacturan_1_4-alpha-galacturonidase|))</Instances>
      <Instances>((?A |http://a.com/ontology#Phospholipid-translocating_ATPase|))</Instances>
      <Instances>((?A |http://a.com/ontology#Acetoacetyl-CoA_hydrolase|))</Instances>
      <Instances>((?A |http://a.com/ontology#Adenylylsulfatase|))</Instances>
      <Instances>((?A |http://a.com/ontology#Formyl-CoA_hydrolase|))</Instances>
```

Fig. 4. Export format showing the query and result generated by OntoIQ

This exported file can be uploaded to OntoIQ and re-read. The 'Import' button located on the main query panel facilitates the loading of OntoIQ XML files (Fig. 2). Fig. 5 shows the Query Sentence Import panel where exported queries can be examined. Selecting the button marked 'Open' provides the user with the main query panel preloaded with the selected query for further modification or resubmission to RACER given that the corresponding ontology is loaded into OntoIQ. If the imported query does not correspond to the ontology file loaded by the user, only the query pattern is loaded without the domain specific content.

No.	rRQL Syntax	Description	Pattern S...
1	[retrieve [?a][?a]http://a.com/ontology#With_oxygen_as_acceptor])	What instances belonging to the...	Open
2	[retrieve [?vendor ?industry][?vendor ?industry]http://a.com/ontology#Producing_enzyme_for])	Which instances are related by I...	Open
3	[retrieve [?Enzyme ?Substrate ?industry] [?industry ?Enzyme]http://a.com/ontology#Is_using]) [?Substra...	What instances belonging to the...	Open
4	[retrieve [?Fungi][?Fungi]http://a.com/ontology#Laccase[ ]http://a.com/ontology#Has_been_reported_t...	Which instances are related to I...	Open

Fig. 5. Query Sentence Import panel for selection of available stored queries.

3   Conclusion

To determine the utility of an ontological conceptualization for a given application it is necessary to examine it based on its concepts, axioms and instances. This remains a time consuming challenge for domain experts who are not ready to learn new syntax in order to pose queries to ontologies or browse very large visualizations.

Despite the fact that OntoIQ requires users to learn a new approach to querying a knowledge resource it makes a significant step in reducing the technical barriers in knowledge mining. This new approach involves the following challenges: (i) how can the user identify the boundaries of the ontological conceptualization (what is included and what is not), (ii) how can users map their queries into patterns that can match the conceptualisation's axioms in order to retrieve the desired results. The first challenge requires users to take the time browse or interrogate the ontology identifying familiar concepts and vocabulary. The second challenge can be summarized as follows; users must become familiar with the properties, the domains and ranges, used in the conceptualisation as well as the capabilities of each of the query patterns so that they can construct complex queries. We note domain experts have expressed concerns about the shift in thinking that requires the selection of a pattern before formulating the content of a query. This sometimes seems counterintuitive for the beginner. However we considered this challenge in the design of the tool and provide the functionality to save query patterns with a natural language description such that they can be reused at a later time by the same or less advanced users.

More advanced users appear to be challenged by the need to compose new patterns to answer what may seem simple queries. Both challenges can be addressed by developing an additional tier onto the query process, namely a natural language query-answer interface which can translate natural language into query patterns. Simple axioms in the FungalWeb Ontology such as those listed below could be formulated in a number of additional ways depending on the scientific vocabulary of the user or ontology engineer. Consequently an NLP based free-text query to query pattern 'mapping module' providing faster and simpler access to the ontology content would be highly relevant for Fungal Enzyme Biotechnologists interested solely in mining the FungalWeb Ontology.

- *Enzyme - Has_been_reported_to_be_found_in - Fungus*
- *Substrate - Is_activated_by - Enzyme*

In summary DL-based 'semantic mining' is a new paradigm where OntoIQ makes the existing functionality of nRQL and RACER available to non-technical knowledge worker, albeit with a learning curve. As such it makes a relevant contribution to the evolution and uptake of knowledge discovery technology.

Acknowledgements

This work was financed in part through the Génome Québec funded project *Ontologies, the semantic web and intelligent systems for genomics*

References

1. Alani, H. (2003) TGVizTab: An Ontology Visualisation Extension for Protégé. In Proceedings of Knowledge Capture (K-Cap'03), Workshop on Visualization Information in Knowledge Engineering, Sanibel Island, Florida, USA. ACM Press, New York, NY, USA.
2. Birte Glimm and Ian R. Horrocks. Query answering systems in the semantic web. In Sean Bechhofer, Volker Haarslev, Carsten Lutz, Ralf Moeller (Eds) CEUR workshop proceedings of KI-2004 Workshop on Applications of Description Logics (ADL 04), Ulm, Germany, Sep 24 2004. Available online as CEUR Workshop Proceedings Volume 115.
3. FaCT, http://www.cs.man.ac.uk/%7Ehorrocks/FaCT/ - last accessed 2006-01-16
4. Growl, http://www.uvm.edu/~skrivov/growl/ - last accessed 2006-01-16.
5. Haarslev V., Moeller R., Wessel M., Querying the Semantic Web with Racer + nRQL In Sean Bechhofer, Volker Haarslev, Carsten Lutz, Ralf Moeller (Eds) CEUR workshop proceedings of KI-2004 Workshop on Applications of Description Logics (ADL 04), Ulm, Germany, Sep 24 2004.
6. Haarslev V., Möller R. (2001). RACER System Description. R. Goré, A. Leitsch, T. Nipkow (Eds.), Proceedings of International Joint Conference on Automated Reasoning, IJCAR. 2001, Siena, Italy. Springer-Verlag, Berlin, pp. 701-705.
7. nRQL Tab Plugin, http://www.cs.concordia.ca/ /~k_bhoopa/nrql.html - last accessed 2006-01-16.
8. Protégé, http://protege.stanford.edu/ - last accessed 2006-01-16.
9. Shaban-Nejad A., Baker C.J.O., Haarslev V., and Butler G. (2005). The FungalWeb Ontology: Semantic Web Challenges in Bioinformatics and Genomics 4th International Semantic Web Conference (ISWC) November 6-10, 2005, Galway, Ireland. Lecture Notes in Computer Science, Vol. 3729, pp. 1063-1066.
10. Smith B., et al. Relations in biomedical ontologies. Genome Biology, 2005, 6(5).

11. The   New   Racer   Query   Language,   URL   = www.cs.concordia.ca/~haarslev/racer/racer-queries.pdf - last accessed 2006-01-16.

12. Wessel M., Möller R. (2005). A High Performance Semantic Web Query Answering Engine. In Horrocks, I., Sattler, U., Wolter, F., (Eds.) Proceedings of the 2005 International Workshop on Description Logics (DL2005), Whistler, BC, Canada, 2005. Available online as CEUR Workshop Proceedings Volume 147.

Datalog^{DL}: Datalog Rules Parameterized by Description Logics

Jing Mei[1], Harold Boley[3], Jie Li[2,3], Virendrakumar C. Bhavsar[2], and Zuoquan Lin[1]

[1]Department of Information Science, Peking University
Beijing 100871, China {mayyam, lz} AT is.pku.edu.cn
[2]Faculty of Computer Science, University of New Brunswick
Fredericton, NB, E3B 5A3, Canada {Jie.Li, bhavsar} AT unb.ca
[3]Institute for Information Technology - e-Business
National Research Council of Canada Fredericton, NB, E3B 9W4, Canada
{Harold.Boley, Jie.Li} AT nrc.gc.ca

Abstract: Combining ontologies with rules has become a central topic in the Semantic Web. Bridging the discrepancy between these two knowledge representations, this paper introduces Datalog^{DL} as a family of hybrid languages, where Datalog rules are parameterized by various DL (description logic) languages ranging from $\mathcal{ALC}$ to $\mathcal{SHIQ}$. Making Datalog^{DL} a decidable system with complexity of EXPTIME, we propose independent properties in the DL body as the restriction to hybrid rules, and weaken the safeness condition to balance the trade-off between expressivity and reasoning power. Building on existing well-developed techniques, we present a principled approach to enrich (RuleML) rules with information from (OWL) ontologies, and develop a prototype system integrating a rule engine (OO jDREW) with a DL reasoner (RACER).

1 Introduction

Alternative architectures for the Semantic Web were proposed by several groups at the W3C Workshop on Rule Languages for Interoperability, and follow-up discussions helped to establish the Rule Interchange Format Working Group [20]. Whether, in the Semantic Web's layered structure, there should be only one homogeneous hierarchy for ontologies and rules [13], or these should stand heterogeneously (hybridly) side by side under a logic framework [10], the combination of ontologies and rules, within a practical and feasible framework, is an interesting topic deserving more investigation.

Description logics (DLs) have been recognized as the logical foundation of ontologies in the Semantic Web, and the Web Ontology Language, namely OWL [18], has two species: OWL-Lite and OWL-DL, closely related to the DL languages $SHIQ(D)$ and $SHOIN(D)$, respectively. On the other hand, Datalog is a wide-spread rule-based language, even popular in the industry. That is, both of these two knowledge representations have reached a certain level of maturity, which make them suitable candidates for combination.

Among the integration frameworks for combining rules and DLs (see Table 1), one is the homogeneous approach (like DLP [8], SWRL [11], and KAON2 [17]), while the other is the hybrid approach (like AL-log [6], CARIN [14], dl-programs [7], and r-hybrid KBs [19]). However, there exists the usual tradeoff between the expressivity of languages and the complexity of their reasoning services.

Table 1. Comparison of Approaches

		Safeness Condition		Information Flow		Strategy
		Strong	Weak	Uni-directional	Bi-directional	
Homogeneous	DLP		X		X	Reduction
Approach	SWRL		X		X	-
	KAON2	X			X	Reduction
Hybrid	AL-log	X		X		SLD-resolution
Approach	CARIN		X	X		Entailment
	dl-programs	X			X	Fixpoint iteration
	r-hybrid KBs	X			X	-
	Datalog^{DL}		X	X		SLD-resolution

AL-log, the earlier and simpler case, integrates standard Datalog rule inference procedures with intermediate ALC DL satisfiability checking. It adopts backward chaining (based on SLD-resolution), first collecting the disjunction of the obtained DL-queries, and then using classical DL tableaux algorithms to check the consistency of those DL atoms. As a result, AL-log is a complete and sound system, whose complexity is ExpTime stemming from those of ALC and Datalog. But, the binary predicates (i.e., properties) are not considered in AL-log, and it requires that each variable appearing in the DL component also appears in the Datalog component (we call this a *strong* safeness condition, and a formal definition is presented below), s.t. only unary predicates without variables (i.e., ground classes) will be submitted to the DL tableaux reasoner.

More generally, CARIN is a family of languages, each of which combines (a sublanguage of) ALCNR DL and Datalog rules. Unlike AL-log, CARIN first computes the entailments of the DL component based on DL tableaux algorithms, and one step of the standard forward chaining is then done for each augmented rule component, using the added DL assertions as new facts. Besides, CARIN allows ground or open DL-queries with unary and binary predicates, and the variables appearing in the head of a rule are required also to appear in the body but not necessary of being in the DL body (we call this a *weak* safeness condition, and a formal definition is presented below) -- this is a general safeness condition for rule-based languages, weaker than that of AL-log. As to non-recursive CARIN-ALCNR , a sound and complete inference procedure has been established, while reasoning in recursive CARIN-ALCNR is un-decidable, and there are two ways of restricting expressivity to regain soundness and completeness: one is to remove some DL constructors and allow an acyclic terminology only, and the other is to make the safeness condition strong.

It should be pointed out that bi-directional information flows are not permitted in the above two systems, and the predicate symbols in the head of hybrid rules are disjoint from those in the DL component. Two other well-known hybrid systems, dl-programs and r-hybrid KBs, are less restricted, and the stable model semantics performs well for both systems; also, they each provide a decidable strategy. In these systems, negation as failure is investigated as an important feature, which is beyond this scope of the current paper.

Being homogeneous approaches, DLP and SWRL share all of the predicate symbols between the rule component and the DL component. However, DLP has more expressivity restrictions, while SWRL is undecidable. KAON2 seems a novelty as to reasoning support for both OWL-DL and rules, reducing the DL knowledge bases to disjunctive programs. But such reduction pushes the task of DL reasoning completely into rule engines, not gaining the benefits from the existing tableaux DL reasoners. Also, a strong safeness condition, similar to the one in AL-log and r-hybrid KBs, is required by KAON2, where this restriction covers some of the common usages of DL expressivity.

In this paper, our objective is to generalize the framework of AL-log, combining (any sublanguage of) a decidable DL system with Datalog, and provide less restricted hybrid rules with DL-query to both classes and properties. Although CARIN is similar in this respect, it requires some built-in coding into a DL reasoner, to obtain a complete entailment for hybrid rules; otherwise, anonymous individuals (e.g., introduced by existence restrictions) and uncertain assertions (e.g., derived from disjunction descriptions) in the DL component will just be kept inside of the primitive DL reasoner, with no access to rule engines. Aiming at developing a feasible strategy for the reasonable Semantic Web community by employing existing techniques as much as possible, we attempt to balance the trade-off of the expressivity and the reasoning power, and consider $SHIQ$ as our bottom line, whose practical and efficient tools are available (such as RACER [9]). Here, we adopt the weak safeness condition, and the problems introduced by the *pure-DL* variables in DL-queries, beyond the strong safeness condition, will be handled cautiously, provided that those expressive statements would be kicked out by the bottom line of $SHIQ$ DL. By defining *independent* properties, we clarify our current reasoning services: hybrid rules with DL-query to classes and independent properties in weak safeness condition are fully supported.

As a result, this paper presents Datalog^{DL} as a family of hybrid representation languages, where Datalog rules are parameterized by a specific DL language L, namely Datalog^{L}, where L ranges from ALC to $SHIQ$. On the theoretical side, we show a sound and complete algorithm for reasoning in Datalog^{DL}, with the complexity of ExpTime in any case of its parameterized DL language L. On the practical side, while keeping a DL reasoner unchanged, a typical rule engine (e.g., OO jDREW [4]) will be extended to incorporate hybrid rules, where the collection of DL-queries, after a so-called constrained SLD-resolution for hybrid rules, will be submitted to an external DL reasoner (e.g., RACER).

Next, Datalog^{DL} will be introduced in Sect. 2 with its syntax and semantics, while its reasoning will be described in Sect. 3 together with proofs of soundness and completeness. Sect. 4 is meant to clarify technical problems of decidability underlying in hybrid rules, and finally conclusions are drawn in Sect. 5.

2 The Datalog^{DL} Languages

The matured languages, Datalog and DL, will be combined in a hybrid approach: Datalog^{DL} is a family of languages, each of which parameterizes Datalog with some variety of DL-query.

Consider the main layers of the DL family bottom-up [3], ALC is a basic and simple language, permitting class descriptions via $C ó D$, $C ò D$, $\neg C$, $\forall R.C$, and $\exists R.D$ where C, D are classes and R is a property. Augmented by transitive properties, ALC becomes ALC_R, in the following denoted by S.

SI is an extension to S with inverse properties, followed by SHI with property hierarchies. It becomes $SHIF$ if extended by functional restrictions, $SHIN$ if extended by cardinality restrictions, and $SHIQ$ if extended by qualified number restrictions. Support for datatype predicates (e.g. string, integer) leads to the concrete domain of D, and using nominals O allows to construct classes from singleton sets.

Assuming the usual definitions of DLs and rules are familiar to readers, we introduce the syntax and semantics for Datalog^{DL} with no need for preliminaries. However, we adopt the so-called *unique named assumption* (UNA), a convention of Datalog not normally used by DLs.

2.1 Syntax

In order to preserve decidability, we fix the rule language to Datalog, so that terms must be variables or constants. Undecidable extensions to Horn logic, where terms can also be function applications, have been considered as well, but are beyond the scope of this paper.

Given a decidable DL language L (here, it ranges from ALC to $SHIQ$), we denote by Datalog^L a subset of the function-free first-order Horn logic language over an alphabet of predicates $A = A_T \cup A_P$, with $A_T \cap A_P = \varnothing$, and an alphabet of constants C. Note that, the predicates in A_P can be of arbitrary arity, while those of A_T should be either unary (also called class in DL) or binary (also called property in DL).

Definition 1. A Datalog^L knowledge base K is a pair (Σ, Π), where: Σ is a L-based description logic knowledge base with predicates in A_T ; Π is a Datalog program with DL-query to Σ, s.t. each hybrid rule r in Π is

$$h(X) : -b_1(Y_1), \cdots, b_m(Y_m) \& q_1(Z_1), \cdots, q_n(Z_n)$$

where X, Y_1, ..., Y_m are n-ary sequences of terms while Z_1, ..., Z_n are unary/binary sequences of terms, h(X) and $b_i(Y_i)$ ($1 \leq i \leq m$) are Datalog atoms with predicates in A_P

while each $q_j(Z_j)$ ($1 \leq j \leq n$) is a DL-query with a predicate in A_T .

Two safeness conditions are introduced for hybrid rules:
Weak safeness: a variable occurring in X must occur in one of the $Y_i | Z_j$'s.
Strong safeness: a variable occurring in r must occur in one of the Y_i's.

For simplicity, in the rest of the paper "rule" means "hybrid rule", while "Datalog rule" refers to a hybrid rule after deletion of the DL body. Besides, making rules strongly safe has been introduced in [17], that is: (1) For each rule r whose variable w does not occur in any of the Y_i's, we add an atom O(w) to the Datalog body of r, where O is a special predicate symbol, $O \in A_P$; (2) For each constant c occurring in K = (Σ, Π), we add a fact O(c) to Π.

As mentioned in Sect. 1, we prefer to the weak safeness condition rather than the strong one. Below, *pure-DL* variables are defined.

Definition 2. A pure-DL variable in a rule r is a variable that only occurs in one of the Z_j's.

Pure-DL variables lead to the violation of the strong safeness condition in cases where the weak safeness condition is obeyed. Note that, without the presence of pure-DL variables (i.e., under the strong safeness condition), our system appears to be Datalog extended with ground DL-queries, which is a simple and straightforward extension to AL-log.

According to the classical SLD-resolution with rules, non-pure-DL variables in (the DL body of) r will be bound to ground values, still leaving pure-DL variables free in the DL body. This situation is similar to conjunctive query answering in DL containing both constants and variables [12]. Instantiation ("Is an individual an instance of a class?") can be reduced to KB unsatisfiability by transforming the query into a negated assertion. However, queries involving properties and variables are non-trivial given that the negation of properties is not supported by most DLs. Hence, a candidate technique is *folding* (called *rolling-up* in [12]), whose objective is to eliminate properties from queries.

Following this route, we encounter another problem: the simple procedure of folding cannot be applied to parts of the query that contain cycles, or where more than one arc enters a node that corresponds to a variable (e.g. P(u, x)∧ Q(v, x)). Tree-shaped DL queries appear to be a solution to this problem by exploiting the tree model property of the DL [12]; however, the undecidability of an unrestricted combination of DLs with rules is exactly due to the fact that adding rules to DLs causes the loss of any form of tree model property [17]. Hence, strong safeness is imposed by DL-safe rules [17] and other approaches [6, 7, 19], while we define *independent* properties, which address the trade-off as mentioned above.

Definition 3. A property P is said to be independent in a rule r, if no P occurrence shares any pure-DL variable with other property occurrences (including other P occurrences).

Now, suppose r is a hybrid rule violating the strong safeness condition, γ being its head, α being its Datalog body, and β being its DL body. Specifically, it has the form γ:-α&β, where β contains a pure-DL variable x having a class description C (C can be the DL top class). We classify the possibilities for β into four cases:

1. If x does not participate (as the first or second argument) in any property, then the DL-query of C(x) is reduced to checking whether C is nonempty.
2. If there exists exactly one property occurrence of P relating x with a term u, then the DL-query of P(u, x)∧ C(x) or P(x, u)∧ C(x) becomes its *folding* result ∃P.C(u) or ∃P⁻.C(u), respectively.
3. If there exists exactly two property occurrences of P and Q relating x with terms u and v, respectively, where P and Q, u and v can be identical, then the DL-queries become the results of following *foldings* (chaining can start with either u or v):

   (a) P(u, x)∧ Q(v, x)∧ C(x) becomes

   ∃P.(∃Q⁻.{v} ⊓ C)(u) or ∃Q.(∃P⁻.{u} ⊓ C)(v)

   (b) P(u, x)∧ Q(x, v)∧ C(x) becomes

   ∃P.(∃Q.{v} ⊓ C)(u) or ∃Q⁻.(∃P⁻.{u} ⊓ C)(v)

   (c) P(x, u)∧ Q(v, x)∧ C(x) becomes

   ∃P⁻.(∃Q⁻.{v} ⊓ C)(u) or ∃Q.(∃P.{u} ⊓ C)(v)

(d) $P(x, u) \wedge Q(x, v) \wedge C(x)$ becomes

$$\exists P^{-}.(\exists Q.\{v\} \circ C)(u) \text{ or } \exists Q^{-}.(\exists P.\{u\} \circ C)(v)$$

4. If there exists three or more property occurrences, nested foldings might be employed by iterating case 3 chainings.

Case 3 requires support by using nominals O (i.e., classes with a singleton extension), as known from the DL literature, whose interaction with cardinality restrictions N and inverse properties I makes the complexity jump from ExpTime (for $SHIN$) to NExpTime (for $SHOIN$). Although the operator $\{u\}$ could be 'simulated' by its *representative* concept C_u [12], we still focus on cases 1 and 2 in this paper, not introducing different fresh concept names for different individuals. Another consideration is following the requirement of independent properties in a hybrid rule r, which is fulfilled by cases 1 and 2, excluding cases 3 and 4 where the pure-DL variable x is a variable shared among properties in r.

Proposition 1. For hybrid rules with independent properties according to case 2, the folding results are equivalent to the original DL-queries.

Proof. For a set of closed formulas S and a closed formula F of a first order language, F is a logical consequence of S iff $S \cup \{\neg F\}$ is unsatisfiable. Applied to logic programming, consider a Datalog program Π with a goal G of the form $\leftarrow G_1 \wedge \ldots \wedge G_n$ with variables $y_1, \ldots, y_m$. Showing that the set of clauses $\Pi \cup \{G\}$ is unsatisfiable is exactly the same as showing that $\exists y_1 \ldots \exists y_m (G_1 \wedge \ldots \wedge G_n)$ is a logical consequence of Π. Note that DL languages are variable-free, where any free variables are hidden within $\forall$, $\exists$, etc., such as $u \in \exists P.C$ meaning $u \in \{x \mid \exists y. P(x, y) \wedge C(y)\}$. So, the folding results, e.g., $\exists P.C(u)$, are equivalent to the original DL-queries, e.g., $\leftarrow P(u, x) \wedge C(x)$ with an independent property of P.

2.2 Semantics

The semantics of Datalog^{DL} derives in a natural way from the semantics of its component languages, based on the first-order semantics. As follows, we define an interpretation and a model of our language Datalog^L, including the satisfying conditions for ground Datalog atoms, ground DL-queries, and hybrid rules. We direct readers to the description logic handbook [3] and the foundations of logic programming [16] for those related definitions.

Definition 4. An interpretation $I = (\triangle, \bullet^I)$ of a language Datalog^L consists of the following: (1) A nonempty domain $\triangle$; (2) For each constant a in C, the assignment of an element in $\triangle$, i.e., $a^I \in \triangle$; (3) For each n-ary predicate p in the alphabet of predicates $A = A_T \cup A_P$, the assignment of a relation of arity n over the domain $\triangle$, i.e., a relation on $\triangle^n$.

Definition 5. Let I be an interpretation for a language Datalog^L, and for a given hybrid rule r,
A variable assignment V_r w.r.t I is an assignment to each variable in r of an element in the domain of I.
A term assignment T_r w.r.t I is defined: (1) Each variable is given its assignment according to V_r; (2) Each constant is given its assignment according to I.

Definition 6. Let I be an interpretation for a language Datalog^L. (1) A ground Datalog atom $\alpha = p(C)$, $p \in A_P$, is satisfied by I if $C^I \in p^I$, written as $I \models \alpha$. (2) A ground DL-query $\beta = q(C)$, $q \in A_T$, is satisfied by I if $C^I \in q^I$, written as $I \models \beta$. (3) A hybrid rule r that $h(X) : -b_1(Y_1), \cdots, b_m(Y_m) \& q_1(Z_1), \cdots, q_n(Z_n)$ is satisfied by I if, whenever T_r is a term assignment w.r.t I, such that $T_r(Y_i) \in b_i^I$ and $T_r(Z_j) \in q_j^I$ ($1 \leq i \leq m$, $1 \leq j \leq n$) for every atom in the body of r, then $T_r(X) \in h^I$ for the head of r, written as $I \models r$.

Definition 7. Let I be an interpretation for a language Datalog^L. I is a model of the Datalog^L knowledge base (Σ, Π), consisting of a Datalog program Π with DL-queries to Σ, if I satisfies each hybrid rule in Π and I is a model of Σ according to the description logic L.

3 Reasoning in Datalog^{DL}

Deviating from AL-log, the algorithm in CARIN is meant to test DL entailment but not satisfiability, resulting in forward chaining being employed as the strategy for the rule component. On the other hand, not concerned with the internals of DL's tableaux calculus, our Datalog^{DL} family is in the tradition of AL-log, making use of the constrained SLD-resolution, so that backward chaining plays the role of our principal reasoning strategy.

3.1 Algorithm

Below is the definition of an algorithm, in pseudo-code, for reasoning in Datalog^L, where L is a DL language ranging from ALC to $SHIQ$, restricted to independent properties in the DL body of hybrid rules under the weak safeness condition.

Input: Datalog^L KB K=(Σ,Π) and a query q.
Output: TRUE if q is satisfied by K, FALSE otherwise.
BEGIN:
1. Apply SLD-resolution for q with Datalog rules. Use the resulting substitution to ground the hybrid rules (no assignment can be made to pure-DL variables). If there is no such grounded version, then return FALSE. Otherwise, collect the disjunction of the obtained DL-queries, after folding in step-2 for each rule r having pure-DL variables left.
2. For each pure-DL variable x in the rule r, where C is a class description of x, and P is an independent property relating x with a term u, output the folding results

   of $\exists P.C(u)$ from $P(u, x) \wedge C(x)$, and of $\exists P^-.C(u)$ from $P(x, u) \wedge C(x)$.

3. Apply the DL tableaux algorithm to (the step-2 folding results of) the DL-queries from step-1. We build a disjunctive DL class $D_1 \grave{o} \cdots \grave{o} D_m$ such that its class descriptions D_i are collected from the involved hybrid rules r_i, where $1 \leq i \leq m$. For an individual a, the separate DL-queries $D_i(a)$ will be replaced by a single new one, $D_1 \grave{o} \cdots \grave{o} D_m(a)$. If the DL-query $D_1 \grave{o} \cdots \grave{o} D_m(a)$ in addition to at least one of the remaining disjuncts are satisfiable in every model, then return TRUE, else return FALSE.

END.

The hybrid rules from the Datalog^L KB K input obey the restriction of only having independent properties, as imposed by our definition of K, s.t. step-2 produces ground rules under the weak safeness condition. For rules fulfilling the strong safeness condition, step-2 will be skipped due to the non-appearance of pure-DL variables. That is, our algorithm introduces a method to re-establish strong safeness by eliminating all pure-DL variables, while a collection of ground DL-queries will be submitted to a DL reasoner for satisfiability checking.

Instead of processing the rule bodies separately, step-3 evaluates them as a single disjunction. As a simple example consider a DL TBox with one axiom
• $\grave{o}$ $A \grave{o} B$ as well as two hybrid rules that C(x) :- & A(x). and C(x) :- & B(x). In addition, there is an individual a in the DL top class • . Given a

query C(a), neither A(a) nor B(a) holds, while step-3 allows to finalize this query via $A \grave{o} B(a)$ to which the DL reasoner replies 'True'.

3.2 Query Answering

In general, a substitution θ is a finite set of the form $\{X_1/t_1, ..., X_n/t_n\}$, where X_i is a variable, t_i is a term, and $X_i \neq X_j$ for $i \neq j$. A ground substitution is a substitution where t_i is a constant for every $i \in \{1, ..., n\}$. Below is the technical details for query answering, using the notions inherited from AL-log but with extensions to DL properties.

Definition 8 [Constrained SLD-resolution]. Let L be a specific DL language, $K=(\Sigma,\Pi)$ be a Datalog^L knowledge base, $q = \alpha_1,...,\alpha_s \& \beta_1,..., \beta_t$ be a query to K where α_i is a Datalog atom and β_j is a DL atom, and r be a hybrid rule of the form α' :- $\alpha'_1,...,\alpha'_m \& \beta'_1,..., \beta'_n$. Suppose θ is the most general substitution such that $\alpha'\theta = \alpha_k\theta$, where α_k is one of $\{\alpha_1,...,\alpha_s\}$. The resolvent of q and r with substitution θ is the query $q'=\mu\&v$, where $\mu=(\alpha_1,...,\alpha_{k-1}, \alpha'_1,...,\alpha'_m, \alpha_{k+1},...,\alpha_s)\theta$ and $v=(\beta_1,..., \beta_t, \beta'_1,..., \beta'_n)\theta$ with simplification: if there are two constraints of the form t:C, t:D, they are replaced by the equivalent constraint t: $C \grave{o} D$.

Definition 9 [Constrained SLD-derivation]. A constrained SLD-derivation for a query q_0 in K is a derivation constituted by:
1. A sequence of queries $q_0, q_1, ..., q_n$
2. A sequence of hybrid rules $r_1, ..., r_n$
3. A sequence of substitutions $\theta_1, ..., \theta_n$
such that for each $i \in \{0, 1, ..., n-1\}$, q_{i+1} is the resolvent of q_i and r_{i+1} with substitution θ_{i+1}. We call n the length of the derivation.

A derivation may terminate with the last query of the form $q_{DL} = \varnothing \& \beta_1,...,\beta_l$, which is called *constrained empty clause*. For strong safeness conditions, the constrained empty clause should have not any variable, while for weak safeness conditions, pure-DL variables appear as being existentially quantified in some of "$\beta_1,...,\beta_l$". In this sense, we currently only consider independent properties in hybrid rules, with folding results fully supported by existing DL reasoners.

Proposition 2. Let $q_0, q_1, ..., q_n$ be a constrained SLD-derivation for q_0 in K. If I is a model of K such that $I \models q_{i+1}$, then $I \models q_i$, for i= 0, ..., n-1.
Proof. It follows from the soundness of SLD-resolution as well as the fact that the simplification of constraints preserves validity. In particular, Proposition 1 states the

folding results are equivalent to the original DL-queries, also applying to the last query q_n, i.e., the constrained empty clause q_{DL} with pure-DL variables. Together with DL classical tableaux algorithms, it holds that

$K \mid\text{-} \varnothing \& C(x)$ iff C^I is nonempty, where I is the model of K

$K \mid\text{-} \varnothing \& P(u, x) \wedge C(x)$ iff $K \models \exists P.C(u)$

$K \mid\text{-} \varnothing \& P(x, u) \wedge C(x)$ iff $K \models \exists P^-.C(u)$

Definition 10 [Constrained SLD-refutation]. A constrained SLD-refutation for a query q in K is a finite set of constrained SLD-derivations $d_1,...,d_m$ for q in K such that, denoting as $q_0^i,...,q_{ni}^i$ the sequence of queries of the ith derivation d_i, the following conditions hold:

1. For each i, q_{ni}^i is one of the form "$\varnothing \& \beta_1^i,...,\beta_{li}^i$", i.e., the last query of each derivation is a constrained empty clause.
2. For each q_{ni}^i with pure-DL variables, obtain the folding results of q_{ni}^i.
3. For each model I of K, there exists at least one $i \in \{1,...,m\}$ s.t. $I \models q_{ni}^i$; we write this condition $K \models disj(q_{n1}^1, ..., q_{nm}^m)$.

We write $K \mid\text{-} q$, if there is a constrained SLD-refutation for q in K.

Lemma 1. Let q be a ground query to a Datalog^L knowledge base $K = (\Sigma, \Pi)$. $K \mid\text{-} q$ if and only if $K \models q$.

Proof. With restriction to independent properties in hybrid rules, we present our proof based on the correctness and completeness of SLD-resolution and DL tableaux algorithms, similar as AL-log does.

=>: Suppose $K \mid\text{-} q$, i.e., the ground query q has a constrained SLD-refutation. Then, for each derivation, if I is a model of K that satisfies the constrained empty clause q_{DL} then it satisfies q (by repeated application of Proposition 2 with q_{DL} as q_n and q as q_0); moreover, each model I of K satisfies at least one of the constrained empty clauses. Then each model of K satisfies q, that is $K \models q$.

<=: Suppose $K \mid\text{-} q$ fails, we have no constrained SLD-refutation for q in K, resulting from three possibilities according to Definition 10.

1. If there is no constrained empty clause, then from the completeness of SLD-resolution, we have the failure of $K \models q$.
2. If there is no folding results of the constrained empty clause, then this query q is beyond our consideration, having a natural conflict with $K \models q$.
3. If there is a model I of K, then for any derivation of q whose last query is a constrained empty clause (written as $q_{ni}^i = \varnothing \& \beta_1^i,...,\beta_{ni}^i$), it makes $I \models q_{ni}^i$ a failure. That is, there is a model I of Σ such that $I \models \beta_1^i,...,\beta_{ni}^i$ fails. Characterized by I, we can construct another model J, and it can be shown -- by induction on the construction of J -- that $J \models q$ fails, and $K \models q$ fails.

Referring to AL-log, Datalog^L also provides a decidable procedure. Note that satisfiability of an ALC class (without any TBox) is PSPACE-complete; while the same problem is ExpTime -complete, if a TBox with general inclusion axioms is present [3]. For the rule component, Datalog is data complete for P while program complete for ExpTime [5]. As a result, the computational complexity of Datalog^L is ExpTime, where L ranges from ALC to SHIQ.

Theorem 1. Query answering in Datalog^L is a decidable problem in ExpTime.

4 Re-obtaining Decidability

As pointed in CARIN, the problem of determining whether K |= q is undecidable, where K is a Datalog^L knowledge base with recursive Datalog rules, and its L-based DL component allows arbitrary inclusion statements while L itself includes only the constructor ∃P.C. In short, the recursive Datalog rules extended with cyclic TBox including only one DL constructor of ∃P.C will destroy decidability, while ∃P.C is the most basic DL constructor, introduced first by the simpler ALC DL. This theorem has been proved in [14], by reducing the halting problem of a Turing machine to the entailment problem of K. Below, we rewrite them:

- DL ABox: integer(1)
- DL TBox: integer ô ∃succ.integer
- rule-primitive: lessThan(x, y) :- & succ(x, y).
- rule-recursive: lessThan(x, y) :- lessThan(z, y) & succ(x, z).

Below, we identify two ways of restricting the expressivity in the knowledge base as to re-obtain a decision procedure, where the first one is in the view of DL and the second is of rules:

(1) To remove some DL constructors: Not obtaining the benefits from the current mature DL techniques as much as possible, we backtrack to the systems of nearly 10 years ago -- actually, CARIN has a (maximal) decidable sublanguage, namely CARIN-MARC, which includes the constructors ó ,ò ,(≥ nR),∃R.C and negation on primitive classes, with the terminology consisting of acyclic class definitions (i.e., no inclusions or property definitions). DLP has another solution: it requires that the existential DL constructor of ∃P.C can only occur on the left hand side of an inclusion axiom, that is, it allows the form of being ∃P.C ô D but disallows that of D ô ∃P.C.

(2) To enforce stronger safeness conditions: Generally speaking, rules are required to be safe, i.e., a variable that appears in the head must also appear in the body -- we call it as the weak safeness condition in this paper, and the above undecidable encoding is a case of weakness. As mentioned in Table 1, CARIN, DLP and SWRL obey this weak safeness, but either CARIN or DLP has its respective restrictions under other considerations as to obtain decidability, while SWRL admits itself undecidable. For the other systems, strong safeness conditions have to be emphasized, such as r-hybrid KBs and KAON2 (demanding that "x" must occur in "lessThan(z, y)" given our above KB example); moreover, AL-log only permits DL-query to classes without admission to DL properties. Regarding our proposal of Datalog^{DL}, weak safeness conditions are fine, but the above rules will obtain such DL queries as "succ(x, z), succ(z, y)" provided by "lessThan(x, y)" with length of two steps. Here, no independent properties are guaranteed, due to sharing the pure-DL variable of "z", s.t. a folding result like $\exists$succ.$\exists$succ.$\{y\}(x)$ will be submitted to a DL reasoner. Considering that it lacks full provision to the nominals O in existing DL systems, and our framework conforms to the available techniques, we exclude the above hybrid rules with requirement of independent properties. Thus, we also define some expressivity restrictions to avoid undecidability, driven by considerations to existing DL reasoners rather than strong safeness conditions. Actually, for simplicity, we deal little with the recursive rules in our prototype system [1], but having been scoped in our ongoing work, this aspect will be paid more attention.

5 Conclusion

AL-log has combined Datalog with ALC, regarded as Datalog^{ALC} in our proposal. To provide an efficient tool in practice and a sound and complete system in theory, our Datalog^{DL} concerns any sublanguage L of $SHIQ$ as its parameter, namely Datalog^{L}, and the practical SLD-resolution and DL tableaux algorithms act well in an integrated framework, beyond what AL-log has done. Like CARIN, both class and property predicates are allowed in DL-queries, with weak safeness conditions instead of strong ones. And the unique requirement is the admission of independent properties in hybrid rules, which conforms to support for reasoning in existing DL reasoners. Besides, different from CARIN, which prefers to forward chaining for modeling an entailment completion, our prototype system [1] performs query answering in backward chaining with improvements to a rule engine (e.g., OO jDREW), making the hybrid rules processable, while keeping the DL reasoner (e.g., RACER) unchanged to act as an external service. And we assume such adaptation is more straightforward to users that the non-trivial DL algorithms would be regarded as a black box.

It should be pointed out how our folding technique is related to 'rolling-up' in [12]. There, (conjunctive) queries to the ABox of a DL knowledge base, perhaps containing variables in DL classes or DL properties, can be rewritten s.t. query answering is reduced to the problem of knowledge base satisfiability. Here, this kind of technique is used to bridge the gap between query answering in hybrid rules and testing satisfiability in the DL component. Furthermore, the usage of our "independent properties" to some extent corresponds to a particular case of tree-shaped (or acyclic) DL queries as described in [12].

We are currently investigating DL query languages in support of hybrid rules on the practical level. The expressivity and reasoning power of Datalog^{DL} were explored with a suite of previous examples from AL-log, CARIN, DL-safe rules, and our use case RuleML FOAF [15]. This suite covers much of the expressiveness currently discussed for hybrid rules, e.g. in the W3C RIF WG [20]. The entire suite is implemented in our hybrid rule engine [1] coupling OO jDREW with RACER.

For the serialization of hybrid rules, the RuleML <Implies> element with its <head> role for h(X) and its <body> role for the $b_i(Y_i)$ can be extended with a <neck> role for the $q_j(Z_j)$. The *neck* of a rule may also be generally used to query other (non-DL) external decidable provers.

In this paper, we enriched rules with information from ontologies, but not vice versa. Sharing common predicates in both components is attractive, while the problems it causes, such as decidability, are open challenges for the Semantic Web. Also, Datalog$^{\neg v}$ was investigated in dl-programs and r-hybrid systems as a more expressive rule component; such rules with disjunction and negation are also considered in our future work.

Acknowledgements

We would like to thank the anonymous CSWWS2006 reviewers for their helpful suggestions.

References

1. *Hybrid Rules in OO jDREW.* http://www.jdrew.org/oojdrew/exa /hybridrules.html.
2. Grigoris Antoniou, Carlos Viegas Damasio, Benjamin N. Grosof, Ian Horrocks, Michael Kifer, Jan Maluszynski, and Peter F. Patel-Schneider (2005) *Combining Rules and Ontologies - A survey.* http://rewerse.net /deliverables/m12/i3-d3.pdf.
3. Franz Baader, Diego Calvanese, Deborah McGuinness, Daniele Nardi, and Peter F. Patel-Schneider (2003) *The Description Logic Handbook: Theory, Implementation and Applications.* Cambridge University Press.
4. Marcel Ball, Harold Boley, David Hirtle, Jing Mei, and Bruce Spencer (2005) *The OO jDREW Reference Implementation of RuleML.* In: International Conference on Rules and Rule Markup Languages for the Semantic Web, pp 218--223.
5. Evgeny Dantsin, Thomas Eiter, Georg Gottlob, and Andrei Voronkov (2001) *Complexity and Expressive Power of Logic Programming.* ACM Computing Surveys, pp 374--425.
6. Francesco M. Donini, Maurizio Lenzerini, Daniele Nardi, and Andrea Schaerf (1998) *AL-log: Integrating Datalog and Description Logics.* Journal of Intelligent Information Systems, pp 227-252.
7. Thomas Eiter, Thomas Lukasiewicz, Roman Schindlauer, and Hans Tompits (2004) *Combining Answer Set Programming with Description Logics for the Semantic Web.* In: The Ninth International Conference on the Principles of Knowledge Representation and Reasoning, pp 141-151.
8. Benjamin N. Grosof, Ian Horrocks, Raphael Volz, and Stefan Decker (2003) *Description Logic Programs: Combining Logic Programs with Description Logic.* In: The Twelfth International World Wide Web Conference, pp 48--57.
9. Volker Haarslev and Ralf Mller (2001) *RACER System Description.* In: International Joint Conference on Automated Reasoning, pp 701--706.
10. Ian Horrocks, Bijan Parsia, Peter F. Patel-Schneider, and James A. Hendler (2005) *Semantic Web Architecture: Stack or Two Towers?* In: Workshop on Principles and Practice of Semantic Web Reasoning, pp 37-41.
11. Ian Horrocks, Peter F. Patel-Schneider, Harold Boley, Said Tabet, Benjamin N. Grosof, and Mike Dean (2004) *Semantic Web Rule Language.* http://www.w3.org/Submission/2004/SUBM-SWRL-20040521/.

12. Ian Horrocks and Sergio Tessaris (2002) *Querying the Semantic Web: a Formal Approach*. In: Workshop on Principles and Practice of Semantic Web Reasoning, pp 177--191.
13. Michael Kifer, Jos de Bruijn, Harold Boley, and Dieter Fensel (2005) *A Realistic Architecture for the Semantic Web*. In: International Conference on Rules and Rule Markup Languages for the Semantic Web, pp 17-29.
14. Alon Y. Levy and Marie-Christine Rousset (1996) *CARIN: A Representation Language Combining Horn Rules and Description Logics*. In: The Twelfth European Conference on Artificial Intelligence, pp 323-327.
15. Jie Li, Harold Boley, Virendrakumar C. Bhavsar, and Jing Mei (2006) *Expert Finding for eCollaboration Using FOAF with RuleML Rules*. In: The Montreal Conference on eTechnologies, May 2006. To Appear.
16. John W. Lloyd (1987) *Foundations of Logic Programming (second, extended edition)*. Springer series in symbolic computation.
17. Boris Motik, Ulrike Sattler, and Rudi Studer (2005) *Query Answering for OWL-DL with Rules*. Journal of Web Semantics, pp 41-60.
18. Peter F. Patel-Schneider, Patrick Hayes, and Ian Horrocks (2004) *OWL Web Ontology Language Semantics and Abstract Syntax*. http://www.w3.org/TR /owl-absyn/.
19. Riccardo Rosati (2005) *On the decidability and complexity of integrating ontologies and rules*. Journal of Web Semantics, pp 61-73.
20. W3C (2005) *Rule Interchange Format Working Group*. http://www.w3.org /2005/rules/wg.html.

Resolution Based Explanations for Reasoning in the Description Logic $\mathcal{ALC}$

Xi Deng, Volker Haarslev, and Nematollaah Shiri

Department of Computer Science and Software Engineering, Concordia University, Montreal, Quebec, Canada

Abstract. With the increasing number of applications of description logics (DLs), unsatisfiable concepts and inconsistent terminologies become quite common, especially when the knowledge bases are large and complex. Even for an experienced knowledge engineer, it can be extremely difficult to identify and resolve the origins of these unsatisfiabilities and inconsistencies. Thus it is crucial to provide services to explain how and why a result is derived. Motivated by the possibilities of applying resolution technique in first-order logic to construct explanations for description logics, we extend our previous work and present an algorithm that generates explanations for unsatisfiability and inconsistency reasoning in the description language $\mathcal{ALC}$. The main advantage of our approach is that it is independent of any specific DL reasoners.

1 Introduction

In recent years, description logics (DLs) have found a wide range of applications in computer science, such as domain modeling, software engineering, configuration, and the semantic web [3]. With increasing complex applications, unsatisfiability and inconsistency become quite common. For example, the DICE (Diagnoses for Intensive Care Evaluation) terminology [17] contains more than 2400 concepts, out of which about 750 concepts were unsatisfiable due to migration from other terminological systems. Unsatisfiability and inconsistency may also arise due to unintentional design defects in the terminology or changes in the process of ontology evolution. However, existing DL reasoners, such as Racer [7] and FaCT [10], do not provide explanation services; they merely provide "Yes/No" answer to a satisfiability or consistency query with no information about the reasons. In addition to such answers, it is desirable that DL reasoners also provide reasons for their answers and identify the sources of inconsistencies to further help knowledge engineers and ontology developers. It is therefore crucial and also challenging to provide explanation services as a useful feature and facility for DL reasoners.

In our previous work [4], we proposed a framework of constructing explanations for the description logic language $\mathcal{ALC}$ using resolution proofs. The approach works as follows:

1. Firstly, if a DL reasoner provides a negative answer to a satisfiability/ consistency query, i.e., a concept is unsatisfiable or a TBox/ABox is inconsistent, the axioms and assertions in the knowledge base will be translated into first-order formulae.
2. Then a resolution based automated theorem prover (ATP) is used to generate the resolution proof, taking the translated formulae as inputs.
3. At last, the resolution proof is transformed into its corresponding refutation graph [6]. Our algorithm traverses the graph and "reads" the proof to generate explanations. Later, the clauses involved in each traversal step are traced back to the contributing axioms/assertions in the original DL knowledge base.

Our approach has two main advantages. The first is that it is independent of any specific DL reasoners. Most implemented DL reasoners use tableau algorithms as the underlying reasoning calculus. Tableau rules are designed to render the results faster but not necessarily easier for the users to understand. Furthermore, some DL optimization techniques, such as absorption[1], are adopted to make reasoning more efficient, however they may make it more difficult for general users to understand if presented as explanations. In order to give explanations, the internal reasoning procedures should be tailored with performance penalties. Since the explanations are constructed based on resolution proofs in our approach, no modification of the internal of a DL reasoner is needed. This makes it possible to provide explanations for any DL reasoner. The second advantage of our approach of using resolution, compared to natu-

---

[1] The basic idea of absorption is to transform a general axiom, e.g., $C' \sqsubseteq D$, to the form of a primitive definition $A \sqsubseteq D'$, where A is an atomic concept name and D' is a non-atomic concept.

ral deduction proofs or tableau proofs, is that it is more focused, as all the literals in the clauses involved in a proof contribute to the proof. In other words, the resolution technique filters and excludes from a proof, the axioms and assertions in the knowledge base that are irrelevant to the query and hence unused in the process.

Since for our explanation, we use a proof that is different from the original proof, a question that may naturally arise at this point is concerned with correctness of the explanation procedure. In this paper, our focus is to study soundness and completeness of our algorithm. In order to guarantee termination of the resolution procedure and hence our explanation technique, we adopt a structural transformation during translation.

The rest of the paper is organized as follows. Sect.2 discusses related work in explanations. In Sect.3, we introduce our explanation algorithm and establish its soundness and completeness. Sect.4 includes an illustrative example. Sect.5 includes concluding remarks and discusses some future work.

2 Related Work

There have been several proposals to provide explanations for DL reasoning. The earliest work is [13] which provides an explanation facility for subsumption and non-subsumption reasoning in CLASSIC [2]. CLASSIC is a family of knowledge representation systems based on description logics. It allows universal quantification, conjunction and restricted number restrictions. Since disjunction is not allowed in CLASSIC, explanations are given based on structural subsumption comparisons. Lengthy explanations are decomposed into smaller steps and a single step explanation is followed by more detailed explanations. This work is extended in [1] by using sequent rules to explain subsumption in $\mathcal{ALC}$. The sequent rules are modified to imitate the behavior of tableau calculus as well as the behavior of human reasoning. In contrast to these works, [17] provides algorithms to pinpoint unsatisfiable concepts and related axioms. This approach first excludes axioms which are irrelevant to the inconsistency and then provide simplified definitions which highlight the exact position of the contradiction. This work is extended in [16] to debug OWL ontologies. This approach consists of two parts: glass box and black box. Glass box relies on information from internals of the reasoners. It traces back to the last clash to give the source of inconsistency. Black box approach uses reason-

ers as oracles and relies on the users to perform navigational search to show
unsatisfiability dependency. On the other hand, most existing explanation facilities in resolution based automated theorem proving transform the proofs
into natural language style explanations [11, 12, 14]. They are specifically designed to solve problems in theorem proving, particularly mathematical theorems. They focus on proving conclusions using theorems, lemmas and prem-
ises and in general not suitable for indirect proofs.

3 Preliminaries

3.1 Description Logics

Description logics are a family of concept-based knowledge representation
formalisms. It represents the knowledge of a domain by first defining the relevant concepts of the domain. These concepts are then used to specify properties of the objects and individuals in the domain. Typically a DL language has
two parts: *terminology* (TBox) and *assertion* (ABox). The TBox includes intensional knowledge in the form of axioms whereas the ABox contains the extensional knowledge that is specific to elements in the domain, called individuals.

Among DL frameworks, $\mathcal{ALC}$ ($\mathcal{AL}$ stands for *Attribute language* and $\mathcal{C}$
stands for *Complement*) has been considered as a basic DL language of inter-
ests in numerous studies in DL. In $\mathcal{ALC}$ and other DL languages as well, basic
descriptions are *atomic concepts*, designated by unary predicates, and *atomic
roles*, designated by binary predicates to express relationships between concepts. Arbitrary concept descriptions such as C and D are built from atomic
concepts and roles recursively according to the following rules:

$$
\begin{array}{ll}
C, D \to A| & \text{(atomic concept)} \\
\neg C| & \text{(arbitrary concept negation)} \\
C \sqcap D| & \text{(intersection)} \\
C \sqcup D| & \text{(union)} \\
\forall R.C| & \text{(value restriction)} \\
\exists R.C & \text{(existential quantification)}
\end{array}
$$

where A denotes an atomic concept and R denotes an atomic role. The *intersection* (or *union*) of concepts, which is denoted $C \sqcap D$ (or $C \sqcup D$), is used to restrict the individuals to those that belong to both C and D (or either C or D). The *value restriction*, denoted $\forall R.C$, requires that all the individuals that are in the relationship R with an individual of the value restriction belong to the concept C. The *existential quantification*, written $\exists R.C$, defines that for all individuals of the existential quantification there must exist an individual in the relationship R that belongs to the concept C. The *universal concept* $\top$ is a synonym of $A \sqcup \neg A$. The *bottom concept* $\bot$ is a synonym of $A \sqcap \neg A$.

An interpretation $\mathcal{I}$ defines a formal semantics of concepts and individuals in $\mathcal{ALC}$. It consists of a non-empty set $\Delta^{\mathcal{I}}$, called the domain of the interpretation, and an interpretation function, which maps every atomic concept A to a set $A^{\mathcal{I}} \subseteq \Delta^{\mathcal{I}}$, and maps every atomic role R to a binary relation $R^{\mathcal{I}} \subseteq \Delta^{\mathcal{I}} \times \Delta^{\mathcal{I}}$. In addition, $\mathcal{I}$ maps each individual name a to an element $a^{\mathcal{I}} \in \Delta^{\mathcal{I}}$. The interpretation $\mathcal{I}$ is extended to concept descriptions, as shown in Table 1.

Constructors	Semantics
A	$A^{\mathcal{I}}$
$\neg C$	$\Delta^{\mathcal{I}} \backslash C^{\mathcal{I}}$
$C \sqcap D$	$C^{\mathcal{I}} \cap D^{\mathcal{I}}$
$C \sqcup D$	$C^{\mathcal{I}} \cup D^{\mathcal{I}}$
$\forall R.C$	$\{a \in \Delta^{\mathcal{I}} \mid \forall b.(a,b) \in R^{\mathcal{I}} \rightarrow b \in C^{\mathcal{I}}\}$
$\exists R.C$	$\{a \in \Delta^{\mathcal{I}} \mid \exists b.(a,b) \in R^{\mathcal{I}} \land b \in C^{\mathcal{I}}\}$
$a : A$	$a^{\mathcal{I}} \in A^{\mathcal{I}}$
$(a,b) : R$	$(a^{\mathcal{I}}, b^{\mathcal{I}}) \in R^{\mathcal{I}}$

Table 1. Interpretations of constructors in $\mathcal{ALC}$.

Axioms express how concepts and roles are related to each other. Generally, an axiom is a statement of the form $C \sqsubseteq D$ or $C \equiv D$, where C and D are concept descriptions. An interpretation $\mathcal{I}$ satisfies $C \sqsubseteq D$ if $C^{\mathcal{I}} \subseteq D^{\mathcal{I}}$. It satisfies $C \equiv D$ if $C^{\mathcal{I}} = D^{\mathcal{I}}$.

The basic inference services in TBoxes include satisfiability, subsumption, equivalence, and disjointness. A concept in a TBox T is said to be *satisfiable* w.r.t T if there exists an interpretation $\mathcal{I}$ that is a model of T. A model for T is an interpretation that satisfies it. The other three inference services can all be reduced to (un)satisfiability. Another important reasoning service in TBoxes is to check whether a TBox T is *consistent*, i.e., whether there exists a model for T. The basic reasoning tasks in ABoxes are instance check, realization, and retrieval. The instance check verifies if a given individual is an instance of a specified concept. The instance realization computes the most specific concepts that an individual is an instance of. The instance retrieval returns all the individuals in the knowledge base that are instances of a given concept. An ABox A is *consistent* w.r.t a TBox T, if there is an interpretation that is a model of both A and T. Similar to the inference services in TBoxes, the other three inference services in ABoxes can also be reduced to the consistency problem of ABoxes. Further details of description logics can be found in [3].

3.2 Resolution

We assume that the readers are familiar with standard definitions of first-order logic (FOL) and clausal theorem proving. Resolution is one of the most widely used calculi for theorem proving in first-order logic. Resolution proves a theorem by negating the statement to be proved and adding this negated goal to the sets of axioms that are known to be true. It then uses the following inference rules to show that this leads to a contradiction.

Positive factoring:

$$C \vee A \vee B$$
$$\overline{}$$
$$C\sigma \vee A\sigma$$

where σ = MGU(A, B),

Resolution:

$$C \vee A \qquad D \vee \neg B$$
$$\overline{}$$
$$C\sigma \vee D\sigma$$

where σ = MGU(A, B).

Resolution is sound and complete: if a set of clauses is saturated up to re-dundancy by the inference rules, then it is satisfiable if and only if it does not contain the empty clause.

4 Preprocessing

In [4], the translation between DL and FOL is straightforward based on the semantics of DL. For $\mathcal{ALC}$, concepts can be translated into the first order predicate logic over unary and binary predicates with two variables, say x, y, which is denoted as $\mathcal{L}^2$. Table 2 shows such a translation from $\mathcal{ALC}$ into $\mathcal{L}^2$. An atomic concept A is translated into a predicate logic formula $\phi_A(x)$ with one free variable x such that for every interpretation $\mathcal{I}$, the set of elements of $\Delta^{\mathcal{I}}$ satisfying $\phi_A(x)$ is exactly $A^{\mathcal{I}}$. Similarly, a role name R can be translated into binary predicate $\phi_R(x, y)$. An individual name a is translated into a constant a. However, in order to guarantee complete and terminating reasoning, a simple direct translation based on the standard first order logic semantics is not ap-propriate. Hence we adopt the structural transformation as shown in [8, 15].

DL Constructor	FOL Formula
A	$\phi_A(x)$
$\neg C$	$\neg\phi_C(x)$
$C \sqcap D$	$\phi_C(x) \wedge \phi_D(x)$
$C \sqcup D$	$\phi_C(x) \vee \phi_D(x)$
$C \sqsubseteq D$	$\forall x(\phi_C(x) \to \phi_D(x))$
$R \sqsubseteq S$	$\forall x(\phi_R(x) \to \phi_S(x))$
$\exists R.C$	$\exists y(\phi_R(x, y) \wedge \phi_C(y))$
$\forall R.C$	$\forall y(\phi_R(x, y) \to \phi_C(y))$
$a : A$	$\phi_A(a)$
$(a, b) : R$	$\phi_R(a, b)$

Table 2 . Translation from $\mathcal{ALC}$ into $\mathcal{L}^2$

The structural transformation is a kind of conjunction normal form trans-formation of first-order predicate logic formulae by replacing the subformulae with some new predicates and adding a suitable definition for these predicates.

We choose the structural transformation because: Firstly, it would avoid the exponential blow up of the size of the clauses. Consider the axiom $E \sqsubseteq F$, where E and F are complex concept descriptions. If n is the number of clauses generated by E and m is the number of clauses generated by F then the above formula generates $n \times m$ clauses. The reason for the exponential explosion is the duplication of subformulae obtained by the exhaustive application of the distributivity law. If we replace F by a fresh concept, say C, then the above axiom transforms into two: $E \sqsubseteq C$ and $C \sqsubseteq F$. The number of clauses generated by these two axioms is $n+m$. Secondly, it helps to preserve original structures of DL axioms after first-order logic formulae are transformed into their conjunction normal forms. Consider the axiom $\forall R.E \sqsubseteq \exists S.F$, without this transformation, the LHS and RHS of this axiom are distributed into four clauses, making it difficult to generate explanations.

A formal definition of the transformation is shown below.

Definition 1 C is a *qualified concept expression* if and only if C is of the form $\ominus R.D$ with $\ominus \in \{\forall, \exists\}$ and D is an arbitrary concept.

Definition 2 [15] A *position* is a word over the natural numbers. The set $pos(\varphi)$ of positions of a given formula φ is defined as follows: (i) the empty word $\varepsilon \in pos(\varphi)$ (ii) for $1 \le i \le n$, $i.p \in pos(\varphi)$ if $\varphi = \varphi_1 \bullet \ldots \bullet \varphi_n$ and $p \in pos(\varphi_i)$ where $\bullet$ is a first-order operator. If $p \in pos(\varphi)$, $\varphi|_{i.p} = \varphi_i|_p$ where $\varphi = \varphi_1 \bullet \ldots \bullet \varphi_n$. We write $\varphi[\phi]_p$ for $\varphi|_p = \phi$. With $\varphi[p/\phi]$ where $p \in pos(\varphi)$ we denote the formula obtained by replacing $\varphi|_p$ with ϕ at position p in φ. The *polarity* of a formula occurring at position π in a formula φ is denoted by $Pol(\varphi, \pi)$ and defined as: $Pol(\varphi, \varepsilon) = 1$; $Pol(\varphi, \pi.i) = Pol(\varphi, \pi)$ if $\varphi|_\pi$ is a conjunction, disjunction, formula starting with a quantifier or an implication with $i = 2$; $Pol(\varphi, \pi.i) = -Pol(\varphi, \pi)$ if $\varphi|_\pi$ is a formula starting with a negation symbol or an implication with $i = 1$ and, $Pol(\varphi, \pi.i) = Pol(\varphi, \pi)$ if $\varphi|_\pi$ is an equivalence.

Definition 3 Let φ be a formula and $\phi = \varphi|_\pi$ be a subformula of φ at position π. For position q which is just one position below π, the DL counterpart of $\varphi|_q$ is a qualified concept expression. Let $x_1, \ldots, x_n$ be the free variables in ϕ and let R be a new predicate. Then the formula

$$\varphi[\pi / R(x_1, \ldots, x_n)] \wedge Def_\pi^\varphi$$

is a structural transformation of φ at position π. The formula Def_π^φ is a polarity dependent definition of the new predicate R:

$$Def_\pi^\varphi = \quad \forall x_1,\dots, x_n [R(x_1,\dots, x_n) \to \phi] \text{ if } Pol\,(\varphi,\pi) = 1$$

$$\forall x_1,\dots, x_n [\phi \to R(x_1,\dots, x_n)] \text{ if } Pol\,(\varphi,\pi) = -1$$

It is easy to see the following result after structural transformation.

Definition 4 There are four types of clauses after normalization:

1. $\bigvee X_i$

2. $\bigvee X_i \vee R(x, f(x))$

3. $\bigvee X_i \vee Y$

4. $\bigvee X_i \vee \neg R(x, y) \vee Z$

where $X_i \in \{C_i(x), \neg C_i(x)\}$, $Y \in \{D(f(x)), \neg D(f(x))\}$ and $Z \in \{D(y), \neg D(y)\}$.

Specifically, clause type (1) is translated from axiom $C \sqsubseteq D$, and both C and D are complex concepts. Type (2) and (3) are translated from axioms $C \sqsubseteq \exists R.D$ or $\forall R.C \sqsubseteq D$. Type (4) is translated from axioms $C \sqsubseteq \forall R.D$ or $\exists R.C \sqsubseteq D$.

The correctness of the translation is proved as follows.

Theorem 1 Let T be a TBox in $\mathcal{ALC}$ and C be a named concept in T. T is consistent. Let $\theta\,(T)$ and $\theta\,(C(a))$ be the resulting set of FOL formulae of T and $C(a)$ after the translation, a being a newly introduced individual. Then C is unsatisfiable if and only if the empty clause is derived under resolution given $\theta\,(T) \cup \theta\,(C(a))$.

Proof. As mentioned in [8], the structural transformation does not affect satisfiability, it is easy to see T and $\theta\,(T)$ are equisatisfiable. Since T is consistent as the known fact, $\theta\,(T)$ is also consistent. Since C is unsatisfiable, C does not admit any instance, i.e., $C(a)$ is false. Hence $\theta\,(T) \cup \theta\,(C(a))$ is inconsistent. According to the refutational completeness of resolution, the empty clause can be derived. Similarly, we can prove that if the empty clause is derived for $\theta\,(T) \cup \theta\,(C(a))$, C is unsatisfiable. ∎

We can also easily prove the following result.

Theorem 2 Let T be a TBox and A be an ABox (either T or A can be empty). Let $\theta\,(T)$ and $\theta\,(A)$ be the resulting set of FOL formulae of T and A after the translation. Then $T \cup A$ is inconsistent if and only if the empty clause is derived under resolution given $\theta(T) \cup \theta(A)$.

5 The Algorithm to Generate Explanations

Our approach uses a refutation graph [6] to reconstruct the resolution proof in order to support explanation. Generally speaking, a refutation graph is a graph whose nodes are literals (grouped together in clauses) and its edges connect complementary nodes/literals which correspond to the resolution steps in the resolution proof. In a refutation graph, complementary literals between input clauses are directly visible. We give the fundamental definition about refutation graphs as below. Further details can be found in [4]. The algorithm of transforming a resolution proof to its refutation graph is shown in Fig.1.

Definition 5 A *refutation graph* is a quadruple $G = (L; C; M_L; K)$, where L is a finite set of literal nodes in G. C is a partition of the set of literal nodes. Its members are clause nodes in G. M_L is a mapping from L to a set of literals. The set of links K is a partition of a subset of L. There are no pure literal nodes in a refutation graph, i.e., every literal node belongs to some link in K.

Input: a resolution proof   **Output**: its corresponding refutation graph

---

For all the steps in the resolution proof
  For all the literals that are involved in a step
    If its literal node does not exist
        create its corresponding clause (literal) node and add it into the refutation graph
    add a link between the literal nodes that are resolved (factored) together
Return the refutation graph

Fig. 1. The Transformation Algorithm.

The main idea of explanations based on the refutation graph is to start from a literal node (or nodes) and traverse the graph. After the traversal is completed, each clause node involved in each step is translated into an entry in an explanation list consisting of its source axioms in DL. After some clean-up, e.g., deleting duplicate line, this explanation list can be further transformed into natural language style explanations.

The traversal algorithms of unsatisfiability reasoning can be described as follows: Start from the literal node corresponding to the unsatisfiable concept, follow the links to its complementary literal nodes L_i, $i = 1, ..., n$. For each of the literal nodes that are in the same clause node as L_i, follow its untraversed link. Stop when there is no untraversed link left. The algorithm to explain the inconsistency reasoning is similar to the unsatisfiability case, except that the traversal will begin with one of the literal nodes involved in the first step of the resolution proof.

The pseudo code of the algorithm is shown in Fig.2. It uses a stack, called SOT, which includes the literal nodes which are yet to be traversed.

Input: a refutation graph   **Output**: an explanation list

If it is an unsatisfiable problem
  start from the unsatisfiable concept C
  else start from a concept C involved in the first step of the resolution proof
SOT ← the associated literal node of C
For all the literal nodes L_i in SOT
  mark L_i as "traversed"
  put the corresponding DL axiom of L_i into the explanation list
  For all the links that are adjacent to L_i
  If the link was created from a factoring step
      mark the literal node at the opposite side of the link as "traversed"
  else
  For all the literal nodes L_k that in the same clause node as the opposite side of the link
      SOT ← L_k
  Remove L_i from SOT
Return the explanation list

Fig. The Traversal Algorithm.

Theorem 3 The unsatisfiability and inconsistency traversal algorithms are complete and can terminate with an explanation.

Proof. Termination: In each step of the traversal, we decrease the number of literal nodes that remain untraversed, since once a literal node is traversed, it will not be traversed again. As the number of literal nodes in a refutation graph is finite, the traversal algorithm will terminate.

Completeness: The completeness in our case means that at the end of the algorithm, no literal node is left untraversed. That we cannot reach a blocked situation follows from the fact that every literal node in the refutation graph has a complementary literal node connected by a link, i.e., every literal node is reachable through other nodes. ∎

6 Example

To help understand the algorithms, we show an example KB as follows:

---

1. $Physician \sqsubseteq \exists hasDegree.BS$
2. $HappyPerson \sqsubseteq Doctor \sqcup \exists hasChild.(PhD \sqcap \neg Poor)$
3. $HappyPerson \sqsubseteq \forall hasChild.Married$
4. $MD \sqsubseteq \neg BS$
5. $Married \sqsubseteq Person \sqcap \exists hasSpouse.Person$
6. $Doctor \sqsubseteq \forall hasDegree.MD \sqcap Physician$
7. $PhD \sqcap Married \sqsubseteq Poor$

After being fed into Racer, HappyPerson is reported to be unsatisfiable. We set KB to be as below and show it to be inconsistent.

$$KB \equiv KB \cup \{HappyPerson(a)\}$$

where a is a fresh individual.

Since Axiom 1, 2, 3, 5 and 6 contain qualified concept expressions. But as the structural transformation does not either decrease the number of the clauses or simplify the explanations for 1, 3, 5 and 6, we only show how it is converted to FOL formulae based on structural transformation for axiom 2. We introduce new names Q for this subconcept and get

$$HappyPerson \sqsubseteq Doctor \sqcup \exists hasChild.Q$$

$$Q \sqsubseteq PhD \sqcap \neg Poor$$

By applying unit resolution to this clause set and by converting the resolution proof to its refutation graph in our prototype system, we get the graph as shown in Fig.3.

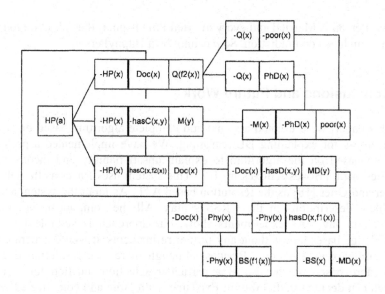

Fig.3. The Refutation Graph of the Example.

By applying the algorithm to explain unsatisfiable concepts, we get an explanation list as follows:

---

1. $HappyPerson(a)$
2. $HappyPerson \sqsubseteq Doctor \sqcup \exists hasChild.(PhD \sqcap \neg Poor)$
3. $Doctor \sqsubseteq \forall hasDegree.MD \sqcap Physician$
4. $Physician \sqsubseteq \exists hasDegree.BS$
5. $MD \sqsubseteq \neg BS$
6. $HappyPerson \sqsubseteq \forall hasChild.Married$
7. $PhD \sqcap Married \sqsubseteq Poor$

It reads as: if a is a HappyPerson, then it can either be a Doctor or has a child which is Q (PhD and not Poor). First, if it is a Doctor, then all its degree is MD and it is a Physician. Every Physician has a BS degree, however, BS is disjoint with MD. So there is a contradiction within the branch of Doctor. Secondly, if a has a child which is a PhD and not poor, since every child of a

HappyPerson is Married and every married PhD is poor, then a's child must be poor, which is a contradiction. So a cannot be a HappyPerson.

7 Conclusions and Future Work

In this paper, we presented a sound and complete algorithm based on resolution proofs for explaining DL reasoning. We have implemented a prototype system based on the algorithm to explain unsatisfiability and inconsistency queries w.r.t TBoxes/ABoxes in $\mathcal{ALC}$. This system uses Racer as the DL reasoner and Otter [18] as the resolution based ATP. As input the system accepts problem descriptions in the KRSS syntax. All the components are implemented in Java. As experiments show, our approach is suitable for small knowledge bases but, without any further refinements, it would generate long and complex explanations. Besides, although there is a resolution decision procedure based on the use of a particular selection function for $\mathcal{ALC}$ [5], which can decide satisfiability in ExpTime, with large and complicated examples, first-order resolution based provers will choke on such input, especially when considering to extend $\mathcal{ALC}$ to include number restrictions or transitive roles. To ensure that the first-order prover will finish, more sophisticated translations and resolution technique should be used.

Acknowledgments

This work was supported in part by Natural Sciences and Engineering Research Council (NSERC) of Canada, by Genome Quebec, and by ENCS Concordia University.

References

1. Borgida A, Franconi E, Horrocks I, McGuiness DL and Patel-Schneider PF (1999) Explaining $\mathcal{ALC}$ subsumption. In Proceedings of 1999 International Workshop on Description Logics. CEUR-WS.org, pp 37-44
2. Brachman RJ, McGuiness DL, Patel-Schneider PF, Resnick LA (1990) Living with CLASSIC: when and how to use a KL-ONE-like language. In

Sowa J (ed) Principles of semantic networks. Morgan Kaufmann, San Mateo, US, pp 401--456

3. Baader F, Nutt W (2003) Basic description logic. In Baader F, Calvanese D, McGuinness DL, Nardi D, and Patel-Schneider PF (eds) The Description Logic Handbook: Theory, Implementation, and Applications. Cambridge University Press, Cambridge, pp 5-44

4. Deng X, Haarslev V, Shiri N (2005) A framework for explaining reasoning in description logics. In Proceedings of the AAAI Fall Symposium on Explanation-aware Computing. AAAI Press, Menlo Park, US, pp 55-61

5. De Nivelle H, De Rijke M (2003) Deciding the guarded fragments by resolution. J Symbolic Computation 35(1):21-58

6. Eisinger N (1991) Completeness, confluence, and related properties of clause graph resolution. Morgan Kaufmann San Francisco, US

7. Haarslev V, Möller R (2001) Racer system description. In T Nipkow R Gori, A Leitsch (eds) Proceedings of International Joint Conference on Automated Reasoning (IJCAR). Springer-Verlag, London, UK, pp 701-705

8. Hustadt U, Motik B, Sattler U (2005) Data complexity of reasoning in very expressive description logics. In Proceedings of Nineteenth International Joint Conference on Artificial Intelligence (IJCAI). Morgan Kaufmann, San Francisco, US, pp 466-471

9. Hustadt U, Schmidt RA (1999) Issues of decidability for description logics in the framework of resolution. In Caferra R and Salzer G (eds) Automated Deduction in Classical and Non-Classical Logics. Springer-Verlag, London, UK, pp 191-205

10. Horrocks I (1998) The FaCT system. In De Swart H (ed) Automated Resoning with Analytic Tableaux and Related Methods: International Conference Tableaux. Springer-Verlag, Berlin, Germany, pp 307-312

11. Huang X (1994) Reconstructing proofs at the assertion level. In Bundy A (ed) Proceedings of 12th Conference on Automated Deduction. Springer-Verlag, London, UK, pp 738-752

12. Lingenfelder C (1996) Transformation and structuring of computer generatedproofs. Ph.D. thesis, University of Kaiserslautern

13. McGuinness DL and Borgida A (1995) Explaining subsumption in description logics. In Proceedings of the tenth International Joint Conference on Artificial Intelligence (IJCAI). Morgan Kaufmann, San Francisco, US, pp 816-821

14. Meier A (2000) TRAMP: Transformation of machine-found proofs into natural deduction proofs at the assertion level. In McAllester D (ed) Proceedings of the 17th Conference on Automated Deduction (CADE). Springer-Verlag, Berlin, Germany, pp 460-464
15. Nonnengart A, Rock G, Weidenbach C (1998) On generating small clause normal forms. In Kirchner C and Kirchner H (eds) Proceedings of the 15th International Conference on Automated Deduction. Springer-Verlag, London, UK, pp 397-411
16. Parsia B, Sirin E, Kalyanpur A (2005) Debugging OWL ontologies. In The 14th Interntional World Wide Web Conference (WWW). ACM Press, New York, US, pp 633-640
17. Schlobach S and Cornet R (2003) Non-standard reasoning services for the debugging of description logic terminologies. In Proceedings of the eighteenth International Joint Conference on Artificial Intelligence (IJCAI). Morgan Kaufmann, San Francisco, US, pp 355-362
18. WosMcCune M and Wos L (1997) Otter - the CADE-13 competition incar-nations. J Automated Reasoning 18(2):211-220

Completion Rules for Uncertainty Reasoning with the Description Logic $\mathcal{ALC}$

Volker Haarslev, Hsueh-Ieng Pai, Nematollaah Shiri

Department of Computer Science and Software Engineering, Concordia University, Montreal, Quebec, Canada

Abstract. Description Logics (DLs) are gaining more popularity as the foundation of ontology languages for the Semantic Web. On the other hand, uncertainty is a form of deficiency or imperfection commonly found in the real-world information/data. In recent years, there has been an increasing interest in extending the expressive power of DLs to support uncertainty, for which a number of frameworks have been proposed. In this paper, we introduce an extension of DL ($\mathcal{ALC}$) that unifies and/or generalizes a number of existing approaches for DLs with uncertainty. We first provide a classification of the components of existing frameworks for DLs with uncertainty in a generic way. Using this as a basis, we then discuss ways to extend these components with uncertainty, which includes the description language, the knowledge base, and the reasoning services. Detailed explanations and examples are included to describe the proposed completion rules.

1 Introduction

Uncertainty is a form of deficiency or imperfection commonly found in real-world information/data. A piece of information is uncertain if its truth is not established definitely [10]. Modeling uncertainty and reasoning with it have been challenging issues for over two decades in database and artificial intelligence research [2,10,12,13]. In recent years, uncertainty management has attracted the attention of researchers in Description Logics (DLs) [1]. To highlight the importance of the family of DLs, we describe its connection with ontologies and Semantic Web as follows.

Ever since Tim Berners-Lee introduced the vision of the Semantic Web [3], attempts have been made on making Web resources more machine-interpretable by giving them a well-defined meaning through semantic mark-ups. One way to encode such semantic mark-ups is using ontologies. An ontology is "an explicit specification of a conceptualization" [5]. Informally, an ontology consists of a set of terms in a domain, the relationship between the terms, and a set of constraints imposed on the way in which those terms can be combined. Constraints such as concept conjunction, disjunction, negation, existential quantifier, and universal quantifier can all be expressed using ontology languages. By explicitly defining the relationships and constraints among the terms, the semantics of the terms can be better defined and understood.

Over the last few years, a number of ontology languages have been developed, most of which have a foundation based on DLs. The family of DLs is mostly a subset of first-order logic (FOL) that is considered to be attractive as it keeps a good compromise between expressive power and computational tractability.

Despite the popularity of standard DLs, it has been realized that they are inadequate to model uncertainty. For example, in the medical domain, one might want to express that: "It is very likely that an obese person would have heart disease", where "obese" is a vague concept that may vary across regions or countries, and "likely" shows the uncertain nature of this information. Such expressions cannot be expressed using standard DLs.

Recently, a number of frameworks have been proposed which extend DLs with uncertainty, some of which deal with vagueness while others deal with probabilistic knowledge. It is not our intention to discuss which extension is better. In fact, different applications may require different aspects to be modeled, or in some cases, it may even be desired to model different aspects within the same application [14].

Following the approach of the parametric framework [11], we propose in this paper a generic DL with uncertainty as a unifying umbrella for several existing frameworks of DLs with uncertainty. This approach not only provides a uniform access over theories that have been expressed using DL with various kinds of uncertainty, but also allows one to study various related problems, such as syntax and semantics of knowledge bases, reasoning techniques, design and implementation of reasoners, and optimization techniques in a framework-independent manner.

The rest of this paper is organized as follows. Sect. 2 provides an overview of the standard DL framework and presents a classification of existing frameworks of uncertainty in DL. In Sect. 3, we present our generic framework for DL with uncertainty in detail along with examples. We discuss how to represent uncertainty knowledge in a general way, as well as how to perform reasoning services. Finally, concluding remarks and future directions are presented in Sect 4.

2 Background and related work

This section first gives an overview of the classical DL framework. Then, a classification of existing frameworks of uncertainty in DL is presented.

2.1 Overview of classical DL framework

The classical DL framework consists of three components:

1. *Description Language*: All description languages have elementary descriptions which include atomic concepts (unary predicates) and atomic roles (binary predicates). Complex descriptions can then be built inductively from concept constructors. In this paper, we focus on the description language $\mathcal{ALC}$ [1].
2. *Knowledge Base*: The knowledge base is composed of both intensional knowledge and extensional knowledge. The intensional knowledge includes the Terminological Box (TBox) consisting of a set of terminological axioms, and the Role Box (RBox) consisting of a set of role axioms. On the other hand, the extensional knowledge includes the Assertional Box (ABox) consisting of a set of assertions/facts.
3. *Reasoning Component*: A DL framework is equipped with reasoning services that enables one to derive implicit knowledge.

2.2 Approaches to DL with uncertainty

On the basis of their mathematical foundation and the type of uncertainty modeled, we can classify existing proposals of DLs with uncertainty into three approaches: fuzzy, probabilistic, and possibilistic approach.

The fuzzy approach, based on fuzzy set theory [19], deals with the vagueness in the knowledge, where a proposition is true only to some degree. For example, the statement "Jason is obese with degree 0.4" indicates Jason is slightly obese. Here, the value 0.4 is the degree of membership that Jason is in concept obese.

The probabilistic approach, based on the classical probability theory, deals with the uncertainty due to lack of knowledge, where a proposition is either true or false, but one does not know for sure which one is the case. Hence, the certainty value refers to the probability that the proposition is true. For example, one could state that: "The probability that Jason would have heart disease given that he is obese lies in the range [0.8, 1]."

Finally, the possibilistic approach, based on possibility theory [20], allows both certainty (necessity measure) and possibility (possibility measure) be handled in the same formalism. For example, by knowing that "Jason's weight is above 80 kg", the proposition "Jason's weight is 80 kg" is necessarily true with certainty 1, while "Jason's weight is 90 kg" is possibly true with certainty 0.5.

3 Our DL framework with uncertainty

To support uncertainty, each component of the DL framework needs to be extended (see Fig. 1). To be more specific, the generic framework consists of:

1. *Description Language with Uncertainty*: The syntax and semantics of the description language are extended to express uncertainty.
2. *Knowledge Bases with Uncertainty*: A knowledge base is composed of the intensional knowledge (TBox and RBox) and extensional knowledge, both extended with uncertainty.
3. *Reasoning with Uncertainty*: The DL framework is equipped with reasoning services that take into account the presence of uncertainties in DL theories during the reasoning process.

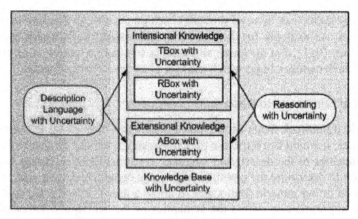

Fig. 1. DL Framework with Uncertainty

In what follows, we discuss each of these three components in detail, along with illustrating examples. Note that this paper extends our previous work [6] by presenting uncertainty inference rules for the reasoning component of the framework.

3.1 Description Language with Uncertainty

To provide a generic extension to a description language, one needs to develop a way to represent certainty values, and assign semantics to each element in the description language.

Representation of Certainty Values

To represent the certainty values, we take a *lattice-based approach* followed in the parametric framework [11]. That is, we assume that certainty values form a complete lattice shown as $\mathcal{L} = \langle \mathcal{V}, \preceq \rangle$, where $\mathcal{V}$ is the certainty domain, and $\preceq$ is the partial order defined on $\mathcal{V}$. We also use $\prec, \succeq, \succ$, and $=$ with their obvious meanings. We use b to denote the bottom or least element in $\mathcal{V}$, and use t to denote the top or greatest value in $\mathcal{V}$. The least upper bound operator (the join operator) in $\mathcal{L}$ is denoted by $\oplus$, its greatest lower bound (the meet operator) is denoted by $\otimes$, and its negation operator is denoted by $\sim$.

The certainty lattice can be used to model both *qualitative* and *quantitative* certainty values. An example for the former is the classical logic which uses the binary values $\{0, 1\}$. For the latter, an example would be a family of multi-valued logics such as fuzzy logic which uses $[0, 1]$ as the certainty domain.

Assignment of Semantics to Description Language

The generic framework treats each type of uncertainty formalism as a special case. Hence, it would be restrictive to consider any specific function to describe the semantics of the description language constructors (e.g., fixing *min* as the function to determine the certainty of concept conjunction). An alternative is proposed in our generic framework to allow a user to specify the functions that are appropriate to define the semantics of the description language element at axiom or assertion level. We elaborate more on this later in Sect. 3.2.

To ensure that the combination functions specified by a user make sense, we assume the following properties for various certainty functions to be reasonable. Most of these properties were recalled from [11], and are reasonable and justified when we verify them against existing extensions of DL with uncertainty. To present these properties, we consider the description language constructors in $\mathcal{ALC}$. We assume that the reader has a basic knowledge about $\mathcal{ALC}$.

Let $\mathcal{I} = (\Delta^{\mathcal{I}}, \cdot^{\mathcal{I}})$ be an interpretation, where $\Delta^{\mathcal{I}}$ is the domain and $\cdot^{\mathcal{I}}$ is an interpretation function that maps description language elements to some certainty value in $\mathcal{V}$.

Atomic Concept. The interpretation of an atomic concept A is a certainty value in the certainty domain, i.e., $A^{\mathcal{I}}(a) \in \mathcal{V}$, for all individuals $a \in \Delta^{\mathcal{I}}$. For example, in the fuzzy approach, the interpretation of an atomic concept A is defined as $A^{\mathcal{I}}(a) \in [0,1]$, that is, the interpretation function assigns to every individual a in the domain, a value in the unit interval that indicates its membership to A.

Atomic Role. Similar to atomic concepts, the interpretation of an atomic role R is a certainty value in the certainty domain, i.e., $R^{\mathcal{I}}(a, b) \in \mathcal{V}$, for all individuals $a, b \in \Delta^{\mathcal{I}}$.

Top/Universal Concept. The interpretation of the top or universal concept $\top$ is the greatest value in $\mathcal{V}$, that is, $\top^{\mathcal{I}} = t$. For instance, $\top$ corresponds to 1 (true) in the standard logic with truth values $\{0,1\}$, as well as in any one of its extensions to certainty domain $[0,1]$.

Bottom Concept. The interpretation of the concept bottom $\perp$ is the least value in the certainty domain $\mathcal{V}$, that is, $\perp^{\mathcal{I}} = b$. This corresponds to false in standard logic with $\mathcal{V} = \{0,1\}$, or corresponds to 0 when $\mathcal{V} = [0,1]$.

Concept Negation. Given a concept C, the interpretation of concept negation $\neg C$ is defined by the negation function $\sim: \mathcal{V} \to \mathcal{V}$, which satisfies the following properties:

1. Boundary Conditions: $\sim b = t$ and $\sim t = b$.
2. Double Negation: $\sim(\sim\alpha) = \alpha$, for all $\alpha \in \mathcal{V}$.

In our work, we consider the negation operator $\sim$ in the certainty lattice as the default negation function. Other properties, such as monotonicity (i.e., $\forall \alpha$, $\beta \in \mathcal{V}$, $\sim\alpha \succeq \sim\beta$, whenever $\alpha \preceq \beta$) may be imposed if desired. A common interpretation of $\neg C$ is $1 - C^{\mathcal{I}}(a)$, for all a in C.

Before introducing the properties of combination functions which are appropriate to describe the semantics of concept conjunction and disjunction, we first identify a set of desired properties which an allowable *combination function f* should satisfy. These functions are used to combine a collection of certainty values into one value. We then identify a subset of these properties suitable for describing the semantics of logical formulas on the basis of concept conjunction and disjunction. Note that, since f is used to combine a collection of certainty values into one, we describe f as a binary function from $\mathcal{V} \times \mathcal{V}$ to $\mathcal{V}$. This view is clearly without the loss of generality and, at the same time, useful for implementing functions in general.

1. Monotonicity: $f(\alpha_1, \alpha_2) \preceq f(\beta_1, \beta_2)$, whenever $\alpha_i \preceq \beta_i$, for $i = 1, 2$.
2. Bounded Above: $f(\alpha_1, \alpha_2) \preceq \alpha_i$, for $i = 1, 2$.
3. Bounded Below: $f(\alpha_1, \alpha_2) \succeq \alpha_i$, for $i = 1, 2$.
4. Boundary Condition (Above): $\forall \alpha \in \mathcal{V}, f(\alpha, b) = \alpha$ and $f(\alpha, t) = t$.
5. Boundary Condition (Below): $\forall \alpha \in \mathcal{V}, f(\alpha, t) = \alpha$ and $f(\alpha, b) = b$.
6. Commutativity: $\forall \alpha, \beta \in \mathcal{V}, f(\alpha, \beta) = f(\beta, \alpha)$.
7. Associativity: $\forall \alpha, \beta, \delta \in \mathcal{V}, f(\alpha, f(\beta, \delta)) = f(f(\alpha, \beta), \delta)$.

Concept Conjunction. Given concepts C and D, the interpretation of concept conjunction $C \sqcap D$ is defined by the conjunction function f_c that should satisfy properties 1, 2, 5, 6, and 7. The monotonicity property is required so that the reasoning is monotone, i.e., whatever that has been proven so far will remain true for the rest of the reasoning process. The bounded value property is included so that the interpretation of the certainty values makes sense. Note that this property also implies the boundary condition (property 5). The commutativity property supports reordering of the arguments of the conjunction operator, and associativity ensures that a different evaluation order of a conjunction of concepts does not change the result. These properties are useful during the runtime evaluation used by the reasoning procedure. Examples of conjunctions include the usual product $\times$ and *min* functions, and bounded difference defined as $bDiff(\alpha, \beta) = max(0, \alpha + \beta - 1)$.

Concept Disjunction. Given concepts C and D, the interpretation of concept disjunction $C \sqcup D$ is defined by the disjunction function f_d that should satisfy properties 1, 3, 4, 6, and 7. The monotonicity, boundedness, boundary condition, commutativity, and associativity properties are required for similar reasons described in the conjunction case. Some common disjunction functions are: the standard *max* function, the probability independent function defined as $ind(\alpha, \beta) = \alpha + \beta - \alpha\beta$, and the bounded sum function defined as $bSum(\alpha, \beta) = min(1, \alpha + \beta)$.

Role Value Restriction. Given a role R and a role filler C, the interpretation of the "role value" restriction $\forall R.C$ is defined as follows:

$$\forall a \in \Delta^{\mathcal{I}},\ \forall R.C^{\mathcal{I}}(a) = \otimes_{b \in \Delta^{\mathcal{I}}} \{f_d(\sim R^{\mathcal{I}}(a, b), C^{\mathcal{I}}(b))\}$$

The intuition behind this definition is to view $\forall R.C$ as the open first order formula $\forall b.\ R(a, b) \to C(b)$, where $R(a, b) \to C(b)$ is equivalent to $\neg R(a, b) \lor C(b)$, and $\forall$ is viewed as a conjunction over certainty values associated with $R(a, b) \to C(b)$. To be more specific, the semantics of $\neg R(a, b)$ is captured using the negation function $\sim$ as $\sim R^{\mathcal{I}}(a, b)$, the semantics of $\neg R(a, b) \lor C(b)$ is captured using the disjunction function as $f_d(\sim R^{\mathcal{I}}(a, b), C^{\mathcal{I}}(b))$, and $\forall b$ is captured using the meet operator in the lattice $\otimes_{b \in \Delta^{\mathcal{I}}}$.

Role Exists Restriction. Given a role R and a role filler C, the interpretation of the "role exists" restriction $\exists R.C$ is defined as follows:

$$\forall a \in \Delta^{\mathcal{I}},\ \exists R.C^{\mathcal{I}}(a) = \oplus_{b \in \Delta^{\mathcal{I}}} \{f_c(R^{\mathcal{I}}(a, b), C^{\mathcal{I}}(b))\}$$

The intuition here is that we view $\exists R.C$ as the open first order formula $\exists b.\ R(a, b) \land C(b)$, where $\exists$ is viewed as a disjunction over the elements of the domain. To be more specific, the semantics of $R(a, b) \land C(b)$ is captured using the conjunction function as $f_c(R^{\mathcal{I}}(a, b), C^{\mathcal{I}}(b))$, and $\exists b$ is captured using the join operator in the lattice $\oplus_{b \in \Delta^{\mathcal{I}}}$.

Additional Inter-Constructor Properties. In addition to the aforementioned properties, we further assume that the following inter-constructor properties hold:

1. De Morgan's Rule: $\neg(C \sqcup D) \equiv \neg C \sqcap \neg D$ and $\neg(C \sqcap D) \equiv \neg C \sqcup \neg D$.
2. Negating Quantifiers Rule: $\neg \exists R.C \equiv \forall R.\neg C$ and $\neg \forall R.C \equiv \exists R.\neg C$

The above two rules are needed to convert a concept description into *negation normal form* (NNF), i.e., the negation operator appears only in front of a concept name. Note that these properties restrict the type of negation, conjunction, and disjunction functions allowed in existing frameworks, and hence in our work.

3.2 Knowledge Bases with Uncertainty

As in the classical counterpart, a *knowledge base* Σ in the generic framework is a triple $\langle \mathcal{T}, \mathcal{R}, \mathcal{A} \rangle$, where $\mathcal{T}$ is a TBox, $\mathcal{R}$ is an RBox, and $\mathcal{A}$ is an ABox.

An interpretation $\mathcal{I}$ *satisfies* a knowledge base Σ, denoted $\mathcal{I} \models \Sigma$, iff it satisfies each component of Σ. We say that Σ is *satisfiable*, denoted $\Sigma \not\models \bot$, iff there exists an interpretation $\mathcal{I}$ such that $\mathcal{I} \models \Sigma$. Similarly, Σ is *unsatisfiable*, denoted $\Sigma \models \bot$), iff $\mathcal{I} \not\models \Sigma$, for all interpretations $\mathcal{I}$.

To provide a generic extension to the knowledge base, there is a need to give a syntactical and semantical extension to both the intensional (TBox and RBox) and extensional knowledge (ABox).

TBox with Uncertainty

A TBox $\mathcal{T}$ consists of a set of terminological axioms expressed in the form $\langle C \sqsubseteq D, \alpha \rangle \langle f_c, f_d \rangle$ or $\langle C \equiv D, \alpha \rangle \langle f_c, f_d \rangle$, where C and D are concepts, $\alpha \in V$ is the certainty that the axiom holds, f_c is the conjunction function used as the semantics of concept conjunction and part of the role exists restriction, and f_d is the disjunction function used as the semantics of concept disjunction and part of the role value restriction. As usual, the concept definition $\langle C \equiv D, \alpha \rangle \langle f_c, f_d \rangle$ is defined as $\langle C \sqsubseteq D, \alpha \rangle \langle f_c, f_d \rangle$ and $\langle D \sqsubseteq C, \alpha \rangle \langle f_c, f_d \rangle$.

In order to transform the axiom of the form $\langle C \sqsubseteq D, \alpha \rangle \langle f_c, f_d \rangle$ into its normal form, $\langle \top \sqsubseteq \neg C \sqcup D, \alpha \rangle \langle f_c, f_d \rangle$, we restrict the semantics of the concept subsumption to be $f_d (\sim C^{\mathcal{I}}(a), D^{\mathcal{I}}(a))$, where $\sim C^{\mathcal{I}}(a)$ captures the semantics of $\neg C$, and f_d captures the semantics of $\sqcup$ in $\neg C \sqcup D$. An interpretation $\mathcal{I}$ satisfies $\langle C \sqsubseteq D, \alpha \rangle \langle f_c, f_d \rangle$ iff for all individuals $a \in \Delta^{\mathcal{I}}$, $(f_d (\sim C^{\mathcal{I}}(a), D^{\mathcal{I}}(a))) \in \alpha$. By defining the semantics for concept subsumption this way, it also allows us to guarantee that some basic properties hold, such as the Negating Quantifiers Rule described in the previous subsection.

RBox with Uncertainty

The RBox $\mathcal{R}$ is similar to the TBox except that we have role axioms instead of terminological axioms. In addition, no conjunction or disjunction functions are specified. Since existing DL frameworks with uncertainty do not allow role conjunction or role disjunction, we do not consider them in the generic framework either. We also remark that since this generic framework supports only $\mathcal{ALC}$, no role hierarchy is allowed. However, we include the definition of a RBox here for completeness.

ABox with Uncertainty

An ABox $\mathcal{A}$ consists of a set of assertions of the form $\langle a{:}C,\ \alpha \rangle \langle f_c, f_d \rangle$ or $\langle (a, b){:}R,\ \alpha \rangle \langle -, - \rangle$, where a and b are individuals, C is a concept, R is a role, $\alpha \in \mathcal{V}$, f_c is the conjunction function, f_d is the disjunction function, and $-$ denotes that the corresponding combination function is not applicable.

An interpretation $\mathcal{I}$ satisfies $\langle a{:}C,\ \alpha \rangle \langle f_c, f_d \rangle$ (resp. $\langle (a, b){:}R,\ \alpha \rangle \langle -, - \rangle$) iff $C^{\mathcal{I}}(a) \in \alpha$ (resp. $R^{\mathcal{I}}(a, b) \in \alpha$).

3.3 Reasoning with Uncertainty

In this section, we describe the reasoning procedure for the generic framework proposed here. Let $\Sigma = \langle \mathcal{T}, \mathcal{A} \rangle$ be a knowledge base, where $\mathcal{T}$ is an acyclic TBox and $\mathcal{A}$ is an ABox.

Satisfiability Problem

To check if a knowledge base Σ is satisfiable, first apply the pre-processing steps (described below) to remove the TBox, $\mathcal{T}$. Then, initialize the extended ABox, $\mathcal{A}_0^{\mathcal{E}}$, with the resulting ABox (i.e., the one after pre-processing steps are performed), and initialize the constraint set, C_0, to the empty set $\{\}$. After that, apply the completion rules (described below) to transform the ABox into a simpler and satisfiability preserving one. The completion rules are applied in arbitrary order as long as possible, until either $\mathcal{A}_i^{\mathcal{E}}$ contains a clash or no further rule could be applied to $\mathcal{A}_i^{\mathcal{E}}$. If $\mathcal{A}_i^{\mathcal{E}}$ contains a clash, the knowledge base is unsatisfiable. Otherwise, an optimization method is applied to solve the system of inequations in C_j. If the system of inequations is unsolvable, the knowledge base is unsatisfiable. Otherwise, the knowledge base is satisfiable.

Entailment Problem

To determine to what degree is an assertion X true, given a knowledge base $\Sigma = \langle \mathcal{T}, \mathcal{A} \rangle$, we are interested in finding the tightest bound for which X is true. As an example, if the certainty values are expressed in a range $[l, u]$, then we would like to find the largest l and the smallest u such that the knowledge base entails X. To do so, we follow the same procedure as the one for checking satisfiability. However, instead of checking whether the system of inequations is solvable, we apply the optimization method to find the tightest bound for which X is true.

Pre-processing Steps

Before performing any inference procedure on the knowledge base, we do the following pre-processing steps.
1. Replace each axiom of the form $\langle C \equiv D, \alpha \rangle \langle f_c, f_d \rangle$ with the following two equivalent axioms: $\langle C \sqsubseteq D, \alpha \rangle \langle f_c, f_d \rangle$ and $\langle D \sqsubseteq C, \alpha \rangle \langle f_c, f_d \rangle$.
2. Transform every axiom in the TBox $\mathcal{T}$ into normal form. That is, replace each axiom of the form $\langle C \sqsubseteq D, \alpha \rangle \langle f_c, f_d \rangle$ with $\langle \top \sqsubseteq \neg C \sqcup D, \alpha \rangle \langle f_c, f_d \rangle$.
3. Transform every concept (including the ones in TBox and ABox) into negation normal form.
4. For each individual a in the ABox $\mathcal{A}$ and each axiom $\langle \top \sqsubseteq \neg C \sqcup D, \alpha \rangle \langle f_c, f_d \rangle$ in the TBox $\mathcal{T}$, add $\langle a : \neg C \sqcup D, \alpha \rangle \langle f_c, f_d \rangle$ to $\mathcal{A}$.
5. Apply the clash trigger (described below) to check if the initial knowledge base is inconsistent.

Completion Rules

As in the classical DL, completion rules are a set of satisfiability preserving transformation rules that allows us to infer implicit knowledge from the explicit one (i.e., the one specified in the original set of assertions in the ABox). In our generic framework, we have specified the following completion rules:

clash triggers, concept assertion rule, role assertion rule, negation rule, conjunction rule, disjunction rule, role exists restriction rule, and role value restriction rule. In what follows, we describe each of these rules in detail.

Let α, β be certainty values in the certainty domain. Also let x_X be the variable denoting the certainty of assertion X, and Γ be either a certainty value in the certainty domain or an expression over certainty variables and values. The completion rules are defined as follows.

Clash Triggers:

$$\langle a : \bot, t\rangle\langle-, -\rangle \in A_i^{\mathcal{E}}$$

$$\langle a : \top, b\rangle\langle-, -\rangle \in A_i^{\mathcal{E}}$$

$$\{\langle a : A, \alpha\rangle\langle-, -\rangle, \langle a : A, \beta\rangle\langle-, -\rangle\} \subseteq A_i^{\mathcal{E}}, \text{ with } \otimes(\alpha, \beta) = \varnothing$$

The purpose of these clash triggers is to detect any possible contradictions in the knowledge base. Note that we use $\bot$ as a synonym for $A \sqcap \neg A$, and $\top$ as a synonym for $A \sqcup \neg A$.

The last clash trigger detects the contradiction in terms of the certainty values specified for the same assertion. To be more specific, in case there is no intersection in the certainty values specified for the same assertion, we have conflicting assertions, hence a contradiction is detected. For example, suppose the certainty domain is defined as $V = C[0,1]$, meaning the set of closed subintervals $[\alpha, \beta]$ in $[0, 1]$ such that $\alpha \preceq \beta$. If a knowledge base contains both assertions $\langle John:Tall, [0.8, 0.9]\rangle$ and $\langle John:Tall, [0.2, 0.4]\rangle$, then the last clash trigger will detect such conflicting information in the knowledge base.

Concept Assertion Rule:

if 1. $\langle a : A, \Gamma\rangle\langle-, -\rangle \in A_i^{\mathcal{E}}$, and

   2. $(x_{a:A} = \Gamma) \notin C_j$, and

   3. Γ is not the variable $x_{a:A}$

then $C_{j+1} = C_j \cup \{(x_{a:A} = \Gamma)\}$

This rule simply adds the certainty value of each atomic concept assertion to the constraint set C_j. For example, if we have the assertion $\langle John:Tall, [0.6, 0.9]\rangle\langle-, -\rangle$ in the ABox, then we add the constraint $(x_{John:Tall} = [0.6, 0.9])$ to the constraint set C_j.

Role Assertion Rule:

if 1. $\langle (a, b):R, \Gamma \rangle \langle -, - \rangle \in \mathcal{A}_i^{\mathcal{E}}$, and
  2. $(x_{(a, b):R} = \Gamma) \notin C_j$, and
  3. Γ is not the variable $x_{(a, b):R}$
then $C_{j+1} = C_j \cup \{(x_{(a, b):R} = \Gamma)\}$

Similar to the Concept Assertion Rule, this rule simply adds the certainty value of each atomic role assertion to the constraint set C_j. For example, if we have the assertion $\langle (John, Diabetes):hasDisease, [0.8, 0.9] \rangle \langle -, - \rangle$ in the ABox, then we add the constraint $(x_{(John, Diabetes):hasDisease} = [0.8, 0.9])$ to the constraint set C_j.

Negation Rule:
if 1. $\langle a : \neg A, \Gamma \rangle \langle -, - \rangle \in \mathcal{A}_i^{\mathcal{E}}$, and
  2. $\langle a : A, \sim\Gamma \rangle \langle -, - \rangle \notin \mathcal{A}_i^{\mathcal{E}}$
then $\mathcal{A}_{i+1}^{\mathcal{E}} = \mathcal{A}_i^{\mathcal{E}} \cup \{\langle a : A, \sim\Gamma \rangle \langle -, - \rangle\}$

The intuition behind the negation rule is that, if we know an assertion has certainty value Γ, then the certainty of its negation can be obtained by applying the negation operator in the lattice to Γ. For example, if the certainty domain is $\mathcal{V} = \mathcal{C}[0,1]$, and the negation operator is defined as $\sim([\alpha, \beta] = [1 - \beta, 1 - \alpha]$. Then, if we have the assertion $\langle John : \neg Tall, [0.4, 0.8] \rangle \langle -, - \rangle$ in the ABox, we could also infer that $\langle John : Tall, [0.2, 0.6] \rangle \langle -, - \rangle$.

Conjunction Rule:
if $\langle a : C \sqcap D, \Gamma \rangle \langle f_c, f_d \rangle \in \mathcal{A}_i^{\mathcal{E}}$
then for each $\Psi \in \{C, D\}$
  if 1. Ψ is atomic, and
    2. $\langle a : \Psi, x_{a:\Psi} \rangle \langle -, - \rangle \notin \mathcal{A}_i^{\mathcal{E}}$
  then $\mathcal{A}_{i+1}^{\mathcal{E}} = \mathcal{A}_i^{\mathcal{E}} \cup \{\langle a : \Psi, x_{a:\Psi} \rangle \langle -, - \rangle\}$
  else if 1. Ψ is not atomic, and
    2. $\langle a : \Psi, x_{a:\Psi} \rangle \langle f_c, f_d \rangle \notin \mathcal{A}_i^{\mathcal{E}}$
    then $\mathcal{A}_{i+1}^{\mathcal{E}} = \mathcal{A}_i^{\mathcal{E}} \cup \{\langle a : \Psi, x_{a:\Psi} \rangle \langle f_c, f_d \rangle\}$
  if $(f_c (x_{a:C}, x_{a:D}) = \Gamma) \notin C_j$,
  then $C_{j+1} = C_j \cup \{(f_c (x_{a:C}, x_{a:D}) = \Gamma)\}$
  if $(f_c (x_{a:C}, x_{a:D}) \preceq x_{a:\Psi}) \notin C_j$,
  then $C_{j+1} = C_j \cup \{(f_c (x_{a:C}, x_{a:D}) \preceq x_{a:\Psi})\}$

The intuition behind this rule is that, if we know an individual is in $C \sqcap D$, we know it is in both C and D. In addition, according the semantics of the description language, we know that the semantics of $C \sqcap D$ is defined by applying the conjunction function to the interpretation of $a{:}C$ and the interpretation of $a{:}D$. Finally, the last part of the rule re-enforces the "bounded above" property of the conjunction function.

For example, if we have the assertion $\langle John{:}Tall \sqcap Thin, [0.6, 0.8]\rangle\langle min, ma\rangle$ in the ABox, then we could infer that $\langle John{:}Tall, x_{John:Tall}\rangle\langle -, - \rangle$ and $\langle John{:}Thin, x_{John:Thin}\rangle\langle -, - \rangle$, with the constraint ($min\,(x_{John:Tall}, x_{John:Thin}) = [0.6, 0.8]$) satisfied. In addition, based on the property of the conjunction function, we also know that $min\,(x_{John:Tall}, x_{John:Thin}) \preceq$ both $x_{John:Tall}$ and $x_{John:Thin}$.

Disjunction Rule:

if $\langle a : C \sqcup D, \Gamma\rangle\langle f_c, f_d\rangle \in \mathcal{A}_i^{\varepsilon}$
then for each $\Psi \in \{C, D\}$
    if 1. Ψ is atomic, and
       2. $\langle a : \Psi, x_{a:\Psi}\rangle\langle -, - \rangle \notin \mathcal{A}_i^{\varepsilon}$
    then $\mathcal{A}_{i+1}^{\varepsilon} = \mathcal{A}_i^{\varepsilon} \cup \{\langle a : \Psi, x_{a:\Psi}\rangle\langle -, - \rangle\}$
    else if 1. Ψ is not atomic, and
       2. $\langle a : \Psi, x_{a:\Psi}\rangle\langle f_c, f_d\rangle \notin \mathcal{A}_i^{\varepsilon}$
      then $\mathcal{A}_{i+1}^{\varepsilon} = \mathcal{A}_i^{\varepsilon} \cup \{\langle a : \Psi, x_{a:\Psi}\rangle\langle f_c, f_d\rangle\}$
  if $(f_d\,(x_{a:C}, x_{a:D}) = \Gamma) \notin \mathcal{C}_j$,
  then $\mathcal{C}_{j+1} = \mathcal{C}_j \cup \{(f_d\,(x_{a:C}, x_{a:D}) = \Gamma)\}$
  if $(f_d\,(x_{a:C}, x_{a:D}) \succeq x_{a:\Psi}) \notin \mathcal{C}_j$,
  then $\mathcal{C}_{j+1} = \mathcal{C}_j \cup \{(f_d\,(x_{a:C}, x_{a:D}) \succeq x_{a:\Psi})\}$

The intuition behind this rule is that, if we know an individual is in $C \sqcup D$, we know it is in either C, D, or in both. In addition, according the semantics of the description language, we know that the semantics of $C \sqcup D$ is defined by applying the disjunction function to the interpretation of $a{:}C$ and the interpretation of $a{:}D$. Finally, the last part of the rule re-enforces the "bounded below" property of the disjunction function.

For example, if we have $\langle John{:}Rich \sqcup CarFanatic, [0.6, 0.8]\rangle\langle min, max\rangle$ in the ABox, then we could infer $\langle John{:}Rich, x_{John:Rich}\rangle\langle -, - \rangle$ and $\langle John{:}\ CarFanatic, x_{John:CarFanatic}\rangle\langle -, - \rangle$, with the constraint ($max\,(x_{John:Rich}, x_{John:CarFanatic}) =$

[0.6, 0.8]) satisfied. In addition, based on the property of the disjunction function, we also know that max $(x_{John:Rich}, x_{John:CarFanatic}) \succeq$ both $x_{John:Rich}$ and $x_{John:CarFanatic}$.

Role Exists Restriction Rule:
if $\langle a : \exists R.C, \Gamma \rangle \langle f_c, f_d \rangle \in \mathcal{A}_i^{\mathcal{E}}$
then if there exists no individual b such that $(f_c(x_{(a, b):R}, x_{b:C}) = x_{a:\exists R.C}) \in C_j$
    then $\mathcal{A}_{i+1}^{\mathcal{E}} = \mathcal{A}_i^{\mathcal{E}} \cup \{\langle (a, b):R, x_{(a,b):R} \rangle \langle -, - \rangle\}$
    if C is atomic
      then $\mathcal{A}_{i+1}^{\mathcal{E}} = \mathcal{A}_i^{\mathcal{E}} \cup \{\langle b:C, x_{b:C} \rangle \langle -, - \rangle\}$
      else $\mathcal{A}_{i+1}^{\mathcal{E}} = \mathcal{A}_i^{\mathcal{E}} \cup \{\langle b:C, x_{b:C} \rangle \langle f_c, f_d \rangle\}$
    where b is a new individual
    $C_{j+1} = C_j \cup \{(f_c(x_{(a,b):R}, x_{b:C}) = x_{a:\exists R.C})\}$
if Γ is not the variable $x_{a:\exists R.C}$
then if $(x_{a:\exists R.C} = \Gamma') \in C_j$
    then if 1. $\Gamma \neq \Gamma'$, and
          2. Γ is not an element in Γ'
        then $(x_{a:\exists R.C} = \Gamma') \leftarrow (x_{a:\exists R.C} = \oplus(\Gamma, \Gamma'))$
            where $\oplus$ is the join operator of the lattice and
            $\leftarrow$ means whatever is on the LHS is
            replaced by the RHS
    else $C_{j+1} = C_j \cup \{(x_{a:\exists R.C} = \Gamma)\}$

The intuition behind this rule is that we view $\exists R.C$ as the open first order formula $\exists b. R(a, b) \wedge C(b)$, where $\exists$ is viewed as a disjunction over the elements of the domain. That is, the semantics of $R(a, b) \wedge C(b)$ is captured using the conjunction function as $f_c(R^{\mathcal{I}}(a, b), C^{\mathcal{I}}(b))$, and $\exists b$ is captured using the join operator in the lattice $\oplus_{b \in \Delta^{\mathcal{I}}}$.

For example, if the join operator is sup (supremum), and we have the assertion $\langle John:\exists hasDisease.Diabetes, [0.4, 0.6] \rangle \langle min, max \rangle$ in the ABox. Then, we could infer that $\langle (John, d1):hasDisease, x_{(John, d1):hasDisease} \rangle \langle -, - \rangle$ and $\langle d1:Diabetes, x_{d1:Diabetes} \rangle \langle -, - \rangle$, where $d1$ is a new individual. In addition, the constraints $(min(x_{(John, d1):hasDisease}, x_{d1:Diabetes}) = x_{John:\exists hasDisease.Diabetes})$ and $(x_{John:\exists hasDisease.Diabetes} = [0.4, 0.6])$ must be satisfied. Now, suppose we have yet another assertion $\langle John:\exists hasDisease.Diabetes, [0.5, 0.9] \rangle \langle min, max \rangle$ in the ABox. Then, when we apply Role Exists Restriction Rule, we will not generate a new individual. Instead, we simply replace the constraint $(x_{John:\exists hasDisease.Diabetes} = [0.4, 0.6])$ in C_j with the constraint $(x_{John:\exists hasDisease.Diabetes} = sup\ ([0.5, 0.9], [0.4, 0.6]))$, where sup is the join operator in the lattice. This new constraint takes into account the certainty value of the current assertion as well as that of the previous assertion.

Role Value Restriction Rule:

if $\{\langle a : \forall R.C, \Gamma\rangle\langle f_c, f_d\rangle, \langle (a, b):R, \Gamma'\rangle\langle -, -\rangle\} \subseteq \mathcal{A}_i^{\mathcal{E}}$
then if 1. C is atomic, and
      2. $\langle b : C, x_{b:C}\rangle\langle -, -\rangle \notin \mathcal{A}_i^{\mathcal{E}}$
     then $\mathcal{A}_{i+1}^{\mathcal{E}} = \mathcal{A}_i^{\mathcal{E}} \cup \{\langle b : C, x_{b:C}\rangle\langle -, -\rangle\}$
else if 1. C is not atomic, and
      2. $\langle b : C, x_{b:C}\rangle\langle f_c, f_d\rangle \notin \mathcal{A}_i^{\mathcal{E}}$
     then $\mathcal{A}_{i+1}^{\mathcal{E}} = \mathcal{A}_i^{\mathcal{E}} \cup \{\langle b : C, x_{b:C}\rangle\langle f_c, f_d\rangle\}$
if $(f_d\ (\sim x_{(a,b):R}, x_{b:C}) = x_{a:\forall R.C}) \notin C_j$
then $C_{j+1} = C_j \cup \{(f_d\ (\sim x_{(a,b):R}, x_{b:C}) = x_{a:\forall R.C})\}$
if Γ is not the variable $x_{a:\forall R.C}$
then if $(x_{a:\forall R.C} = \Gamma'') \in C_j$
    then if 1. $\Gamma \neq \Gamma''$, and
        2. Γ is not an element in Γ''
      then $(x_{a:\forall R.C} = \Gamma'') \leftarrow (x_{a:\forall R.C} = \otimes(\Gamma, \Gamma''))$
          where $\otimes$ is the meet operator of the lattice and
          $\leftarrow$ means whatever is on the LHS is
          replaced by the RHS
    else $C_{j+1} = C_j \cup \{(x_{a:\forall R.C} = \Gamma)\}$

The intuition behind this rule is to view $\forall R.C$ as the open first order formula $\forall b.\ R(a, b) \to C(b)$, where $R(a, b) \to C(b)$ is equivalent to $\neg R(a, b) \vee C(b)$, and $\forall$ is viewed as a conjunction over certainty values associated with $R(a, b) \to C(b)$. That is, the semantics of $\neg R(a, b)$ is captured using the negation function $\sim$ as $\sim R^{\mathcal{I}}(a, b)$, the semantics of $\neg R(a, b) \vee C(b)$ is captured using the disjunction function as $f_d\ (\sim R^{\mathcal{I}}(a, b)$, and $\forall b$ is captured using the meet operator in the lattice $\otimes_{b \in \mathcal{I}'}$.

For example, if the meet operator is inf (infimum), and we have assertions $\langle John:\forall hasPet.Dog, [0.4, 0.6]\rangle\langle min, max\rangle$ and $\langle (John, d1):hasPet, [0.5, 0.8]\rangle\langle -$

, $-\rangle$ in the ABox. Then, we could infer that $\langle d1{:}Dog, x_{d1:Dog}\rangle\langle-, -\rangle$. In addition, the constraints $(max\ (\sim x_{(John,d1):hasPet},\ x_{d1:Dog}) = x_{John:\forall hasPet.Dog})$ and $(x_{John:\forall hasPet.Dog} = [0.4, 0.6])$ must be satisfied. Now, suppose we have yet another assertion $\langle John{:}\forall hasPet.Dog, [0.5, 0.9]\rangle\langle min, max\rangle$ in the ABox. Then, when we apply Role Value Restriction Rule, we simply replace the constraint $(x_{John:\forall hasPet.Dog} = [0.4, 0.6])$ in $\mathcal{C}_j$ with the new constraint $(x_{John:\forall hasPet.Dog} = inf\,([0.5, 0.9], [0.4, 0.6]))$, where inf is the meet operator in the lattice. Note that the new constraint takes into account the certainty value of the current assertion as well as that of the previous assertion.

3.4 Illustrative Example

Most of the proposed fuzzy DLs ("most" because our framework supports only $\mathcal{ALC}$) can be represented in the generic framework by setting the certainty lattice as $\mathcal{L} = \langle V, \preceq \rangle$, where $V = C[0,1]$ is the set of closed subintervals $[\alpha, \beta]$ in $[0, 1]$ such that $\alpha \preceq \beta$. The negation operator in this case is defined as $\sim([\alpha, \beta]) = [1 - \beta, 1 - \alpha]\}$. In [7,15,17,18], the meet operator is inf (infimum) and the join operator is sup (supremum). On the other hand, in [16], min is used as the meet operator, and max is used as the join operator. The conjunction function used in all these proposals is min, whereas the disjunction function used is max. As an example, suppose we have the following fuzzy knowledge base:

$\mathcal{T} = \{\langle \exists owns.Porsche \sqsubseteq (Rich \sqcup CarFanatic), [0.8, 1]\rangle\langle min, max\rangle,$
   $\langle Rich \sqsubseteq Golfer, [0.7, 1]\rangle\langle-, max\rangle\}$
$\mathcal{A} = \{\langle Tom : \exists owns.Porsche, [0.9, 1]\rangle\langle min, -\rangle,$
   $\langle Tom : \neg CarFanatic, [0.6, 1]\rangle\langle-, -\rangle\}$

Then, we first transform all the axioms into normal form:

$\mathcal{T} = \{\langle\top \sqsubseteq ((\forall owns.\neg Porsche) \sqcup (Rich \sqcup CarFanatic)), [0.8,1]\rangle\langle min,$
   $max\rangle,$
   $\langle\top \sqsubseteq (\neg Rich \sqcup Golfer), [0.7, 1]\rangle\langle-, max\rangle\}$

After that, we could remove the axioms in the TBox $\mathcal{T}$ by adding the corresponding assertions to the ABox $\mathcal{A}$. To be more specific, for each individual a in the ABox (in this case, we have only one individual, Tom, in the ABox) and for each axiom of the form $\langle\top \sqsubseteq \neg C \sqcup D, \alpha\rangle\langle f_c, f_d\rangle$ in the TBox, we add an assertion $\langle a{:}\neg C \sqcup D, \alpha\rangle\langle f_c, f_d\rangle$ to the ABox. Hence, in this step, we add the following two assertions to the ABox:

   $\{\langle Tom : ((\forall owns.\neg Porsche) \sqcup (Rich \sqcup CarFanatic)), [0.8,1]\rangle\langle min,$

$max\rangle$,

$\langle Tom : (\neg Rich \sqcup Golfer), [0.7, 1] \rangle\langle -, max\rangle\}$

Now, we can initialize the extended ABox to be:

$\mathcal{A}_0^{\mathcal{E}} = \langle Tom : \exists owns.Porsche, [0.9, 1]\rangle\langle min, -\rangle$,

$\quad\langle Tom : \neg CarFanatic, [0.6, 1]\rangle\langle -, -\rangle$,

$\quad\langle Tom : ((\forall owns.\neg Porsche) \sqcup (Rich \sqcup CarFanatic)), [0.8,1]\rangle\langle min,$

$\quad max\rangle$,

$\quad\langle Tom : (\neg Rich \sqcup Golfer), [0.7, 1] \rangle\langle -, max\rangle\}$

and the constraint set to be $\mathcal{C}_0 = \{\}$.

Note that, according to the clash triggers, there is no trivial contradiction in the knowledge base. So, once the pre-processing steps are over, we are ready to apply the completion rules to construct the model. For sake of brevity, we show only how to apply the Role Exists Restriction Rule to the first assertion.

According to the first assertion, $\langle Tom : \exists owns.Porsche, [0.9, 1]\rangle\langle min, -\rangle$, Tom must own at least one Porsche, with certainty more than 0.9. Indeed, when we apply the Role Exists Restriction Rule to this assertion, we get:

$\mathcal{A}_1^{\mathcal{E}} = \mathcal{A}_0^{\mathcal{E}} \cup \{\langle (Tom, p_1) : owns, x_{(Tom, p1):owns}\rangle\langle -, -\rangle$,

$\quad\langle p_1 : Porsche, x_{p1:Porsche}\rangle\langle -, -\rangle\}$

where p_1 is a new individual

$\mathcal{C}_1 = \mathcal{C}_0 \cup \{(min\,(x_{(Tom, p1):owns}, x_{p1:Porsche}) = x_{Tom:\exists owns.Porsche}\}$

$\mathcal{C}_2 = \mathcal{C}_1 \cup \{(x_{Tom:\exists owns.Porsche} = [0.9, 1])\}$

After applying the Role Exists Restriction Rule to the first assertion, we can continue applying other completion rules to the rest of assertions in the extended ABox until either we get a clash or no further rule could be applied. If a clash is obtained, the knowledge base is inconsistent. Otherwise, a linear programming technique is applied to check if the system of inequations is solvable, or to find the tightest bound for which an assertion is true.

Now, suppose we want to reason about the same knowledge base using basic probability instead of fuzzy logic. Then, we may replace the conjunction function in the knowledge base with the algebraic product $(\times(\alpha, \beta) = \alpha\beta)$, and the disjunction function with the independent function $(ind\,(\alpha, \beta) = \alpha + \beta - \alpha\beta)$ if desired. For example, the first terminological axiom in the above knowledge base can be interpreted using simple probability as: $\langle \exists owns.Porsche \sqsubseteq (Rich \sqcup CarFanatic), [0.8, 1]\rangle\langle \times, ind\rangle$, which asserts that the probability that someone owns a Porsche is Rich or CarFanatic is at least 0.8. Once the knowledge base is defined and the pre-processing steps are followed, the appropriate completion rules can be applied to perform the desired inference. Note that, since reasoning with probability requires extra information/knowledge about the events and facts in the world (Σ), we are investigating ways to model knowledge bases with more general probability theory, such as positive/negative correlation [9], ignorance [9], and conditional probability [4,8].

It is important to note that, unlike other proposals which support only one form of uncertainty for the entire knowledge base, our framework allows the user to specify different combination functions (f_c, f_d) for each of the axioms and assertions in the knowledge base. For example, for a given knowledge base, an axiom may use $\langle min, max \rangle$ as the combination functions, while another axiom may use $\langle \times, ind \rangle$. This is in addition to the fact that our generic framework can simulate the computation of many DLs with uncertainty, each having different underlying certainty formalism.

4 Conclusion and Future Works

We introduced a generic framework which allows us to incorporate various forms of uncertainty within DLs in a uniform way. In particular, we abstracted away the underlying notion of uncertainty (which could be fuzzy, probability, possibilistic, etc.), the way in which the constructors in the description language are interpreted (by flexibly defining the conjunction and disjunction functions), and the way in which the inference procedure proceeds. An implementation of the proposed generic framework is underway. In addition, on the basis of the finite model property and disallowing terminological cycles, we can guarantee termination of the proposed reasoning procedure. We are working to establish this and the completeness of this procedure. As future work, we plan to further extend the generic framework to a more expressive fragment of DL (e.g., $\mathcal{SHOIN}$), and study optimization techniques for the extended framework.

Acknowledgements

This work is supported in part by Natural Sciences and Engineering Research Council (NSERC) of Canada, Genome Québec, and by ENCS, Concordia University, Montreal, Québec, Canada. We also thank the anonymous reviewers for their helpful comments.

References

1. Baader F, Calvanese D, McGuinness DL, Nardi D, Patel-Schneider PF, eds (2003) The description logic handbook: theory, implementation, and applications, Cambridge University Press.
2. Bacchus F (1990) Representing and reasoning with probabilistic knowledge - a logical approach to probabilities, MIT Press.
3. Berners-Lee T, Hendler J, Lassila O (2001) The semantic web. Scientific American 284(5).
4. Giugno R, Lukasiewicz T (2002) P-SHOQ(D): A probabilistic extension of SHOQ(D) for probabilistic ontologies in the semantic web. In: Proceedings of the European conference on logics in artificial intelligence, Cosenza, Italy, pp 86–97.
5. Gruber TR (1993) A translation approach to portable ontology specifications. Knowledge acquisition 5(2):199–220.
6. Haarslev V, Pai HI, Shiri N (2005) A generic framework for description logics with uncertainty. In: Proceedings of uncertainty reasoning for the semantic web, Galway, Ireland, pp 77–86.
7. Hölldobler S, Khang TD, Störr HP (2002) A fuzzy description logic with hedges as concept modifiers. In: Proceedings of the 3rd international conference on intelligent technologies, Science and Technics Publishing House, Hanoi, Vietnam, pp 25–34.
8. Koller D, Levy AY, Pfeffer A (1997) P-CLASSIC: A tractable probablistic description logic. In: Proceedings of the 14th national conference on artificial intelligence, AAAI Press, Providence, Rhode Island, pp 390–397.
9. Lakshmanan LVS, Sadri F (1994) Probabilistic deductive databases. In: Proceedings of workshop on design and implementation of parallel logic programming systems, MIT Press, Ithaca, NY, pp 254–268.
10. Lakshmanan LVS, Shiri N (2001a) Logic programming and deductive databases with uncertainty: A survey. Encyclopedia of computer science and technology, vol 45, Marcel Dekker, New York, pp 153–176.
11. Lakshmanan LVS, Shiri N (2001b) A parametric approach to deductive databases with uncertainty. IEEE transactions on knowledge and data engineering, 13(4):554–570.
12. Motro A, Smets P, eds. (1997) Uncertainty management in information systems - from needs to solutions, Springer-Verlag.

13.Parsons S (1996) Current approaches to handling imperfect information in data and knowledge bases. IEEE transactions on knowledge and data engineering, 8(3):353–372.
14.Ross TJ, Booker JM, Parkinson WJ, eds (2002) Fuzzy logic and probability applications: bridging the gap, SIAM.
15.Sánchez D, Tettamanzi, AGB (2004) Generalizing quantification in fuzzy description logics. In: Proceedings of the 8th Fuzzy Days, Springer-Verlag, Dortmund, Germany.
16.Straccia U (1998) A fuzzy description logic. In: Proceedings of the 15th national conference on artificial intelligence, AAAI Press, Menlo Park, CA, USA, pp 594–599.
17.Straccia U (2001) Reasoning within fuzzy description logics. Journal of artificial intelligence research 14:137–166.
18.Tresp C, Molitor R (1998) A description logic for vague knowledge. In: Proceedings of the 13th European conference on artificial intelligence, John Wiley and Sons, Brighton, UK, pp 361–365.
19.Zadeh LA (1965) Fuzzy sets. Information and control, 8:338–353.
20.Zadeh LA (1978) Fuzzy sets as a basis for a theory of possibility. Fuzzy Sets and Systems 1(1):3–28.

Author Index